AMORAL THOUGHTS
ABOUT MORALITY

ABOUT THE AUTHOR

Howard H. Kendler's career has been varied and distinguished. He received his B.A. from Brooklyn College and his M.A. and Ph.D. in psychology from the University of Iowa. He served in the U.S. Army during World War II and was the Chief Clinical Psychologist at Walter Reed General Hospital. From 1946 to 1948 he was an assistant professor at the University of Colorado and from 1948 to 1963 he was associated with New York University, where in 1951 he became Professor of Psychology and Chair of the Department of Psychology of University College. Since 1963 he has been Professor of Psychology at the University of California, Santa Barbara. Dr. Kendler has been a Fellow at the Center for Advanced Studies in the Behavioral Sciences as well as Visiting Professor at the University of California, Berkeley; Hebrew University in Jerusalem; and Tel-Aviv University. He is the author of *Basic Psychology, Psychology: A Science in Conflict, Historical Foundations of Modern Psychology,* co-editor of *Essays in Neobehaviorism: A Memorial Volume to Kenneth W. Spence,* and has written more than 150 professional articles. In addition to serving as consultant to governmental agencies, Dr. Kendler has held the office of President of the Western Psychological Association, Chairman of the Board of Governors of the Psychonomic Society, and President of the American Psychological Association. He is also a member of the Society of Experimental Psychologists.

Second Edition

AMORAL THOUGHTS ABOUT MORALITY

The Intersection of Science, Psychology, and Ethics

By

HOWARD H. KENDLER

University of California, Santa Barbara

CHARLES C THOMAS • PUBLISHER, LTD.
Springfield • Illinois • U.S.A.

Published and Distributed Throughout the World by

CHARLES C THOMAS • PUBLISHER, LTD.
2600 South First Street
Springfield, Illinois 62794-9265

© 2008 by CHARLES C THOMAS • PUBLISHER, LTD.

ISBN 978-0-398-07791-4 (hard)
ISBN 978-0-398-07792-1 (paper)

Library of Congress Catalog Card Number: 2007037936

With THOMAS BOOKS *careful attention is given to all details of manufacturing
and design. It is the Publisher's desire to present books that are satisfactory as to their
physical qualities and artistic possibilities and appropriate for their particular use.*
THOMAS BOOKS *will be true to those laws of quality that assure a good name
and good will.*

Printed in the United States of America
MM-R-3

Library of Congress Cataloging in Publication Data

Kendler, Howard H., 1919–
    Amoral thoughts about morality : the intersection of science, psychology,
and ethics / by Howard H. Kendler.–2nd ed.
        p. cm.
    Includes bibliographical references and index.
    ISBN 978-0-398-07791-4 (hbk.)–ISBN 078-0-398-07792-1 (pbk.)
    1. Psychology–Moral and ethical aspects. 2. Psychology, Applied–Moral
and ethical aspects. 3. Psychology–Social aspects. 4. Psychology, Applied–
Social aspects. I. Title.

BF76.4.K47 2008
174'.915–dc22   2007037936

Dedicated to my grandchildren:
Jenny, Seth, and Nathan
Remember!

PREFACE

The purpose of *Amoral Thoughts About Morality* has not changed in its second edition. Consequently, the original preface is still appropriate. However, there are two important additions that can be briefly described. One is the updating of empirical evidence and theoretical development occurring during the recent past. The second is an attempt to extend the analysis of the relationship between scientific facts and moral principles beyond the boundaries of a democratic society for which it was originally designed. By examining the differences between experimental and historical analyses, an attempt is made to clarify the nature of the conflict between political democracies and Islamic societies and identify potential sources of reconciliation and persistent conflict.

My great indebtedness to those mentioned at the end of the Preface to the First Edition still remains. The preparation of the second edition profited from an illuminating correspondence with Gerald Zuriff, the helpful editorial assistance of Karen Aldenderfer, and the counsel and support of Madeline Hanrahan.

H.H.K.

PREFACE TO THE FIRST EDITION

Since the birth of psychology as an independent discipline in 1879, controversy has raged as to whether it is a prescriptive or descriptive science. Can psychology advocate moral principles and prescribe public policies (e.g., bilingual education, affirmative action, pro-abortion) or is psychological knowledge value-free, lacking any logical implications for moral principles or public policies? Perhaps more importantly, can psychology, without endorsing any moral position or public policy, provide reliable information about the consequences of competing policies so that informed decisions can be made about which policy best serves the needs of society.

The debate about the prescriptive or descriptive status of psychology has remained unresolved, partly because the conflict has rarely been analyzed by examining the epistemological basis of the relationship between psychological evidence and moral principles. Consequently, when psychology is required to address moral issues, particularly in the realm of public policy, the profession speaks with conflicting voices. Some psychologists presume that they can identify public policies that are right, good, and just. Others consider such moral judgments to be inconsistent with the ethics of science that demand empirical facts be reported without any moral implications or spin. Others, probably the majority of psychologists, have ignored the issue, or refuse to deal with it.

The controversy about facts and values cannot be resolved because it reflects conflicting conceptions of both science and psychology. My aim is to bring the problems into sharp focus by clarifying the issues so that psychologists and their professional organizations can better appreciate the consequences of their views, for the benefit of both the discipline and a democratic society. To achieve my goal, the relationship between facts and values will initially be analyzed in the abstract and then the resulting epistemological framework will be applied to controversial issues such as genetic and environmental influences on behavior, the concept of racial superiority, affirmative action, and multiculturalism. The general analysis brings to the surface underlying ethical, legal, and scientific problems that have tended to be ignored by those social scientists who believe that empirical data, or what are regarded as such, can logically validate public policies. The book will touch upon many emotional problems that generate social strife. The hope, as well as the expectation, is that exposing these sensitive issues to critical examination will help more than harm a moral pluralistic society.

Although the views expressed are my own, I must acknowledge my indebtedness to John Dewey, Karl Popper, Imré Lakatos, Ernest Nagel, and Isaiah Berlin for shaping them. I wish to thank Tracy S. Kendler, Bob Silverman, Tom Bouchard, and Brewster Smith for their contributions to my book.

H.H.K.

CONTENTS

AMORAL THOUGHTS
ABOUT MORALITY

Chapter 1

SCIENCE, PSYCHOLOGY, AND PUBLIC POLICY

The study of ethics is concerned with human values and moral conduct; what is good and bad and right and wrong. Science is a method that collects data through observations and experiments and offers systematic interpretations of the results. Psychology is the science of the mind and behavior. The three—ethics, science, psychology—obviously interact but in a manner that is far from clear. The reason for this ambiguity is that much more must be known about ethics, science, and psychology to understand their reciprocal interactions. As of now one would be hard-pressed to answer the following questions. Can science determine a moral truth such as abortion is *wrong* or affirmative action is *right?* Does the scientific method employed in physics, chemistry, and biology consist of an exact set of rules, for example the games of chess and checkers? Can psychology be a science in the same way as physics and biology? Are there different kinds of sciences? Can science, psychology, and ethics in combination assist a democracy in formulating and judging the effectiveness of public policies?

This book is focused on the last question. To answer this query, however, demands responding to the prior questions. Only by realizing that ethics, science, and psychology can be interpreted in a variety of ways does it become possible to isolate those aspects of each discipline that in combination can become a tool for effective policy choices. But this project cannot be accomplished swiftly or easily. A few more definitions accompanied by a quickie discussion will not be sufficient! What is required is a carefully constructed epistemological edifice that will reveal how a particular intersection of science, psychology, and ethics can assist a democracy in coping effectively with public policy conflicts. And when this structure is constructed we will be in the position to analyze perceptively a few of the major social problems confronting American society.

Underlying all public policy clashes are moral conflicts. There are times that the very survival of a society depends on its ability to resolve, or at least ameliorate, the divisive, and sometimes destructive, consequences of ethical conflicts. Currently, the daily newspaper is rarely without stories about painful national clashes such as the morality of abortion, affirmative action, socioeconomic inequality, religious and ethnic conflicts, racial differences, gender clashes, sexual harassment, and homosexual marriage. Typically such policy clashes are fought in the political arena where the aim of the participants is usually to win the public debate by hook or crook. Instead of clarifying the basic issues at stake, confusion is encouraged in an effort to gain political advantage. Some would argue that misinformation is an inevitable consequence of the political process; a price that democracy must pay. But the price can be reduced if reliable information becomes available about the consequences of competing social policies. With such knowledge democratic processes can yield educated choices instead of uninformed decisions.

Can one really distinguish between *misinformation* and *accurate information* in the world of politics? Is it possible, in an era when the concept of *objective truth* is being challenged, to distinguish between *truth* and *falsity?* Yes, but the task is not easy. To be successful one must know what truth is and how it can be attained.

THE MEANINGS OF TRUTH

Baruch Spinoza (1632–1677), the great Dutch philosopher who encouraged a life of reason, not passion, suggested "He who would distinguish the true from the false must have an adequate idea of what is true and false." History tells us clearly "an adequate idea" can take many different forms. To make sense of the various kinds of truth that are possible, a distinction between understanding as a psychological process and explanation as an epistemological standard will prove helpful. Understanding is a psychological phenomenon that refers to the personal criteria "truth seekers" use when they report they "understand." Explanation, in contrast, requires a social criterion consisting of explicit epistemological rules that must be met in order for a person to achieve understanding. Understanding is personal, explanation is social, and in a fundamental sense they are separable. The difference is illustrated in the case of the paranoid who understands that he or she is a victim of persecution in the absence of a socially acceptable explanation. In essence, understanding is based upon a radical subjectivity while explanation reflects a social reality.

The justification for the distinction between understanding and explanation is that it shifts attention away from the quixotic search for the true definition of truth to the reasonable task of characterizing different kinds of truth that people employ when interpreting their world. By recognizing that people can conceive truth in different ways, one then can evaluate the social consequences of the different criteria of truth while simultaneously avoiding entrapment in needless disputes about real or true truth.

Forms of Understanding

A tripartite division among three different forms of understanding–*intuitive, rational,* and *scientific*–can help clarify its meaning.

Intuitive: A common theme in the history of philosophy is that humans have a special mental faculty to ascertain truth. Human intuition enables one to grasp truth in an unpremeditated, noninferential manner. A prime example is the belief in God. His existence is intuitively true and no other reason is required. Henry Bergson (1859–1941), a philosopher, psychologist, and recipient of the Nobel Prize for literature, postulated a conflict between a life force (élan vital) and the world of matter. He acknowledged that the human intellect, operating within a scientific framework, is capable of understanding the physical world. Science, however, for Bergson is too restrictive for comprehending all human experience. Intuition, an evolutionary product of animal instincts, is needed to understand purely human events that range from the common to the mystical.

Rational: Rational simply means that understanding is achieved through reason. The existence of God can be supported by both rational and intuitive arguments. One common rational justification for God's existence is that some supernatural power is needed to create the universe and the human race. Rational understanding involves extended cognitive activity as contrasted with the instant flash of intuitive comprehension. Another difference between the two is that one, intuitive, is private while in contrast a rational argument is public, subject to the scrutiny of others.

Scientific. Not only must scientific understanding meet a more demanding standard of rationality than does rational understanding, it also must be consistent with empirical evidence. Whereas rational understanding can justify the conclusion that the earth is flat, such a decision would be rejected by natural science because the mathematical analysis of empirical evidence indicates the shape of the earth approximates a globe. Rational within the context of rational understanding means a reasonable, coherent interpretation, not a mathematical proof. Supreme Court decisions are rarely unanimous but one cannot describe the majority opinion as rational and the contrasting minority opinion as irrational. The Constitution is not a logically organized document that offers a single answer to all legal questions. Instead, in the hands of Justices of the Supreme Court it can generate a wide variety of rational decisions, some that are mutually incompatible. Scientific disagreements occur, but over time they tend to be resolved by a combination of additional evidence and sharper logical analysis. The essential empirical component of science serves as the cutting edge that divides truth from falsehood. Intuitive and rational understandings fail to provide an equivalent rule that distinguishes truth from falsehood.

The classification of different forms of understanding carries a risk of possible misinterpretations. First, it must be emphasized that these three conceptions of understanding are not mutually exclusive, airtight categories that are sharply delineated from each other. Characteristics of one category can operate in another. Within science, intuitive and/or rational understanding can precede the formulation of a scientific explanation. Einstein confessed to knowing that his theory of relativity was correct before being able to demonstrate its scientific (empirical) justification (Wertheimer, 1945).

The major reason for identifying different forms of understanding is to emphasize the point that truth-seekers pursue different kinds of truth. What are the relative merits of the different forms of truth? Many natural scientists would suggest that only scientific truth is valuable because it alone can reveal the nature of reality. Such a position would be challenged by the old philosophical argument that the scientist's reality is an inference, not the "true reality." There is no way to reach beyond our own observations and observe reality directly. For our purposes the metaphysical problems of the true nature of reality is best avoided. Empirical observations, not "reality," will serve as the foundation of our natural science orientation.

Even if one agrees that natural science methodology offers superior knowledge of the world that one intuitively believes exists, this admission of preeminence is limited, not general. Although science can offer impressive answers about the real world, it is inarticulate about questions that are basic to human existence: the meaning and purpose of life, what is a self-fulfilling life, does God exist, what is moral truth? Was the invasion of Iraq right or wrong? Science has no sense of taste when it comes to esthetics! Which is more beautiful: a Rembrandt, a Van Gogh, a Picasso or a Pollock? Neither does science have a moral sense when it comes to judging right from wrong—a proposition soon to be explained fully. Is abortion good or bad?

If our framework for judging contrasting form of understanding is shifted from the specific to the general, then the flaw in the reasoning that one form of comprehension is more valid than others should become obvious. If humans employ different criteria for understanding then the demonstration of the supremacy of one over the others requires a super criterion of true understanding that is independent of all three modes. Such a criterion is unavailable.

Thus the goal of true understanding, in the global sense, appears unachievable. Each form of understanding is "true" within its own context, and by implication wanting within the framework of other forms. We are left with the stark conclusion that there is no universal truth, but only limited truths that fit limited criteria. This conclusion has both a positive and negative consequence. It offers a variety of ways for the flexible human intellect to achieve understanding of the myriad events to which humans are exposed. At the same time it creates conflicting truths that have the potential, as the history of humankind vividly demonstrates, of one group forcefully imposing their truth on those who resist acceptance.

The Consequences of Scientific Understanding

Science has been amazingly successful in providing empirical information and in answering theoretical questions about the nature of the world. Nevertheless, natural science methodology is limited in its ability to answer directly important questions about the human condition. In contrast, other modes of inquiry such as intuitive and rational understanding can answer questions that science is impotent to address, but such responses, it must be noted, fall far short of the level of agreement that natural science answers achieve.

The fact that competing modes of understanding cannot be judged in terms of any absolute value does not imply they are equally valuable. When it comes to understanding the world, science has been overwhelmingly effective in providing information that can be employed in such practical endeavors as enhancing health, increasing agricultural yields, providing improved shelter, disease control, facilitating communication and transportation, increasing longevity, exposing more people to great works of art, and so forth. At the same time scientific creations such as the atomic bomb, the internal combustion engine, mass-produced cigarettes, atomic waste, climate change, and others have raised the issue of whether so-called scientific progress is desirable. It would be difficult to deny that the natural science interpretation of the world has led to a mixed bag of consequences. How can these consequences be evaluated? An answer will be forthcoming by first reducing the size of the question to the relationship between psychology and public policy.

The Relationship between Psychology and Public Policy

Can psychology contribute to the formulation and evaluation of public policy? If psychology can offer reliable information about the consequences of different social policies–abortion, bilingual education, preferential treatment in college admissions–then society would be able to make educated choices about competing programs. The capacity of psychology to provide such useful knowledge depends on its ability to employ the scientific method that has been successful in providing a deep understanding of physics, chemistry, and biology. To determine whether psychology can meet this epistemological demand requires some understanding of both natural science methodology and psychology.

Natural Science Methodology

The common view is that the scientific method that generated Galileo's law of falling bodies, Newton's conception of gravity, Darwin's interpretation of evolution, and Einstein's theory of relativity can clearly be spelled out, is wrong. Whereas naïve observers of poker or chess could discover the rules that govern the game and agree about their conclusions, a similar effort by sophisticated philosophers of science over the past centuries has failed to yield complete agreement about the essential nature of the so-called scientific method. In this sense, science is not an exact science. This, however, does not mean it is chaotic. The scientific method represents a shared general orientation that developed over time in the course of human efforts to understand the world in which they live.

Consider the case of solar eclipses. Several centuries before Christ, the Chaldeans, an ancient Semitic people who inhabited Babylonia, discovered that solar eclipses occur approximately every eighteen years and eleven days. This knowledge not only enabled the prediction of solar eclipses, but also encouraged a shift in the prevailing view of the world. Before the realization that solar eclipses occurred in a repetitive cycle, they were believed to be a result of supernatural forces. Only prayer or incantations or other rituals could restore the hidden light. The fundamental conception was that worldly phenomena, like solar eclipses, were mysterious. Discovering that eclipses appeared in a repetitive cycle encouraged the view that natural phenomena were comprehensible. They were expressions of natural forces.

Naturalism did not immediately, or ever completely, overthrow supernaturalism but it did evolve into modern science that led to the expansion of our understanding of physical and biological phenomena. But this development was not an expression of some self-conscious premeditated effort to formalize the scientific method into an explicit procedure that prescribed both rules of scientific conduct and standards for knowledge claims. Instead, the scientific approach to understanding the world developed in response to the immediate needs of the enterprise itself. Reliability of observations, systematic experimentation, mathematical representation of results, theoretical integration, in addition to other ideas, were gradually and casually incorporated into the so-called "scientific method." But these notions were never transformed into precise, universally accepted rules. Thus the meaning of the scientific method has and always will remain open to dispute. One feature of the scientific method is not open to dispute. Empirical evidence is the final authority in science. Speculations are free but facts are sacred.

In spite of the general agreement about the empirical foundation of the natural and biological sciences, contrasting opinions about fundamental issues abound in the philosophy of science. Three controversial issues that are central to the role of scientific evidence in the development of public policy are *observational purity* or what may be more whimsically described as *immaculate perceptions,* the meaning of *scientific "truth,"* and the boundary that separates *science from nonscience.*

Observational Purity

Many philosophers of science emphasize the epistemological principle that scientific knowledge is grounded in experience. If the foundation of science is the observations of the scientist the immediate question becomes, "How do such observations get communicated to other scientists?" The answer: "By trying to accurately report the original observations without any distortion." Thomas Kuhn's influential *The Structure of Scientific Revolutions* (1962) challenged the assumption that scientific observations could be reported without bias. Kuhn rejected the common-sense notion that scientific progress results from the accumulation of individual discoveries and theoretical refinements. Instead, Kuhn perceived a repetitive pattern in the history of science consisting of two markedly different enterprises: normal science and revolution.

Normal science refers to the accumulation of knowledge within a widely adopted global orientation, labeled by Kuhn as a paradigm and described as a "strong network of commitments–conceptual, theoretical, instrumental and methodological, and quasi-metaphysical" (Kuhn, 1962, 102). Success, during normal science, is not guaranteed. Anomalous results can occur adversely to the expectations of the prevailing paradigm. Such findings may be the first sign of an impending revolution (the second stage of historical development) during which time a prevailing paradigm is overthrown by a new one more competent to interpret the anomalous findings. Revolutions, however, do not occur quickly; the old paradigm does not collapse in the face of embarrassing data, thus encouraging the immediate acceptance of the new paradigm. Those who were trained and worked within the old paradigm do not readily abandon it. These paradigmatic "loyalists" resist the new paradigm by persistently making ad hoc modifications to their theory to accommodate the new data.

A case history that illustrates Kuhn's paradigmatic shift is the revolutionary Copernican heliocentric system that finally overthrew the Ptolemaic geocentric system. The motion of Jupiter's four moons was inconsistent with the prevailing Ptolemaic view that the earth lay at the center of the universe. Tycho Brahe (1564–1601), the Danish astronomer who observed the stars and planets with unprecedented positional accuracy "salvaged" the geocentric theory with the ad hoc assumption that the planets revolve around the sun as the sun revolves around the earth. Although not successful in rejecting the Copernican theory, Brahe's modification proved effective in maintaining the allegiance of the supporters of the old paradigm. The younger scientists, whose attachment to the prevailing paradigm is less deep or enduring, recognize the superiority of the new paradigm in its capacity to absorb the anomalous results and encourage promising new lines of research. The struggle between the old and new paradigm requires many years to settle, and its final resolution is more a result of the mortality of humans than any set of data or compelling logic. To sum up, according to this Kuhnian analysis, science is not a cumulative discipline as suggested by the traditional conception; scientific revolutions are "noncumulative episodes in which an older paradigm is replaced in whole or in part by an incompatible new one" (Kuhn, 1962, 91).

Kuhn's suggestion that the history of science is characterized by paradigm shifts has challenged the assumption that unbiased scientific observations are always possible. He essentially claimed that scientific observations tend to be biased in the direction of paradigmatic expectations. To support his contention Kuhn cites the results of psychological experiments that demonstrate that perceptions are influenced by a person's preconceptions. This evidence is used to support the contention that one cannot separate the scientific observer from what is observed, an adverse conclusion to both the general notions of scientific objectivity and scientific progress.

In a study cited to support Kuhn's position (Bruner and Postman, 1949), college students were briefly shown individual playing cards with instructions to identify them. Mixed in with the conventional cards were incongruous ones such as a black four of hearts. Most students identified such a card as a red four of hearts or as a black four of spades. That is, their observations were not determined exclusively by external reality but also by their preconceptions about playing cards–black spades and red hearts. The conclusion of this study, and similar perceptual experiments, is that presuppositions can influence observations. Such evidence is consistent with the notion that a scientist's observations can be contaminated by the investigator's preconceptions.

Was Kuhn too gullible interpreting such evidence as being representative of the observations of the scientist? He mistakenly assumed that the observational conditions of the Bruner-Postman subjects are analogous to those of the scientist when doing research. The dramatic effects were obtained when the anomalous playing card was briefly exposed. Longer exposure times enabled the subject to correctly identify the anomalous card. If the experiment had been designed to replicate scientific practices, optimal conditions of observations would have been employed to encourage accurate identification. And if an error were made, and no doubt observational errors are more likely to occur when events are at odds with prevailing expectations, then the self-correcting procedures of good research practices, such as the use of several observers and/or the replication of the study, would uncover the observational error. In sum, although preconceptions may influence empirical observations, they do not necessarily have to, especially when precautions are taken.

One can also fault Kuhn for employing the wrong perspective. The proper framework to interpret the relevance of the study to the methodological problem of immaculate perceptions is not from the position of the subject, but from the position of the experimenter. Was any confusion generated about the nature of the experimental situation? Difficulty was not encountered by the scientific community in knowing that anomalous playing cards were employed in the Bruner-Postman study. Any experimenter would be able to replicate their experiment without difficulty regardless of his or her theoretical persuasion.

When analyzing whether unbiased observations are possible, one must distinguish between the influences of a scientist's interest on his scientific observations from the scientist's capacity to make unbiased observations. It appears trivial to note a scientist's motivation will dictate what he or she will observe, thereby refuting the notion, transparently naïve, that scientific observations are completely independent of the scientist's preconceptions. Scientists have different interests and therefore will observe different phenomena. But do such instances justify the unqualified conclusion that the "Observer and observed are not separable" (Kessel, 1969, 1002)? Is it not possible that scientists, with conflicting theoretical conceptions, will be able to report common observations when observing the same phenomenon? An affirmative response is demanded by one who views the history of science as a constant interaction between theoretical speculation and empirical evidence. Only if scientists had agreed about bedrock observations could Newton's law of universal gravitation or Darwin's theory of evolution finally been adopted. The issue of unbiased observations, "immaculate perceptions," has been the source of such confusion that it becomes essential to clearly illustrate how and why they are possible. The problem is not whether scientists are encouraged by different backgrounds and interests to observe different events, but instead to understand how observational agreement is possible when scientists, even with different theoretical orientations and philosophies of life, are observing the same event.

Paul Meehl (1920–2003), who achieved professional eminence as a psychologist, philosopher, psychometrician, and clinician puts it this way:

> I often hear and read the flat statement, "As Kuhn has shown, all observation is theory laden." Kuhn has not shown that, he has merely asserted it; and only a minority of philosophers and scientists agree with him . . . Consider the protocol "Rat 13 locomoted to the right side goal box, where he drank some water." What is theory laden about that? Nothing. But isn't the term goal theory-laden? It looks so, but it is not . . . But in the neutral observation language . . . it's the box at the right end of the T-cross-bar where rat 13 has encountered water and ingested it. You may be thinking, "Well, Meehl makes it easy for himself by picking simple cases from animal behavior . . . But as a clinician he should know better" . . . Take a clinical example: "In Alabama, students with 9'4 MMPI profile are twice as likely to ignore a letter from the college dean as are those with a 7'2 profile" . . . Theory-laden? No. Or, behind the couch, "After reporting a dream of squirting a garden hose on a fire, this (male) patient spoke the words "shame," "proud," "ambition," and "embarrass." Again, nothing theory-laden at all. (Meehl, 1993, 709–710)

In spite of our criticism of Kuhn's suggestion that unbiased observations are impossible, his emphasis on paradigm shifts is particularly relevant to psychology where contrasting paradigms have influenced the course of its early history (e.g., natural science, psychoanalytic, humanistic, and so on).

Scientific "Truth"

Scientists and philosophers of science have different conceptions of scientific "truth," or what may be more accurately designated as verisimilitude, the appearance or semblance of truth. Philosophers of science, as well as scientists, are not in complete agreement as to the criteria that should be employed to define scientific truth.

Ernst Mach (1838–1916) was a distinguished physicist who became interested in the philosophical underpinnings of science. Mach's aim was to rid science of metaphysical notions that were, for him, any event or concept that could not be directly observed by the senses. For Mach, the demonstration of a functional relationship among directly observed variables–taking two Tylenol and the disappearance of a headache–represents the ultimate form of scientific explanation. In psychology, B. F. Skinner (1904–1990) adopted a Machian view that rejected the notion that theories were necessary. For him, only facts are important. Thus if one can eliminate the fear of high places among acrophobics by appropriate conditioning procedures, then one understands the effectiveness of the therapy. In sum, a plain description of an empirical relationship for some scientists is sufficient to reveal scientific truth.

Although most scientists and philosophers would not deny that an established empirical relationship is true, they would nevertheless suggest that simple descriptions do not represent the whole truth. Darwin, in his naturalistic observations of animal and plant life, as well as coral reefs, expressed the opinion that facts alone were not sufficient in the scientific enterprise. He wrote in a letter:

> About 30 years ago there was much talk that geologists ought only to observe and not to theorize, and I well remember someone saying that at this rate a man might as well go into a gravel pit and count the pebbles and describe the colours. How odd it is that anyone should not see all observations must be for or against some view–if it is to be of any service. (Darwin & Seward, 1903, 195)

Darwin was essentially arguing in favor of a theoretical conception of truth; to really understand empirical events one must deductively explain them. A classic example of the achievement of scientific truth through deductive explanation is gravitational theory. Everybody had observed that apples fell, and stones tossed up ultimately came down, and that the waters of the seas periodically rose and fell. It was also noted that pendulums of all lengths took the same amount of time to swing back and forth regardless of the size of the arc and that planets followed the same orbits in their trips around the sun. Initially individual explanations were offered for each of these events. However, theoretical physicists like Galileo and Newton saw a basic similarity among the various phenomena. The theory of gravitation, the attraction that masses of matter have for each other, was formulated to deductively explain all of these formerly "isolated" events. The truth value of the theory of gravitation was later enhanced by a novel prediction. In the early nineteenth century, it was noted the planet Uranus followed a peculiar path around the sun. Astronomers deduced from the theory of gravitation that some unknown body must be exerting a gravitational pull on Uranus. The location of the unknown planetary body was predicted from gravitational theory that in turn led to the discovery of the planet Neptune. For some people, particularly natural scientists, understanding is equated with a process analogous to logical proof with the precision of the deductive process varying from mathematical verification to rigorous use of ordinary language.

In recent years, partly as a result of the great advances made in the biological sciences, including medicine, the deductive model of scientific truth has been found wanting. Simply deducing the increased frequency of the occurrence of depression in a group of women is not sufficient. Identifying the causal mechanism, the responsible neurological and chemical changes, is the ultimate goal of science (Losee, 2001; Woodward, 2003).

While recognizing different views of scientific truth occur among philosophers of science it should be understood these disagreements do not affect the distinction between science and other methods of interpreting the world (e.g., religious, intuitive, rational). Scientific explanations, however defined–descriptive, deductive, or causal–must be consistent with empirical evidence. It should not be forgotten an essential component in scientific discourse is publicly observable events.

The Boundary between Science and Nonscience

The acceptance of empiricism as the sine qua non of natural science does not resolve all methodological issues. Is astrology a science? It deals with empirical phenomena. It assumes that the pattern of celestial bodies determines the course of human events. An empirical relationship is postulated to exist between astronomical conditions at the time of one's birth and future events in one's life. Interestingly, such illustrious scientists as Copernicus, Kepler, Galileo, and Newton were practicing astrologers.

One proposal to distinguish science from nonscience is the *verifiability principle* that equates a scientific theory with one that can be verified by determining whether its logical implications match empirical events. Astrology flunks this test on two counts. The theoretical expectations are usually couched in such vague terms (e.g., "you will have unorthodox views") that prevent them from being empirically evaluated. What is more important, theories based on astrology have failed to achieve empirical verification. The exact time of one's birth does not determine one's future behavior.

Another proposal to distinguish science from nonscience is the *falsifiability principle*. Rather than emphasize empirical confirmation as the hallmark of scientific theories, Karl Popper (1902–1994) chose to stress the importance of falsifiability as a standard that scientific theories must meet. Popper's enunciation of the falsifiability principle was encouraged by his early association with psychoanalytic theories (e.g., Freud, Adler) in his native Vienna. He concluded that they were epistemologically defective because they could not be falsified. Because they were able to explain everything, they were unable to explain anything. Consider, for instance, the case of a man's unresolved Oedipus complex, his presumed desire to achieve sexual gratification with his mother. Combined with a variety of Freudian defense mechanisms, an unresolved Oedipus could be expressed in such widely diverse behaviors as homosexuality, marrying a woman who resembled his mother, marrying a woman who is totally unlike his mother, not marrying, avoiding all sexual contacts, and ignoring or being obsessed with sexual desires. Freudian theory was incapable of generating an empirical deduction that could, in principle, be falsified. Popper's point of view is neatly captured in the comments of a fictional detective,

In my experience . . . [being a psychoanalyst] does not necessarily con-
fer expertise in understanding the motives of men, only some skill in
designing explanations of their behavior, which may or may not be true
and which can't be proved one way or another. (Kemelman, 1976, 64)

Popper, employing the same line of reasoning, drew the shocking
conclusion, at least for devotees of Freud and Adler, that psychoanalytic theories are no better than the pseudoscientific theories of astrology and phrenology because, like them, they "explain" everything
while being protected against possible refutation.

Popper (1965) suggested that the characteristic of falsifiability could
be used to strategic advantage when developing scientific theories.
The theorist has a choice between testing safe predictions or those that
strongly challenge the theory. Rather than focus on potential confir-
mations, Popper recommended theorists should deliberately set out to
disprove their conceptions! This tactic represents an efficient method
for achieving theoretical success. If the attempt to falsify is successful
then the theory is eliminated from consideration and no further time
and effort is wasted. If the attempt to falsify fails, then the theory
retains its credibility, thereby justifying additional exploration.

Not unexpectedly, Popper was unable to convince all philosophers
of science about the superiority of the falsification over the verifiability procedure. In fact, some denied a significant difference between the
two. Although both identified features that distinguished science from
nonscience, neither seemed complete. According to Lakatos (1970a,
1970b), a student of Popper, the reason is that scientific theories evolve
over time and therefore must be judged within a historical context.
According to Lakatos the problem lies with the idea of a theory. Is a
theory a single formulation or a set of formulations that share common
assumptions? Are two theories that postulate slightly different environ-
mental-genetic interactions in cognitive functioning only slightly different, distinctly different, or essentially similar? In attempting to answer these questions Lakatos concluded that the proper unit for historical analysis of scientific development is a research program, not a specific theory. A research program contains an infinite number of specific theories with a common cluster of core assumptions. If a test of a
specific theory yields embarrassing evidence, then ad hoc modifications of the research program can be made to accommodate the new
evidence. Such modifications can persist forever because, in principle,

a research program contains an infinite number of possible theories.

Lakatos suggests research programs can be judged in terms of their historical development, whether they degenerate or progress. Recall Brahe's effort to repair the Ptolemaic view with the ad hoc assumption that the planets revolve around the sun as the sun revolves around the earth (p. 11). Although this modification was able to interpret the paths of Jupiter's four moons, it was unable to generate new predictions that would expand the deductive capacity of Ptolemaic theory. In striking contrast was the progressive development of the revolutionary Copernican theory. Johannes Kepler (1571–1630) used Tycho Brahe's data to replace the circular orbits of planets in the Copernican system with elliptical orbits. Later, the Copernican theory progressed further when Newton was able to explain the actual orbits of the planets with his theory of gravitation. In sum, a progressive change occurs when an ad hoc modification of a theory not only copes with an unexpected result but also predicts the occurrence of novel events. In contrast, a research program is degenerating if an ad hoc modification does nothing more than accommodate the anomaly.

Thus, the conclusion can be drawn that the methodological-historical analysis proposed by Lakatos has considerable merit in clarifying the procedures that actually operate in the evaluation of scientific theories. The process of evaluation is not precise, that there is much room for disagreement, and should not be seen as a deficiency in Lakatos's framework, but instead as a reflection of the intrinsic nature of the scientific enterprise. The scientific method is not a system that exists in nature, but is a human creation that emerged from a variety of their efforts to understand the nature of the world in which they live. As such, different views about the nature of the innovation that is called the scientific method are to be expected. The crucial question, for the present discussion, is whether the scientific method is so ill defined, laden with so many subjective judgments, as to make it indistinguishable from other methods of interpreting the world as postmodern rhetoric suggests. Our unmatched scientific knowledge of physics, chemistry, and biology forcefully rejects such a conclusion. Natural science methodology, although far from being exactly defined, is clearly distinguishable from the other methods humans use–intuition, religious, rational–to interpret the world. The distinctive feature that sets natural science methodology apart from other modes of understanding is the combined requirement that scientific data be publicly observable and logically related to the theoretical explanation.

It is impossible at a given time to foretell the future of any theoretical formulation. Thus Popper can be challenged when he equates Freudian theory with astrology because at a given time both were unfalsifiable. The basic assumptions of astrology, it can be argued, are definitely false, whereas Freudian theory, some would suggest, contain kernels of truth that, if properly organized into an empirically meaningful theory could, in principle, become a viable scientific formulation. As time goes by many tough-minded scientists believe this possibility is remote.

PSYCHOLOGY

Psychology is a science in conflict (Kendler, 1981). The unity that characterized its birth as an independent science by Wilhelm Wundt (1832–1920) at the University of Leipzig in 1879 has collapsed. Psychology is burdened with fundamental disputes about what it is, what it should be, and what it can be. Bitter arguments surround the issue as to whether natural science methodology or a distinctly different kind of human science procedure is the appropriate method for psychology. This disagreement has spilled over into controversies about the proper professional role of psychologists. And finally, when the problem of psychology's potential contribution to public policy is approached, harsh clashes make it impossible for the discipline of psychology to speak with one voice about its professional responsibilities and social obligations in a democratic society.

There are several reasons for the chaotic condition in contemporary psychology. Foremost is the dualistic heritage of the mind-body problem. By assuming that human beings represent a union between a psychological mind and a mechanical body, Descartes (1596–1650) set the stage for two kinds of psychology, one of the mind and the other of bodily activity, or behavior. Two centuries later, Wilhelm Wundt established his psychological laboratory, burdened with the task of transforming a dichotomous subject matter into a viable, productive science.

Natural Science Psychology

The mind-body dualism becomes less confusing when it is relocated from armchair philosophy into empirical psychology. Should psychology study private conscious experience or publicly observed behavior? Or can psychology study both within a common scientific orientation? Wundt thought it possible to observe one's own private conscious experience (e.g., an image) as accurately as a physicist observes physical events (e.g., a pointer on a measuring scale). William James (1842–1910) was also optimistic about the precision of self-observation (introspection) that he defined as "looking into our minds and reporting what we there discover" (James, 1890, 185). James believed self-observation would be able to provide a reliable body of facts that could lead to a scientific understanding of the workings of the mind. Although early psychologists disagreed about what was observed in consciousness, James confidently anticipated a harmony of views about the nature of mental events would ultimately be achieved. His optimistic forecast was never realized.

Psychology, during the period the direct examination of consciousness was the main investigatory procedure, was constantly mired in disputes. One prime example was the imageless thought controversy. Introspectors at some laboratories reported that thinking was always accompanied by mental images, while imageless thought was reported at other research centers (Kendler, 1987). Can thought occur without images? A direct answer was not possible because the different methods of self-observation used at different laboratories could confound the influences of the observer with what is observed. Reports of imaged or imageless thought could not result from consciousness itself but instead from different methods of self-observation. If neuroscientists were able to develop an independent neurological measure of imagery then perhaps the question of whether images always accompany thought could be answered. The lack of a publicly verifiable observational base prevents knowledge claims based only on self-observation of mental events from meeting the epistemological requirements of natural science methodology. Natural science methodology demands public–that is, objective–observations. Flimsy data cannot serve as a foundation of a solid science.

The methodological limitations of observing consciousness encouraged a revolutionary conception of psychology among many academic psychologists. For them consciousness exists but cannot serve as the foundation of a natural science psychology. John Watson (1913), self-described *behaviorist,* maintained that psychology is a branch of natural science concerned with the prediction and control of behavior. Later, B. F. Skinner (1904–1990) assumed the mantle of behaviorism by formulating a conception of psychology that had worldwide appeal. He shared with Watson the goal of creating a body of reliable knowledge about the behavior of individual organisms, both animals and humans. Skinner achieved this objective by adopting a Machian view (p. 14) that rejected the notion that theories are necessary to explain behavior. For Skinner, a plain description of an empirical law between the organism's environment and its behavior is sufficient to reveal scientific truth. Reduced to its barest minimum, Skinner formulated a descriptive model of behavior in which an organism's responses are selected by their consequences. When followed by reinforcement, the probability of a response increases. If the response is not reinforced, the probability of its occurrence decreases. What operates as reinforcement is an empirical question that research must answer. For Skinner, only facts are important. If you can, by appropriate conditioning procedures, control the bar-pressing responses of a rat or eliminate the fear of high places among acrophobics, then one understands the behavior. Behavioral control becomes the litmus test of understanding.

Skinner's simple descriptive model of behavior became a target for those psychologists who believed that an organism's tendency to respond fails to reflect fully the subject matter of psychology. The strongest opposition to Skinner's atheoretical approach to psychology occurred at Harvard University, where Skinner held his academic post. J. S. Bruner and George Miller believed that psychology required a concept of mind in order to deal with the full range of cognitive phenomena (e.g., knowledge, memory, thinking, language, etc.) that humans and lower animals exhibit. Bruner and Miller helped found *The Center for Cognitive Studies* at Harvard in 1962. The view from Harvard was that these two contrasting conceptions of psychology, behaviorism, and cognitivism, were incompatible

The truth of the matter is that behaviorism and cognitivism are not incompatible but, instead, are complementary. They refer to two different components of psychology; *methodology* and *theory.* Tolman justified psychology's need for a behavioristic methodology because natural science cannot be based on "private and noncommunicable" events of consciousness (Tolman, 1922, 44). Tolman's *Purposive Behavior in Animals and Men* (1932) proposed a cognitive theory that in learning to get food in the goal box of a maze, rats gradually acquire a cognitive map of the physical structure of the apparatus. In essence, he melded a cognitive theory of behavior with a behavioristic methodology. Cognitive psychology, which postulates a theoretical concept of the mind, is a popular form of psychological theorizing.

Behaviorism, as a methodology, attracted a variety of psychologists, who shared the goal of converting their discipline into a natural science. Clark L. Hull (1884–1952), became one of the most influential twentieth-century theorists in psychology. During his early career he did important research on the influence of tobacco smoking in relation to the efficiency of thinking, learning of concepts, aptitude testing, and hypnosis. In 1929 he was invited to become a research professor at Yale University, where he had previously been rejected to enter graduate school. He attracted a large number of talented graduate students in his effort to construct a hypothetico-deductive theory of learning, initially based on Pavlovian conditioning principles. Hull and his fellow psychologists use the term *stimulus* to describe the relevant feature of the environment such as a red traffic light or a bell that is followed by a pellet of food during classical conditioning. *Response* is the term employed to describe behavior such as pressing the brake when seeing the traffic light or a dog salivating when the bell is sounded. He employed stimulus-response associationistic language (S-R) to represent behavior, but assumed other variables, such as motivation, had to be included to provide an adequate account of behavior. His general theory of behavior was presented in his *Principles of Behavior* (1943) and later modified in his *A Behavior System* (1952).

Kenneth W. Spence (1907–1967) later became his closest collaborator, especially in extending his hypothetico-deductive theory to psychological phenomena that were considered cognitive. For example, his expansion of the theory, properly described as the Hull-Spence model, to two developmental levels. This formulation postulated two levels of stimulus-response behavior. In single-unit responding, animals, such as rats, learn to slowly discriminate between brightness cues (e.g., black vs. white) by gradually associating an approach response to the reinforced cue (e. g., black). Adult humans, in contrast, are capable of responding in a mediational manner by rapidly transforming the distinctive cues of a common dimension, such as white and black, into an internal representation of a dimension (e.g., brightness, size) that guides subsequent behavior. This two-stage model was successful in accounting for developmental changes in children of varying ages (H. H. Kendler and Kendler, 1962, 1975). This expanded stimulus-response model involving two levels of behavior raised questions about whether mechanistic stimulus-response formulations were fundamentally different from cognitive theories that conceptually had ties to consciousness. One answer was Tracy Kendler's (1955) level of information processing model that contained features of both and could ultimately be linked to neurophysiological development. There is no unanimous agreement to the controversial question of whether a model of the mind is necessary for a successful theory of psychology. For the present it is important to distinguish clearly between a model of the mind as an objective theory or as a subjective conception of conscious experience.

To complete the review of different forms of behaviorism demands reference to the efforts of Donald O. Hebb (1904–1985), who received less attention than the other leading behaviorists but perhaps most accurately forecasted future trends in psychology. Hebb's neurobehavioristic approach in psychology is distinctively different from that of Skinner, Tolman, and Hull in that he insists that psychological theory must be based on knowledge of neurophysiological processes. The historical roots of Hebb's theory lie in past efforts to relate behavior to brain function. Although Hebb employed the concept of the mind, it served primarily as a metaphor for brain functioning. Psychology, for Hebb, is part of biology.

Although these four leading forms of behaviorism–descriptive model, cognitive, hypothetico-deductive mechanistic theory, biological–represented different strategies for dealing with psychology, all behaviorists were committed to a natural-science psychology that could meet the standards of objectivity. On the simplest level, behaviorism offered a methodological recipe that could provide an objective knowledge base capable of interpreting and predicting the performance of organisms.

Psychology: A Human Science

The inability of private examinations of consciousness to meet the standards of the scientific method led to a bifurcation in the history of psychology. One path was to reject the notion that psychology need-ed to become a science in the same way as physics, chemistry, and biology. Giambattista Vico (1668–1744), a Neapolitan historian and philosopher, denied that the scientific method used to investigate the physical sciences was the only valid method of scientific inquiry. History, Vico argued, requires a different method than physics be-cause physical events must be observed from the outside while human events must be observed from the inside, within the context of human consciousness. For Vico the science of the social sciences, or what may be better described as the human sciences, is a different kind of sci-ence than that of the physical sciences. Humans studying human events are capable of empathizing, sharing experiences, with those who made history and are thus capable of achieving an intimate acquaintance with their subject matter that is denied the physical sci-entist. Consciousness represents the center of the universe for human beings, serving as the only conduit to the physical and social worlds.

Ever since Vico argued that human scientists seek a different kind of understanding than natural scientists, the tantalizing problem has been to elucidate this difference. A popular distinction is that the natural sci-ences investigate phenomena from the outside with the aim of identi-fying their causes, whereas human sciences study human phenomena from the inside with the goal of revealing subjective meaning (Polkinghorne, 1983). Whereas natural scientists understand a phe-nomenon by an ability to control its occurrence, and by a deductive explanation or by identifying its causes, the human scientist achieves a sense of understanding of a person's activities by revealing the mean-ing, "empathic reexperiencing" (Harrington, 1996), on which the actions were based.

Natural scientists and human scientists have different views about precision and ambiguity. Most natural scientists deal with laws—the pressure and volume of a gas are inversely proportional to one another—of objective "reality" that can be understood with near certainty. In contrast, human scientists, for the most part, recognize that the con-scious experience of another cannot exactly be known or completely shared. Therefore the human scientist is forced to tolerate ambiguous and conflicting interpretations of the mind that cannot be resolved. This failure to establish clear and demanding standards to verify knowledge claims is perceived by natural scientists as reflecting a fundamental inadequacy in the human science enterprise. If one seeks truth but has no means to identify it, then truth is unattainable. This criticism of an intrinsic ambiguity in their knowledge base does not faze the human scientist. The precision of natural science psychology, for the human scientist, fails to compensate for its inability to cope with the inexactitude of sharing conscious experience. Whereas truth in natural science is associated with a match between objective empirical data and theoretical expectations, truth in the human sciences is in some way related to the ability of humans to estimate, inevitably imperfectly, the conscious experience of others. In sum, the search for causes and the search for subjective meaning represents a bifurcation in the search for so-called psychological truth.

This conclusion does not imply that science in general and psychology in particular are totally independent of, or have no use for, evidence based on self observations. The limitations of self-observation have been stressed in regard to natural science methodology and only in relationship to its liabilities as an *exclusive* form of knowledge. But observations of consciousness can be viewed in a different light, not as an end in itself, but as a means of providing information that can be helpful in achieving natural science understanding. Subjective reports about memorizing a series of digits–87309425–indicates that they can be remembered better when they are encoded into four pairs of two digits–87 30 94 25–instead of as a series of eight independent numerals. This finding is useful in emphasizing the theoretical importance of organizing information to improve memory.

Technological advances have led to a deeper understanding of neuropsychological events. A variety of electronic recording techniques (e.g., Positron Emission Tomography, commonly referred to as PET) provide objective evidence of brain activity while a person is engaged in subjective experiences such as problem solving, remembering, and imagining. This information provides objective correlates of conscious experience and therefore contributes a public link to scientific analysis of personal knowledge. Today, psychologists are employing a variety of investigatory techniques, many from neuroscience, to integrate subjective experience with objective data. One must not conclude that successes in objectifying subjective experiences will eliminate the need or desire for a human science conception of psychology. Natural science psychology and human science psychology are antithetical in that they represent opposed ways of interpreting the human world.

FACTS AND VALUES

A common belief is that scientific evidence can validate a public policy. If women who abort their fetuses suffer no greater psychological harm than those who bring their pregnancy to term, then a pro-choice policy ought to be adopted. If bilingual education results in lower academic performance than English-only education, then bilingual education should be abandoned. Both conclusions are a result of faulty logic. There is no logical connection between facts and values; one cannot validate moral rules (social policies) on the basis of empirical evidence alone. Because the natural *is* cannot deductively generate the moral *ought,* it becomes a non sequitur to conclude that psychological facts can validate a public policy.

Two compelling philosophical conclusions, centuries old, reject the idea that facts can justify moral positions. David Hume (1717–1776) and G. E. Moore (1873–1958) offered persuasive arguments that an unbridgeable gap exists between facts and values. Hume proposed the *fact/value dichotomy* that insisted "ought" statements cannot be logically derived from "is" propositions. Moore's *naturalistic fallacy* contends moral statements, "good" and "bad," do not have counterparts in physical reality and therefore cannot be justified by natural events. The conclusion is clear. Empirical facts cannot lead *directly* to moral conclusions.

The fact/value dichotomy and the naturalistic fallacy do not imply that empirical facts are irrelevant to society's policy decisions. Knowing the empirical consequences of controversial political policies, such as abortion, would help those who are not committed to either a pro-life or pro-choice position. Major (1998) found that over a two-year span the risk of a depression is no greater than if an unplanned pregnancy is brought to term. This finding contradicted the statements of pro-life politicians who proclaimed that the risk of having a depression following an abortion is high. Major's findings would not influence the opinions of committed pro-choicers except possibly to increase their belief in the moral correctness of their attitude. Similarly the opinion of the impassioned pro-lifers would not be swayed by Major's data because their attitude is purely an expression of deep-seated moral commitment. For the uncommitted, Major's data could be decisive. Such an individual might view abortion purely as a political problem, not a moral one, and therefore favor the policy that would gain the strongest support. Social policy can be "determined in the light of facts, but is not deduced from them" (Passmore, 1953, p. 675). Reliable empirical evidence can assist a democracy in selecting the policy that reflects "the will of the people." In sum, facts alone do not determine public policy but, in combination with a democratic ethic, they can assist in forming political decisions.

Although the logic of the fact/value dichotomy appears impeccable, it is nevertheless unacceptable for many. For them a conviction prevails that nature can offer clues that reveal a valid ethical system. Unfortunately, for most, this assumption is adopted without any attempt to demonstrate its validity.

Nature's Search for Human Values

The search for a moral code within nature has been, and continues to be, an enduring venture. Ancient Greek philosophers proposed that the moral code underlying the legal systems of all societies was dictated by natural law, a pervasive ethical system that is embedded in nature. Natural law is opposed to positive law that assumes that humans create their own morality that is subject to change, in contrast to the eternal moral truths that are prescribed by natural law. The Stoics suggested that moral guidance could be achieved by living in harmony with nature. Thomas Aquinas (1225–1274) proposed that all people, regardless of their religious outlook, were governed by natural law but the revealed law of Christianity provides additional moral insight. Spinoza and Rousseau, both philosophers, assumed rational thought could reveal the principles of human morality that is embedded in natural law. Natural law was considered to be the origin of the democratic and egalitarian ideals that served as the driving force behind the American and French revolutions. In the late nineteenth century, natural law was challenged by the rise of empiricism, positivism, and materialism, all of which questioned, in one way or another, the existential basis of natural law. An obvious limitation of natural law is its intrinsic ambiguity: It has been used to justify incompatible political goals such as a monarchy or a democracy. Without being burdened by meeting some standard of empirical proof, natural law served as an appealing idea to justify one's philosophical predilections. The rigorous thinking that was encouraged during the scientific age helped undermine the popularity of natural law although it still has its adherents.

Although natural law still has an appeal, its justification has been subverted by its contradictory implications. Natural law failed in its mission to offer a positive conception of morality but, nevertheless, left a void that challenged evolutionists, philosophers, and social scientists to fill.

Darwinian evolution has suggested a basis for a natural morality. Endowing evolution with a purpose would generate a moral code consistent with the evolutionary objective. This position has taken many forms varying from evolutionary principles that are interpreted to suggest that survival is the ultimate moral imperative, to the transcendental view that biological organisms strive toward some ideal state. This line of reasoning has been rejected vigorously by Dawkins (1986), an evolutionary biologist.

> Natural selection, the blind, unconscious, automatic process, which Darwin discovered and which we now know is the explanation for the existence and apparently purposeful form of all life, has no purpose in mind. . . . It does not plan for the future. It has no vision, no foresight, no sight at all. (5)

Survival per se is not a universal property of the biological world. Individual organisms die in the struggle for species survival and species expire because of their inability to adapt to their environment. The evolutionary principle of natural selection encourages death and extinction as well as life and survival. Survival and extinction are the opposite sides of the evolutionary coin.

The notion that organisms strive toward an ideal state has no basis in fact or theory. Which one of the fourteen species of the Galapagos finches, all presumably descended from one species, has approximated most closely the ideal finch (Lack, 1947)? Which one of the 300 species of cichlid fishes in Lake Victoria expresses the perfect cichlid (Johnson et al., 1996)? No answer is forthcoming because the anatomical structure of each species has evolved as a function of natural selection, not to achieve a standard of perfection. The past, not the future, determines the structure of species. The evolution of organisms is controlled by ecology, not by some transcendental goal.

John Rawls' *A Theory of Justice* (1971) held high hopes for some of providing a moral code that could be adopted because of its intrinsic decency. The key idea of his idealistic moral theory, proposed for a democracy, is "justice as fairness." The pursuit of the "good" was transformed into an ethical imperative that social reform should maximally benefit the least advantaged, a position that was assumed, as natural law postulated, to be consistent with human nature. Rawls later realized that conflicting moral theories could gain adherents in a democracy and consequently his theory of justice represents a political formulation, not a normative conception.

Rawls' political theory, *Political Liberalism* (1993), assumed that a democratic society ought to be shaped in the direction of caring for the least fortunate. One postulate of his liberal formulation "gives a woman a duly qualified right to decide whether or not to end her pregnancy during the first trimester" (1993, 243). Although I share Rawls' attitude, it will not be considered "reasonable" by those who consider abortion to be a mortal sin or a practice that promotes human coarseness. Although Rawls has proposed a compassionate moral theory, it does not follow that it will be embraced by all.

A persistent idea, too attractive to be abandoned, is that humans have an innate moral code based on their biology. Hauser (2006), a psychologist, essentially adopts this principle. He fails, however, to distinguish between two possible meanings of the biological underpinnings of humans. One is the general idea that cannot be disputed. Everything we do, or don't do, is based on our biological structure. We see colors because of the cones on our retina. We don't fly because our arms cannot function as wings of a bird. A specific biological theory of morality demands identifying the physiological cause of ethical codes such as those that govern western democracies and Islamic autocracies. The basic question is whether such differences are a function of our biological learning mechanisms or our innate physiological structure.

The tantalizing aspect of an innate moral sense is that it presumably identifies a *righteous* moral code. James Q. Wilson (1993), a distinguished and broad-based social scientist, postulates that human nature contains the *seeds* of an ethical code that predisposes people toward certain moral principles and away from others. Unlike many natural law theorists, Wilson denies that humans are predisposed to a specific universal moral code, an ethical system that is demanded by human nature. Instead, he assumes a more cautious stance in suggesting that humans are predisposed toward a variety of moral sentiments, particularly four that he emphasizes and attempts to justify by empirical evidence: sympathy, fairness, self-control, and duty. In essence he proposes:

> People have a natural moral sense, a sense that is formed out of the interaction of their innate dispositions with their earliest familial experiences. To different degrees among different people, but to some important degree in almost all people, that moral sense shapes human behavior and the judgment people make of the behavior of others. (Wilson, 1993, 2)

Although we are not all genetically predestined to adopt a shared universal ethical system, we are nevertheless guided by our heredity to value sympathy, fairness, self-control, and duty.

> To say that people have a moral sense is not the same as saying that they are innately good. A moral sense must compete with other senses that are natural to humans—the desire to survive, acquire possessions, indulge in sex, or accumulate power—in short, with self-interest narrowly defined. How that struggle is resolved will differ depending on our character, our circumstances, and the cultural and political tendencies of the day. But saying that a moral sense exists is the same thing as saying that humans, by their nature, are potentially good. (Wilson, 1993, 12)

Wilson's conclusion brings to mind a comment attributed to Isaac Bashevis Singer, the Yiddish writer and Nobel Laureate. When asked whether he believes in God, he replied, "I'm not sure about God but I know there is a Devil." Singer's comment neutralizes Wilson's potential for human goodness with an equally justified potential for human badness, examples of which abound in this day and age as well as throughout history (e.g., suicide bombers, ethnic cleansing, rape as a political weapon, sadistic murders). A more productive approach than romanticizing human morality would be to discover the variables that influence "moral" predispositions and their behavioral manifestations, both "good" and "bad." Knowledge about such predispositions can be employed in shaping public policy. But the important point, even accepting the empirical validity of Wilson's predispositions, is that they are incapable of logically justifying a social policy. To be specific, would this set of four moral predispositions endorse or reject the policy of legalized abortions or affirmative action? Such social choices in a democracy are a result of political decisions, not empirical evidence.

Psychology's Efforts to Bridge the Fact/Value Gap

Natural science methodology contradicts natural law. Nothing in nature can validate moral principles! In spite of this, natural science has developed an implicit moral code that must be obeyed for science to operate productively. Doesn't this discrepancy suggest that science is capable of generating a moral code? The answer resides in a brief description of science's moral guidelines.

Although there is no written constitution, two interrelated principles are understood by most scientists to be essential in the scientific endeavor. The first is honesty. Science progresses by empirical advancement and theoretical refinement. Lying and cheating can obstruct progress, as has been shown too frequently in the past few years (Couzin and Unger, 2006). False information, however, is not necessarily a result of deception. Without knowing the exact reasons, a researcher can report results that cannot be replicated. Only replicated research should be considered as reliable scientific evidence.

Honesty and the principle of replication are guidelines for scientific research, but their epistemological status is not equivalent to the fact/value dichotomy in natural science methodology. Honesty, for example, is a functional property of the scientific method in that it enables science to function more effectively. The fact/value dichotomy, in contrast, is a logically demanded consequence of natural science methodology.

Another important distinction to be made in the analysis of the foundations of morality is between *moral realism* and *moral pluralism*. As the term implies, moral realism assumes that moral principles exist in the same sense as physical laws; they share a reality status that underlies their truth. A common explanation for a "factual morality" is a Supreme Being who has imposed moral principles on humanity that ought to be obeyed (religious fundamentalism). A realistic foundation of morality can also be an expression of a political philosophy that assumes humanity is preprogrammed to adopt and utilize a given moral system (Nazism, Marxism). Equivalent views operate in dictatorships. Regardless of where they are articulated, the moral system is conceptualized as being valid, right, and true.

Moral pluralism exists in a society that tolerates a variety of ethical positions, both religious and political. An eloquent advocate of this form of social organization is Isaiah Berlin, who was convinced that the absolute claims of one form of moral realism would inevitably be challenged by competing conceptions. Thus moral conflicts, both personal and social, cannot be avoided; they are "an inescapable characteristic of the human condition" (Berlin, 1958, 54). Although unavoidable, their consequences can vary within an open society that allows for free expression of competing moral positions, as contrasted with a closed society that imposes one code on all.

Without minimizing the social importance of ethical systems that are embedded in religious or political conceptions, it must be understood, as has been proposed, that their relationship to science is indirect. Natural science methodology has no evaluative connection to moral principles other than those required for its own functioning. This failure need not be perceived as a misfortune if we acknowledge that moral conflicts are unavoidable. Dictatorships are threatened by rejected codes, while democracies are challenged by irreconcilable disputes.

In spite of psychology's inability to validate a specific morality, numerous segments of the psychological community persist in this effort. Why? Some natural science psychologists with their apparent commitment to objectivity find it difficult to reject the seductive belief that psychology has the capacity to reveal a universal set of moral principles to guide human conduct. Other psychologists do not accept the notion that their discipline is a natural science and, consequently, they believe that they are capable of identifying moral principles that are right for humanity.

An illustration of both reasons will serve as the springboard for our discussion. The "father" of experimental psychology, Wilhelm Wundt, had no hesitation in concluding that Germany was morally justified during World War I. As a psychologist he argued that Germany had attained a better, a morally superior, society than did the Americans and British. Whereas German society had a proper balance between the needs of the state and the individuals, American and British societies were plagued by excessive individualism and materialism.

Wundt's conclusion can be faulted in two ways. First, by failing to develop a scale of social organization, he offered no compelling evidence to demonstrate that Germany had a superior social balance between the needs of individuals and the larger society. Unless one attributed to Wundt a capacity to determine factual truth without empirical investigation, one would be forced to reject his reasoning. Wundt's decision about Germany's "moral superiority" also fails to demonstrate how possible psychological evidence can transform *is* into *ought.* But his argument does suggest a semantic confusion in his belief that facts can justify values. He conflated the meanings of *good* and *better.* Good, an ethical concept, means righteous, virtuous, while better, in an empirical sense, refers to a superior or higher level of some dimensional value. A gross domestic product of 100 billion dollars is better than one of 5 billion while an IQ of 160 is better than one of 120, but the higher (better) value is no more virtuous or righteous than the lower value. Wundt misled himself into believing that a higher level of social organization is morally superior to a lower level.

The theme of identifying what is *truly* human is repeated by one of the founders of humanistic psychology, Abraham Maslow (1908–1970). Although he was trained as an experimental psychologist, he shifted his orientation to humanistic psychology during the early part of his career. He formulated a theory of motivation that assumed a hierarchy of human needs. At the lowest level are the basic motivational drives of hunger, thirst, and sex, followed in ascending order by safety needs, social belonging wants, and a demand to achieve self-respect. At the top rung is the need for self-actualization, "the desire to become more and more what one is, to become everything that one is capable of becoming" (Maslow, 1954, 92). Maslow assumed that self-actualized individuals are the healthiest because they achieved the highest level of the human potential. Consequently their value system, Maslow reasoned, represented "the ultimate values by which humanity should live" (Maslow, 1961, 5). These values were truth, goodness, beauty, gaiety, justice, and joy. In addition, the self-actualized person reports having peak experiences: Feelings of being fused into one with the rest of the world, and living fully in the present, free from thoughts of the past and the future.

Although the empirical base of Maslow's psychological conclusions can be challenged, the present concern is limited to the ethical implications of such evidence. First is the intrinsic ambiguity of Maslow's "ultimate values." Consider *justice, beauty,* and *goodness.* Supreme Court Justices disagree about the meaning of *justice,* art critics clash over their interpretation of *beauty,* and religious leaders and philosophers have different answers to the meaning of *good*. These basic disagreements about the meaning of moral terms become greater among different countries throughout the world.

Maslow (Kendler, 1987) succumbed to the same seductive error as did Wundt by confusing better, in an empirical sense, with good in the moral sense. He, too, created his own data to validate his moral beliefs. He proposed that self-actualized people, those who have achieved the pinnacle of personality development, embrace valid moral commitments (Goble, 1971). Because self-actualized people achieve the highest level of psychological development, their values reflect the ultimate form of human morality. Maslow decided to identify this psychologically valid ethical system by collecting information about a group of self-actualized people: Jefferson, Einstein, Lincoln, Eleanor Roosevelt, and some of Maslow's friends and acquaintance, and probably himself (Kendler, 2002). As a group, Maslow described them as individuals who identified with humankind and were realistic, spiritual in a humanistic sense, accepting of themselves, nonconforming spontaneous, and humorous in a philosophical as opposed to a hostile sense. From this kind of evidence, Maslow drew his conclusions:

> You can find the values by which mankind must live, and for which man has always sought, by digging into the best people in depth. I believe . . . that I can find ultimate values, which are right for mankind, by observing the best of mankind. . . . If under the best conditions and in the best specimens I simply stand aside and describe in a scientific way what these human values are, the old values of truth, goodness, and beauty and some additional ones as well–for instance, gaiety, justice, and joy. (Maslow, 1961, 5–6)

Although Maslow views his conclusions to be scientific, they are actually a self-induced tautology. The "best people" are not determined independently of the moral beliefs they hold. By selecting those he considered the "best people," Maslow guarantees that his own values will prevail as the ones that are right for humankind. Suppose another psychologist, enamored with pragmatism, judged William Gates, Warren Buffet, Henry Kissinger, and Andrew Carnegie to be prime examples of self-actualized individuals. Or perhaps another psychologist, fascinated with the irony of life, selects Woody Allen and Groucho Marx as first-class examples of self-fulfilled characters. Or consider a variation of the present theme. Would Maslow have considered Eleanor Roosevelt to be self-actualized if she had divorced Franklin Roosevelt because of marital infidelities, and become a Republican who espoused a market economy as the most effective economic plan to help the poor and disadvantaged? The conclusion should be clear. Both Wundt and Maslow misled themselves and their audience into believing that psychology is capable of validating moral principles.

Phenomenology is a philosophical orientation that emerged in Western Europe during the twentieth century. It shares with the discipline of psychology a concern with human consciousness. How consciousness should be observed and interpreted, as already noted, has been a source of debate within psychology since its birth as a laboratory science. The basic conflict was whether introspectors, observers of consciousness, require special training. Phenomenology is also involved with the observation of consciousness, but in a manner radically different from introspective psychology. Phenomenologists seek to describe consciousness completely free of preconceptions, especially those stemming from a natural science orientation. Phenomenological psychologists demand that conscious experience be detached from assumptions about reality, causation, existence, and absolute truth. In this way they reject naturalism as appropriate orientations for their field. They focus on historical and cultural factors, seeking to interpret them in an intuitive, reflective fashion. Natural science psychologists can easily find phenomenology incomprehensible because of the difficulty, or impossibility, of suspending one's beliefs about living in a real world.

There are a variety of phenomenological approaches emphasizing different aspects of human existence, e.g., sociology, history, religion, and so forth. They all share a major concern with comprehending and interpreting existence within the context of one's inner world. Although phenomenologists do not directly address problems of morality, it frequently becomes a byproduct of their existential conclusions (Kendler, 2005). Perhaps the best-known conception is Heidegger's treatment of *being*–what it is to be *truly* human. By realizing life's existential meaning, one can live an *authentic life* that is distinguished by such dispositions as commitment, integrity, courage, steadiness, and clear-sightedness. An inauthentic life, in contrast, is disjointed and directionless.

An interesting attempt to validate a moral code emerges from Kohlberg's (1971, 1981) effort to construct a scale of moral development. Instead of pretending to offer empirical evidence as did Wundt and Maslow, Kohlberg offered hard data that traced changes in moral reasoning with age. His results indicated that moral reasoning advanced with age through a series of stages in which initially egocentric concerns dominated, followed by period of acceptance of established authority, and finally a stage in which moral reasoning expressed a concern for a common welfare and a commitment to abstract principles of justice.

Although Kohlberg's scale has not escaped criticism (Gilligan, 1982; Kohlberg, Levine, and Hewer, 1983; Puka, 1994), it can nevertheless serve as a model for evaluating the moral implication of developmental changes in moral reasoning. The blunt question is whether the highest level of moral development, the Golden Rule, (e.g., Do unto others as you would have them do unto you) becomes an ethical imperative simply because it represents the highest level of moral reasoning? According to the principle underlying the naturalistic fallacy, the absence of a logical relationship between facts and values, the answer must be "No." But it must be noted that the denial of a logical relationship does not imply an absence of a functional relationship. Although empirical results cannot logically assign moral authority to an ethical principle, moral imperatives can nevertheless have different psychological and social consequences. To be specific, a scale of moral development would locate the Golden Rule at a higher stage of development than the Old Testament maxim, "An eye for an eye and a tooth for a tooth." Although the Golden Rule is not any more valid than the less mature principle, they obviously encourage different forms of behavior. The Golden Rule, for argument sake, would be more effective in creating cohesiveness among members of a social group, such as a family, than an ethic of retaliation, but such a moral predisposition could be more effective than the Golden Rule in combating a ruthless enemy such as the Nazis during World War II or as some would say, Militant Islam today.

A frontal assault on the fact/value dichotomy appears to be doomed to failure because of the logical impossibility of demonstrating that *is* is equivalent to *ought*. Perhaps an oblique approach, an end run, can accomplish what a direct assault cannot. An intriguing and revealing attempt is that of M. Brewster Smith, a humanistic psychologist, who readily and refreshingly acknowledges that there is "no magic bridge between facts and values" (Smith, 1991, 68) but nevertheless insists that psychology can advocate specific public policies without compromising its detached and unbiased scientific integrity. This becomes possible when one embraces the science of psychology with humanistic values:

> I have struggled to make sense of an emerging three-way commitment: to a psychology that seeks to come to grips with human experience (and in that sense is "humanistic"), to a psychology that broadly abides by the game of science as a public, self critical, and therefore cumulative enterprise aimed at the comprehensive understanding of the phenomenon in its territory, and to one that bears helpfully on the urgent social problems that hinge on an ingredient of human cussedness. (Smith, 1991, xi)

To rephrase Smith's orientation in a less personal fashion, a tripartite approach to psychology has been proposed, which includes methodological commitments to human experience as a core subject matter of psychology, the canons of science as a public form of inquiry to determine empirical truth, and a sense of professional responsibility for psychology to take a stand on matters of public interest.

Conscious experience as a core subject matter of psychology, as already noted, has been a source of debate since psychology gained its status as an independent discipline. Smith offers a fresh slant on the relation between consciousness and ethics.

> From the perspective of each of us, what we regard as desirable or preferable, what we feel we ought to want or do, seems to be objectively given, not a matter of our personal whim. Even if we are tolerant of other people's different values, we are convinced of the rightness of our own. Values as the explicit or implicit standards involved in these occasions of valuing have the quality of objective requiredness. . . . The quality of experienced objectivity seems important in the role that values play in giving sense and direction to our lives. (Smith, 1991, 5–6)

Smith is arguing against a radical cultural relativism that depicts moral values as merely social customs. Such a position ignores the possibility of moral predispositions being expressions of biological evolution. Rather than adopt an environmental-hereditary interactionist viewpoint, Smith goes one step further and suggests a humanistic value system that pervades human consciousness and is objectively required. Although the exact meaning of this phenomenal quality of "objective requiredness" is ambiguous, it nevertheless is sufficiently persuasive to allow Smith to conclude that the American Psychological Association, an organization of which Smith was president, has not only a right, but a duty, to promote social policies that are in the public interest, those that he defines as consistent with "humane values" (1991, 185). The root problem, according to Smith, is that "we psychologists have given the sanction of science uncritically to implicit individualistic values that are, of course, preempirical, not legitimately accessible to 'scientific' support on such lines" (185). In contradiction to his previous renunciation of a bridge between facts and values, Smith entertains the view that individualistic values can be rejected by empirical evidence in favor of communitarian values. Finally, he arrives at this tortured conclusion:

> For better or worse, we are stuck in a pluralistic society and world in which there is little prospect of our agreeing on first premises about abortion, the meaning of gender, or any of the things that people seem still to be ready to fight about, including religion and nationhood. Nevertheless, I want to endorse the essence of Lippman's (1955) conception of public interest and to argue that even without consensus on fundamentals, we can do much better than is usual for us by trying, in our leadership and individually, to emphasize informed, rational, disinterested, benevolent decision making. Just as in our scientific roles we should and most do act as if there were truth "out there" that we only have to be clever enough to discover . . . [that] in our personal, political, and psychologist roles we also do well to act as if there are objective right and wrong, better and worse choices and policies. We are surely mistaken if we have the presumption to believe we are absolutely right about our own choices, just as we are mistaken if we are sure about the absolute truth of our factual beliefs. But we are adrift as persons and useless as citizens if we do not try to find and pursue the right and if we do not take our own convictions—and those of our opponents—seriously as attempts to advance the right and give it reality. We become literally "de-moralized." (Smith, 1991, 188–189)

Smith's fundamental error is that he confuses his position as a scientific psychologist with that of Walter Lippman, a political philosopher. Lippman (1955) in attempting to pin down the meaning of public interest, concludes "that the public interest may be presumed to be what men would choose if they saw clearly, thought rationally, acted disinterestedly and benevolently" (41–42). He then goes on to suggest that the "free political institutions of the Western World were conceived and established by optimistic men who believed that honest reflection on the common experience of mankind would always cause men to come to the same ultimate conclusions" (134). In other words, the political processes of a democratic society can reveal the public interest. This position dovetails with a descriptive psychology that attempts to discover the empirical consequences of different social policies so that a democratic society can make knowledgeable choices among competing social policies. Lippman's position expresses the moral part of the fact/value dichotomy; the moral choice is the democratic choice. Smith's position, in contrast, assigns to psychologists and their professional associations the power to divine the moral choice. For example, the American Psychological Association tells society that the Equal Rights Amendment should have been ratified, that the United States should have agreed to a nuclear freeze with the Soviet Union, that abortion is morally justified, and so forth. Such public-interest declarations are not expressions of democratic processes, as Lippman favors; they are expressions of belief that psychology and psychologists have a pipeline to moral truths. In spite of all Smith's uncertainties about reaching such social policy conclusions–absence of a magic carpet between facts and values, conflicting views of psychologists about social policy issues–he nevertheless commits the science of psychology to operate as a political force without fully appreciating the risks of such actions to psychology and society.

The basic threat may lie with Smith's assumption that we should act as if moral truth can be discovered in our conscious experience. Harrington's (1996) treatment of holism in German culture reveals in frightening detail that the logic that justifies the assumption that moral truths can be directly revealed in conscious experience can also, with equal force, justify Nazi values or those of Militant Islam.

Philip Handler (1980), former President of the National Academy of Science, expressed the principle that when scientists testify about the relevance of scientific information to social policy they "best serve public policy by living within the ethics of science, not those of politics" (1093). Richard C. Atkinson, a theoretical psychologist, formerly Director of the National Science Foundation and past President of the University of California, strongly believes in the Handler principle but regretfully notes that it has failed to be adopted by many socially active psychologists. In an address to the American Psychological Association, he noted:

> There are many reasons behind this country's current attitude toward the social sciences. But I want to emphasize that we as social scientists have contributed to this state of affairs. We have done so by not being careful enough in drawing a sharp distinction between our role as scientists versus another role—that of political advocate and policymaker. The psychologist's job as a scientist is to search for data, principles, and laws that enlarge our understanding of psychological phenomena. But too often, in reporting research findings, we become advocates for a particular public policy. There is no reason why psychologists should not advocate political viewpoints, but they should advocate them only as individual citizens. The psychologist's role as a scientist is to set forth the facts, and to set forth these facts in as value-free fashion as possible. It is the job of the citizens of this country and their elected representatives to use those facts in making policy decisions. Too often I have witnessed psychologists speaking on education, child rearing, social institutions, and mental health, using what they claim is research evidence as a disguise for advocating a particular public policy. Psychologists and social scientists, more so than other scientists, need to distinguish carefully between providing data and making policy. . . . Most disturbing to me is the psychologist who, on the basis of flimsiest data, make pronouncements as if they were backed by the full weight of science. (Atkinson, 1977, 207–208)

Atkinson offered a pessimistic prediction about the continued politicization of psychology that, it should be noted, has accelerated in past decades: "To permit psychology to be misused as an advocate for public policy will lead inevitably to the demise of the field" (1977, 210). All psychological research is viewed with suspicion when only some are designed to achieve political goals. Thus both society and psychology suffer; society loses the benefits of sound psychological knowledge that can guide the formation of social policy, and psychology loses the respect and support of a democratic society that is needed to achieve its scientific potentialities.

The barrier that isolates *is* from *ought* cannot be breached, no matter how much one tries. Instead of seeing it as an obstacle, the barrier should be perceived as a challenge. The human condition, which reflects the enormous range of individual and social differences as well as the impact of a myriad of environmental and genetic interactions, cannot be served by a narrow moral code created by those—political fanatics, religious zealots, methodologically naïve psychologists—who are convinced that they know what is ethically valid. Instead, humankind has to pragmatically create its own moral code to serve its diverse needs. In that endeavor natural science psychology, as well as other social sciences, can help, but not dictate.

Chapter 2

INDIVIDUAL AND GROUP DIFFERENCES
IN PSYCHOLOGICAL ABILITIES

N ow that the intersection of *ethics, science,* and *psychology* has been examined, we are in a position to explore its implications for the adoption of social policies in a democratic society. The major conclusion drawn is that the "combined wisdom" of *ethics, science,* and *psychology* is unable to reveal social policies that are morally right. But the intersection of the three disciplines can hopefully yield information that can encourage judicious choices. Three assumptions will serve as guidelines in one of the most controversial and emotionally-laden topics in American society: Individual and group differences in psychological abilities. One premise is that psychology can provide reliable evidence about human performance. The second thesis is that empirical evidence by itself is incapable of identifying the morally correct social policy. Third, a democracy can make more effective policy decisions in light of trustworthy data.

Can all these assumptions be transformed into effective social programs in a political democracy such as the United States? That depends on the ability of the profession of psychology to provide reliable and valid information about psychological facts and theories. One obstacle in achieving this goal is, as already noted, the fact that psychology is not a unified discipline in regard to a commitment to the tenets of natural science methodology. In addition, of supreme importance, self-confessed natural scientists do not necessarily share a common *ideology* about the interaction between science and society. For the purpose of our discussion, ideology can be defined as a comprehensive vision of the nature and structure of a desirable sociopolitical entity.

Do ideological commitments influence the development of science and the nature of scientific knowledge? History provides an unequivocal answer. The history of the twentieth century, during which time the major part of the author's career was spent (Kendler, 2002), illustrate how science was shaped by ideological goals in both Germany and Russia. Following World War I, Germany developed a creative scientific culture that was destroyed after the Nazis gained control under the leadership of Adolph Hitler. The ideology of an Aryan master race combined with a mission to defend Germany against its enemies, most notably communism, Jews, and nations that challenged Germany's destiny to be supreme, forced science to be subservient to Nazi dogma. Many scientists who failed to qualify as Aryans fled the country, while the education of future scientists was limited to the "racially acceptable." The history of Nazi Germany illustrates how ideological commitments can stunt the growth of science and technology.

The science of genetics was also impeded in the Soviet Union in a direction opposite to what occurred in Germany. The agronomist Trofin Lysenko (1898–1976) proposed a theory of inheritance of acquired characteristics for agricultural crops that denied genes existed in nature. Stalin adopted his position because it was consistent with Marxist ideology that emphasized the importance of environmental influences in the biological and social worlds. In spite of the fact that Lysenkoism was destructive to Soviet agriculture it persisted for three decades because of its ideological virtues.

EGALITARIANISM AND ELITISM

American society is racked by stresses and strains. The clash between *egalitarianism,* all people are equal, and *elitism,* some people are superior to others, tops the list of conflicts that undermine social harmony. Although they appear incompatible, the two concepts are not discordant. They apply to different worlds. Egalitarianism is a moral principle that expresses the democratic ideal, that all individuals, regardless of their social status, should be treated equally before the law. Elitism refers to the world of behavior when it asserts, consistent with empirical evidence, that some individuals are clearly superior to others in specific skills. Albert Einstein, the physicist, and Tiger Woods, the star golfer, are clearly members of the elite of their respective vocations. Albert Einstein is generally considered superior to every physicist of his generation, or any other generation. Tiger Woods is superior to any golfer of his generation, or perhaps any other generation. But Albert Einstein is not superior to Tiger Woods nor is Tiger Woods superior to Albert Einstein. Such a comparison cannot be reduced to a simple empirical comparison because their respective virtues involve different skills. Evaluating their relative merits demands a value judgment as to which skill is more important. One could suggest that Einstein's achievements had a greater historical influence but on the other hand one could argue that Tiger Woods gave more pleasure to more people. But in the final analysis, we should recognize that we are comparing two incommensurable entities like physics and golf, like apples and oranges.

Emphasizing the distinction between moral judgments and empirical events serves as preparation for a rational discussion of such controversial topics as the nature of intelligence, and environmental and hereditary influences on cognitive behavior. The critical issues in this discussion are whether social agreement can be achieved about the meaning of intelligence and whether a democracy can cope with the inevitable debates about the appropriate social policy to adopt in regard to individual differences in intelligence.

APTITUDE TESTS

Soon after I completed my Ph.D. in psychology during World War II, I participated in applied research for the Psychological Corporation, under contract to the governmental Office of Scientific Research and Development. The task was to improve the Navy's training program for radio (Morse) code operators. Morse code is a system of communication in which patterns of auditory signals, consisting of dits and dahs, represent different letters of the alphabet (e.g., A, dit-dah; B, dah-dit-dit-dit).

Learning to send and receive radio code is an exacting task, beyond the capacity of many who try to learn. A two-pronged attack was directed at improving the Navy's program in training this skill. First, a psychological test was constructed in an effort to identify those sailors who could become proficient radio code operators. Second, my responsibility as a specialist in learning theory was to develop a training program superior to the one operating in the Navy. Behind my commitment to the psychology of learning was an attitude that was encouraged by a popular American view. Education was the means by which individuals and society could solve their problems. This position was challenged to some extent by the results of our research project. Whereas my training plan slightly improved the achievement scores at the end of the training, the 30-minute aptitude test dramatically improved the efficiency of the entire Navy's radio code program.

If a group of newly inducted sailors were randomly selected, 40 percent would fail the learning course in radio code. Training 10,000 sailors for approximately five weeks to obtain 6,000 radio code operators would be a doubly wasteful procedure. The school wastes time and effort in training 4,000 failures and these sailors, in turn, waste five weeks that could be better spent acquiring skills for which they had more aptitude, more potential to perform effectively. With the assistance of the 30-minute aptitude test (Kurtz, 1944) the number of failures was reduced to 6 percent. When compared to the 40 percent failure rate for unselected trainees, the test must be judged a great practical success.

This brief description of the radio code aptitude test enables us to focus on problems that are relevant to aptitude tests in general. The first issue is whether the radio code aptitude test can claim to be a product of natural science methodology. In the language of natural science, an empirical law was established between two independent measures: scores on the aptitude test and performance in radio code school. This empirical relationship permitted the use of behavioral measures obtained on the aptitude test to predict behavior exhibited in radio code school. Are the concepts of radio code aptitude and radio code test performance similar to such concepts as asteroid in astronomy or cell in biology? Yes, in the sense they are all publicly observable. One can suggest a difference in that both the asteroid and cell, as contrasted to aptitude test score and school performance, have an independent material existence. An aptitude test score or school performance is an attribute of behavior, not a material physiological and biological entity. One cannot locate the exact neurophysiological site of the radio code aptitude, but a good guess would be that it is located in parts of the auditory system and the brain. But for the present we must acknowledge that the meaning of an aptitude test resides in observations about behavior, scores obtained on a standardized aptitude test.

A possible source of misunderstanding about the empirical relationship between the radio code aptitude test score and radio code test performance must be guarded against. The concept of an aptitude test that measures the potentiality of individuals for performing a particular task is neutral in regard to the cause of the capacity. The more neutral term *assessment* is sometimes substituted for aptitude because it is less suggestive of a genetic basis. Aptitude (assessment) tests measure behavior at a given time in a given situation without providing any clue as to its hereditary or environmental correlates. Such influences can only be determined by additional research.

To convey the social value of aptitude tests, one can briefly summarize their effectiveness in predicting success in graduate schools for the past 80 years, in a variety of disciplines including medicine, law, physics, humanities, biology, psychology, and others. Most assessment tests predict performance in graduate schools better than prior college grades but, in combination, the estimate is improved. These tests also predict research productivity in professional careers (Kuncel and Hezlett, 2007).

Let us now turn to the moral aspects of aptitude testing. For example, does not the effectiveness of the radio code aptitude test automatically justify its use? If it is so effective and efficient then it must be used! If so, then facts logically dictate values! But such a conclusion is too easily drawn. The use of every aptitude test has moral implications. A small percentage of subjects, known as false negatives, whose scores were too low on the aptitude test to qualify for radio code school, could have succeeded, if given the opportunity, to become naval radio code operators. The "defects" of the aptitude test prevented this from occurring, thus forcing these false negatives to be reassigned, perhaps leading to their injury or even to their death. In a similar vein, one might speculate that some of the false positives, the 6 percent who passed the aptitude test and failed in school, suffered a lowered self-esteem that contributed to later adjustment problems. In a larger framework, the aptitude (assessment) test was part and parcel of the entire war effort; thereby its use was consistent with the moral purpose of World War II.

I can be accused of indulging in overkill to demonstrate that moral choices are involved in decisions that for some may appear as an obvious necessity. Toilet training a child represents a moral choice that favors society's conventions over the free expression of a child's needs. But the moral conflicts embedded in a radio code aptitude test and toilet training are overlooked because their consequences are so favored by most of society that their ethical implications are ignored. This discussion prepares us to deal with the question of whether a qualitative difference prevails between a radio code aptitude test and an academic aptitude test that is more commonly referred to as an intelligence test.

Intelligence Testing

Efforts to define intelligence have generated much confusion. The main reason for this turmoil is that intelligence does not exist in nature as do the physical concepts of weight and mass. Recall that Moore pointed to a similar problem when analyzing the term *morality* (p. 26). He formulated the *naturalistic fallacy* that maintained that moral terms do not have counterparts in physical reality and therefore cannot be justified by natural events. The result is that meanings of ethical concepts such as *good* and *bad,* and *right* and *wrong* have to be invented. Inevitably different definitions will be assigned to these ethical concepts and, as a consequence, moral conflicts will occur within cultures and between cultures.

The concept of *intelligence* is similar to that of *morality* in that they are both notional; they are socially created ideas. People differ in their ability to understand, communicate, reason, solve problems, in short, to act intelligently. We observe these differences in the behavior of individuals not in their neurophysiological functioning. In other words, intelligence is an attribute of behavior, not a material entity. Thus, according to intelligence-is-behavior interpretation the first practical step in understanding intelligence is to develop some tentative measure of it.

Although psychological test construction rests on complicated statistical procedure, the basic idea underlying the use of psychological tests is simple. By measuring behavior at one time it becomes possible to predict behavior at a future time. The track coach tests his eight-quarter mile runners on Thursday and selects the fastest four to run in the mile relay race on Saturday. Running speed during a trial race is a good predictor of performance in the track meet. Similarly performance on a radio code or intelligence test provides information that can be useful in predicting subsequent behavior.

An early attempt to construct a "mental test" was made by James McKeen Cattell in 1890. He gave a series of ten tests to students at Columbia College that evaluated their sensory and motor skills such as the speed of their reaction time, their ability to estimate a 10-second interval, the strength of their hand grip, and others (Tuddenham, 1962). The selection of the tests was defended by assuming that the more sensitive and responsive a person is, the greater would be his or her mental ability. The key question is, "How can one know whether this assumption is justified?" This query was initially ignored while many psychologists of that era exuberantly supported Cattell's effort in the belief that it represented a major breakthrough in the measurement of mental abilities. Their optimism was short-lived. Cattell's test scores failed to correlate with academic grades although the grades were correlated among themselves, thus suggesting that some common factor was related to college grades. Psychologists were confronted with a thorny predicament. A test that presumably measured intelligence failed to be correlated with college grades, which presumably reflect intelligence. Which presumption is wrong: Cattell's test of intelligence or college grades as an index of intelligence? It was assumed that intellectual ability was required to do well in demanding college courses in mathematics, science, philosophy, and literature. Why should that assumption be rejected in favor of Cattell's premise that cognitive talent can be measured by sensory and motor tests? Does estimating a 10-second period require more intelligence than solving an algebra problem? Is the strength of one's grip a better index of cognitive ability than the capacity to understand photosynthesis? Psychologists were finally persuaded that the real-life measures of college grades seemed to be a more reasonable measure of intellectual ability than performance on an arbitrary series of sensory and motor tests that some psychologist thought measured intelligence. As a result, Cattell's test was abandoned but the question of the requirements an intelligence test should meet was left hanging.

The historical development of another presumed test of intelligence had a more successful outcome. In 1904, the French Minister of Public Instruction appointed a commission of leading citizens to discover how children, unable to cope successfully with regular work in elementary school, should be taught. The commission in turn consulted Alfred Binet, a psychologist, and his student Theodor Simon, a physician, who had worked in an institution for children who had been judged intellectually retarded.

One may ask why not consult classroom teachers to identify slow students? The answer is that such a procedure may depend too much on subjective judgments: A pupil that one teacher considered dull might be considered inattentive by another. A large number of nonintellectual factors such as students' looks, clothes, manners, and conduct, could influence a teacher's assessment of a student's academic ability. In addition, a student's academic performance might be lowered by nonintellectual factors such as poor hearing or eyesight, or personality problems.

Binet and Simon designed an ingenious test that provided an objective and reliable estimate of a child's intellectual ability based on a simple and clever idea–the age standard method–for measuring a child's intelligence in relation to the intellectual performance of children of different ages. By using the performance of these children on a series of tests ranging from easy to difficult, Binet and Simon calculated the average cognitive performance at each age level. With such specific information, it became possible to measure the intellectual ability of any child in a quantitative manner. For example, after testing an 8-year-old, one could characterize the child's performance as equivalent to the average performance of a particular age group, such as 4 years, 8 years, or 12 years. To simplify interpretation of such results, the concepts of intelligence quotient (IQ), mental age (MA), and chronological age (CA) were later developed. IQ was considered an index of intellectual brightness being a ratio between an individual's mental age and the child's chronological age multiplied by 100. In the example just cited, the IQ of an 8-year-old child with an MA of 4 would be 50, with an MA of 8 would be 100, and an MA of 12 would be 150. With the clear goal of predicting academic performance and the ingenuity to formulate a dimension of intelligence, Binet and Simon were able to identify students whose academic potential was limited, thus enabling the design of more effective educational programs. In a similar fashion, the gifted child could be recognized and placed in classes designed to exploit his or her superior talent. The Binet-Simon test was not a foolproof test in that errors of administration were possible, such as the examiner overlooking a child's hearing defect or illness that could depress test performance. Nevertheless, it was far superior to any other technique for evaluating a child's academic aptitude. Later versions of the Binet-Simon tests proved more effective in predicting academic performance. The Binet-Simon test's dependence on Mental Age encouraged the development of the Wechsler Adult Intelligence Scale (WAIS) that could be used with adults. These tests proved to be useful in selecting successful applicants for a variety of educational programs, as well as a broad range of industrial, commercial, and military positions.

Our concern with the Binet-Simon test of intelligence, and the numerous variations that the test instigated, is not with the technical aspects of intelligence testing, but rather with methodological issues. The contrast between Cattell's approach (a test designed to mirror the presumed nature of intelligence) and Binet and Simon's (a test designed to predict academic performance) reveals the difference between an interpretation of intelligence as a real thing as compared with a socially-constructed behavioral entity. The failure of Cattell's test to catch on reveals the crucial role that a criterion of intelligence plays in the social acceptance of a measure of intelligence. No matter how persuasively one may argue that a particular test represents a valid measure of intelligence, the argument collapses in face of evidence that denies its relation to socially defined intelligent behavior. Thus the lack of success of Cattell's test is not properly attributable to its failure to measure "real intelligence," but is due to its failure to have any pragmatic value in predicting subsequent behavior. The weaknesses of Cattell's test proved to be the strength of Binet-Simon test. Having a specific, limited goal, enabled Binet and Simon to design a test that could be evaluated by its ability to predict academic performance, which was judged to be, not only a socially important form of behavior, but also a reasonable criterion of intelligence.

The socially constructed definition of intelligence did not raise any problem as long as agreement prevailed about academic performance serving as an acceptable criterion of intelligence. As noted, the justification of this gauge of intelligence increased when later versions of the Binet-Simon test, as well as other related intelligence tests, were able to predict behavior in a variety of educational programs and jobs. But no matter how effective they proved to be, they could never escape the criticism that the selection of academic performance as a criterion of intelligence is arbitrary.

But the accusation of arbitrariness loses it force when a crucial aspect of social science research is appreciated. Socially constructed concepts have no valid guidelines to guarantee their potential empiri-cal fruitfulness. Before a concept, like intelligence, can be empirically analyzed, it must be transformed into some measuring instrument. For example, economists who seek to understand factors related to a nation's productivity must construct an index of productivity, such as a gross domestic product. These measures are usually modified over time to enhance their effectiveness in generating systematic knowl-edge. Similarly, psychologists who are interested in understanding what is obvious to most–individual differences in intelligence–must develop a measure of cognitive ability to investigate that attribute of behavior.

Once the validity of the intelligence test is demonstrated by being correlated with reasonable criteria (e.g., academic success, job per-formance) a deeper understanding becomes possible. One obvious goal is to understand the genetic and neurological correlates of intelligence-test performance. Several important chromosomal regions have been identified, and progress in understanding the relation between intelli-gence and brain function is being achieved (Posthuma and de Geus, 2006).

Although the intelligence-is-behavior assumption is pragmatically reasonable, it nevertheless instigates social conflicts. Is it possible that a socially agreed upon criterion of intelligence can be formulated? Since the concept of intelligence must be socially constructed, is it not inevitable that fundamental disagreements among social groups will occur about the meaning of intelligence? Will these disagreements prove irresolvable? History offers an answer but one that is not entire-ly clear.

Criticisms of Intelligence Tests

Intelligence tests have been criticized from the time of their devel-opment. These judgments have their roots in methodological disputes with the pragmatic orientation that gave birth to intelligence tests. One major source of disapproval stems from ideology; intelligence tests undermine principles that some consider socially valid. For example, a common objection to intelligence tests is that it undermines demo-cratic values and goal, particularly the principle of social equality. Another set of common objections stems from the belief that the intel-ligence tests developed by Binet and his successors fall short of being a true or satisfactory test of human intelligence: They are too narrow, intelligence cannot be measured by one number, intelligence tests are culturally biased.

Ideological criticisms. Gould (1981), a paleontologist and popular science writer, insists that ideology influenced psychologists when they constructed intelligence tests. This criticism is based on Gould's own ideological convictions that are revealed in his book, *The Mismeasure of Man* (1981, 1996). Gould suggests that the construction and use of intelligence tests, from Binet's to the modern Wechsler Adult Intelligence Scale, imply a biological determinism that sets a limit on the cognitive behavior of individuals and groups. This, in turn, encourages racial prejudice, the belief of the superiority of some races over others. Intelligence-test researchers, as later discussions will reveal, acknowledge environmental influences on test scores and conduct research designed to reveal them. Gould's fear of intelligence tests supporting the idea of racial superiority seems misplaced. The concept of racial superiority, or inferiority, does not *directly* emerge from IQ scores but results instead from unjustifiably adding a value judgment. The fact that top-notch sprinters of African descent are faster than Japanese sprinters does not imply Africans are superior to Japanese in any general sense.

Sternberg, a former president of APA, seeks to construct an improved test of intelligence that will have "increasing predictive validity, and, at the same time . . . reducing ethnic group differences in scores" (Sternberg, 2006, 323). He shares Gould's ideological concerns about racial differences and seeks to solve the social problem by constructing an intelligence test with preordained empirical relationships. Typically in scientific research involving any concept–intelligence, depression, adjustment–one first defines the concept and then discover its empirical correlates. Sternberg appears to confuse scientific research with political action. Admittedly, one of the most complex and confusing issues in contemporary society is that of intelligence and race. To fully appreciate it one must comprehend scientific research, statistical inference, the meaning of race, and the nature of ethics.

Intelligence tests fail to define intelligence. Sternberg argues that intelligence tests by themselves fail to convey what intelligence really is: "To this day, it is not totally clear what an intelligence test measures, and thus it cannot be clear on the basis of the test to define what intelligence is" (Sternberg, 2006). Wechsler (1958) who did the original work on the Wechsler Adult Intelligence Scale offered the following definition of intelligence, "Intelligence is the aggregate or global capacity of the individual to act purposefully, to think rationally, and to deal effectively with his environment." Although this definition offers an intuitive sense of what Wechsler thought intelligence to be, one can suggest that the test itself and all of its empirical correlates and mathematical properties provides a more accurate and objective description of intelligence. In comparing other tests to Wechsler's the important information will not be differences in definitions but differences in their objective knowledge base.

Intelligence tests are too narrow. Intelligence tests employ academic performance as a gauge of intelligence. The argument has been advanced that the criterion of academic performance is too narrow to reflect the full range of cognitive behavior especially those characteristics–creativity, originality, emotional maturity, humor, esthetic–that are so valuable in the arts, sciences, and the business world. Basically, this criticism reflects a prejudgment about the nature of intelligence; what it really is or should be. True, by its very nature intelligence tests reflect those behaviors that are encouraged in the classroom, such as linguistic ability, mathematical skills, abstract reasoning; a knowledge base that society deems important, and competencies that are judged useful for future personal and social adjustment. But isn't intellectual functioning that generates creative ideas important and isn't its identification critical for society? Rather than design an intelligence test that is as limited as our present ones, shouldn't we try to understand the broad spectrum of intellectual functioning and then forge a test that reflects all-important aspects of intelligence? What is being suggested is that the first task for scholars studying intelligence is to understand the wide range of intellectual behavior and then design a test based upon such a conception. Instead of bowing to the demands of expediency, psychologists should have proceeded more cautiously and imaginatively by developing a test of intelligence based upon a theory of intelligence, instead of the easily accessible but narrow criterion of academic performance. This criticism dissipates when one learns about the historical development of a theory of intelligence once a useful test is constructed. Having a tool to initially measure intelligence enables psychologists to discover its various empirical correlates and fundamental components.

Intelligence cannot be reduced to a single number. A related criticism to the narrowness of intelligence tests is that a single number cannot fully reflect intelligence. Some distinguished nonpsychologists (Gould, 1981; Medawar, 1977) have argued that the whole idea of measuring human intelligence collapses in the face of attempting to reduce intelligence to a single number. Such a criticism ignores the history of intelligence tests. Most psychologists, from Binet on, share the view that a single measure of intelligence cannot fully convey a description of a person's cognitive ability. The picture of intelligence revealed by the statistical method of factor analysis is that intelligence consists of different components. But how these components are distributed has been a source of debate. The most widely held view is the one originally proposed by Charles Spearman (1927), an eminent English psychologist, who concluded that there is a general intelligence, widely known as *g*, in addition to specific intelligences, or *s*'s. The supporting evidence for *g* is that in a wide variety of verbal, numerical, and reasoning tests, a sizable positive correlation is found among the different tests. Spearman, therefore, concluded that such apparently different cognitive abilities as mathematical reasoning, remembering, vocabulary-use, and other intellectual skills, are in part determined by this basic *g* factor. Performance on any specific task is not, however determined solely by general intelligence. A person's performance in mathematics is a combined product of a *g* factor and a specific mathematical ability. Mention also must be made that intelligence tests, such as the widely-used Wechsler Adult Intelligence Scale (Matarazzo, 1972), consist of several subtests that allow for a variety of specific scores, such as verbal and nonverbal IQs, as well as several derived scores that are useful in diagnosing psychological disturbances.

Additional research and improved mathematical procedures have helped to identify superior factor analytic interpretations of human intelligence (Carroll, 1993; Jensen, 1998). Rather than interpret human intelligence as some combination of different capacities, one cognitive psychologist has suggested that it can more productively be thought of as "the process of creating a mental representation of the current problem, retrieving information that appears relevant, and manipulating the representation in order to obtain an answer" (Hunt, 1995, 359). But these various approaches-the pragmatic approach of Binet and Simon, sophisticated factor analytical orientations (Carroll, 1993), theoretical perspective of cognitive processes (e.g., Hunt,

1995)–represent different strategies that supplement, rather than conflict with each other in making empirical and theoretical sense of human intelligence. From the perspective of the social pragmatist, these various approaches to understanding intelligence can be judged by the assistance they provide in the selection and training of individuals.

Intelligence tests are culturally biased. If intelligence tests are socially constructed, does it not follow that they must be culturally biased? Can one expect a child raised in a Latino ghetto, where only Spanish is spoken, to be fairly tested with items designed for English-speaking middle-class American children? Certainly, if the test were given in English, the Spanish-speaking children could not be fairly evaluated. But the accusation that intelligence tests are culturally biased is not limited to language differences. Even if the test has different language versions, as good intelligence tests usually do, the test is nevertheless deemed biased. The cultural-bias criticism essentially states that intelligence is, to some extent, culturally bound (Sternberg, 2004). Intelligence tests cannot properly measure the cognitive ability of a person whose ethnic background is different from that of the society the test reflects. This criticism, in essence, rejects the use of an intelligence test designed in one culture for members of another culture.

The initial purpose of intelligence tests was to predict academic performance. The basic issue is whether intelligence tests are biased in their predictive ability when those tested are members of a culture different from the one in which the test was designed. If a particular intelligence test, for example, *predicts* the cognitive behavior of minorities less successfully than it does for children of the majority, then the test is, in terms of its predictive powers, culturally biased. If, however, a particular intelligence test predicts with equal accuracy the academic performance of minority and majority students, the test is not culturally biased. It is important to recognize this distinction between two possible meanings of a test's cultural bias: an inevitable result of using the same test with different ethnic or racial groups, versus a differential predictive ability.

Summarizing. In essence, all the above criticisms, in one fashion or another, prejudge the nature of intelligence and criticize the pragmatic approach of Binet and Simon and their successors. In light of these criticisms, should intelligence tests be discarded as a failed psychological invention or hailed as a triumph of pragmatism that has provided psychologists and society with fundamental tools to understand important features of cognitive behavior?

The nature of intelligence test scores will now be examined in preparation for a discussion of the emotion-laden controversy about the relative importance of genetic and environmental influences on intelligence. In order to understand the dispute, one cannot avoid dealing with ideological influences on science, in general, and on psychology, in particular.

THE CHARACTER OF INTELLIGENCE TEST SCORES (IQ)

First and foremost in the discussion of the nature of intelligence test scores is to recognize that they measure a "phenotypic behavioral trait" (Humphreys, 1994). *Phenotypic* refers to observable behavior and is used in contrast to *genotype* that refers to the genetic constitution of an organism. Contrary to a common misconception, intelligence tests do not measure innate intelligence. In fact, the concept of innate intelligence, as a measurable phenomenon, is challenged by knowledge that at all stages of development environmental and genetic factors interact to determine behavior. From the moment of conception, when the sperm unites with the egg, environmental and genetic influences interact. Identical twins who share a common heredity can differ markedly at birth because one twin, during the period of gestation, receives less nourishment than the other. Thus any estimate of an innate IQ independent of environmental influences is impossible to approximate with intelligence tests alone. In sum, an intelligence test score measures the observable behavior of an individual at a given time and provides, by itself, no indication of environmental and genetic influences.

To complete our description of intelligence, *trait* must now be defined. Trait is a relatively stable characteristic of an individual's behavior. Investigations of intelligence test scores reveal that they are reliable in that a person tends to obtain similar IQ scores when tests are given on successive occasions. The general rule is that the shorter the interval between successive tests, the more stable the obtained IQs. Another important factor is the age at which the first test occurs. IQs at age 6 and below are not as predictive of future cognitive functioning as IQs tested later. One possible explanation is that at an age around 6 new cognitive processes, intimately related to adult intelligence, begin to operate (T. S. Kendler, 1995). All in all, the IQ is relatively stable for most persons, much more stable than an electrocardiogram, which has nevertheless proved to be a useful medical test.

Intelligence tests are robust tests in that the obtained score is not influenced by minor disturbances.

> If examinees are well motivated–a critical condition–measurement is . . .
> remarkably robust to conditions in the examinee and the environment
> that are considered stressful. Among these are minor illness, fatigue,
> loss of sleep, ambient temperature, and ambient noise. These are not
> excuses for measuring intelligence unpleasantly, but they do show that
> the trait is robust. (Humphreys, 1994, 183)

Are intelligence tests accurate in estimating an individual's cognitive potential? Or are they on target only for those who are raised in environments that provide satisfactory opportunities for cognitive development? No simple answer is possible to these questions because the spectrum of possible environmental influences is so vast, ranging from being raised in a closet without any intellectual stimulation to the other extreme of being exposed to the richest possible intellectual environment. Those who insist that IQ scores are misleading unless the testee had optimal opportunity for cognitive development, or those who argue that the tests are accurate regardless of differences in environmental stimulation are both wrong.

The accuracy of intelligence tests cannot be evaluated by prejudgments. Empirical evidence is demanded. Certainly the potential of the testee is not being measured if the child is not familiar with the language in which the test is given. A child with undetected deafness or psychiatric disorder or attention difficulty will fail to achieve a score that reflects his or her cognitive potential. And if children remain in an intellectually impoverished environment (an inadequate institution for the retarded) their IQ gradually declines, in contrast to the stable IQs of children who develop in a "normal" environment (Stoddard, 1943). In the case of a child whose IQ gradually declines it must be emphasized that the test is not unfair. From a social perspective, the argument could be advanced that the child is being treated unfairly. The test only measures the gradual decline in the child's cognitive ability as a function of an intellectually impoverished environment.

If impoverished environments can depress IQs, can stimulating surroundings raise them? This will prove to be the most important question in the nature-nurture controversy about IQs. Improved educational environments suggest that IQs can be raised. The average IQ of children of various ethnic groups in Hawaii was significantly higher in 1938 than in 1924 (Smith, 1942). During this 14-year period, improved educational opportunities, particularly for learning English, were put into place. Special training of 5-year-old slum children to improve verbal ability and enhance achievement motivation—the social drive to be successful—increased their IQs about six points (Gray and Klaus, 1965). Other studies can be cited that support the idea that intellectually stimulating environments can raise IQ scores, but the increase in most cases is modest. With presently available techniques, a ceiling appears to exist beyond which no amount of special training can produce more than modest gains. While expressing this important qualification, it becomes necessary to also note that, in principle, one cannot rule out the possibility that some future development might produce a technique to enhance a person's IQ by a large amount. But so far this has not been accomplished. And the intriguing question, that is too easily ignored, is whether an ideal intellectually stimulating environment or a neurological elixir would produce greater or smaller differences in the range of IQs that presently exist in the general population. In other words, if all children were raised in such an ideal environment would the range of IQs decrease or increase?

The fact that pockets of intellectually stultifying environments exist should not conceal the fact that most people are raised in surroundings that provide opportunities for cognitive development: compulsory education, public libraries, museums, TV, newspapers, magazines, friends, and so forth. Whether these opportunities are exploited will be determined to some extent by a child's cognitive talent. Science clubs in schools, for example, will attract students who have the cognitive ability to profit from them. Although children may inhabit the same physical environment, their intellectual environment can vary tremendously depending on the child's ability to cope with the intellectual challenges that are available.

The fact that intelligence tests have predictive validities does not imply that our effort to understand intelligence will be satisfied by intelligence tests alone.

Defining intelligence as a phenotypic behavioral trait is not a substitute for understanding how people . . . solve problems that are said to require intelligence. Neither is it a substitute for understanding the anatomical and biochemical mechanisms underlying the behavioral trait. These problems are legitimate and important, but they supplement . . . [the intelligence test approach to intelligence]. Research in those areas, if it is to be related to a behavioral trait, require definition and measurement of the trait. (Humphreys, 1994, 180)

In spite of failing to provide a complete understanding of intelligence, intelligence tests are socially important:

General intelligence is one of many human traits, but it is clearly an important one. It is highly related to educational success and to occupational attainment. . . . It is related to economic productivity, and, although it is a difficult research problem, it is undoubtedly related to the ability of a democratic society to function as such. Remember, in this connection, that there is little difference between functional literacy and general intelligence. (Humphreys, 1994, 189)

The emphasis on the social importance of general intelligence should not be perceived as the exclusive standard by which a democratic society values the worth of individuals. Intelligence is not synonymous with human excellence! Artistic, musical, and athletic abilities are also valued, as indicated by the social prestige and financial rewards they bring for top-level performance. And cognitive ability, as indicated by intelligence test performance, is not usually sufficient by itself, especially in the commercial arena. Intelligence, to be exploited, frequently requires assistance from other traits–personality and temperament–especially when leadership and communication skills are required.

Intelligence can be viewed from the perspective of an individual or from the entire society. In both cases intelligence has economic value (Herrnstein and Murray, 1994). As intelligence increases so does the income of the individual. The correlation is far from perfect for three major reasons: Many bright persons, for a variety of reasons, do not seek high-paying jobs. By choice, accident, or personal limitations, they do not strive for the monetary rewards that are presumably within their grasp. Anastasi and Foley (1958) obtained intelligence scores for different occupations ranging from the low-end pay of farm workers to the high-end of accountants. As one ascended this range the median intelligence scores increased along with the median incomes. Although the median scores vary from occupation to occupation, an enormous amount of overlap between occupations occurred. A small percentage of highly intelligent farm workers matched the intelligence test scores of the low-end of accountants. If given an opportunity, perhaps these farm workers could have become accountants, or perhaps they lacked necessary personality characteristics, or they may prefer being farm workers.

The economic prosperity of a society is enhanced by the achievements of the intellectually gifted. A prime example is the development of computer science, which has benefited our economy and our entire culture. The computer revolution was based on the creativity of people with high IQs. This radical change could not have occurred without an advanced educational system that provided positive opportunities for talented students. Development of improved methods of production, creation of commercially valuable goods, better agricultural techniques, creative efforts in the financial and artistic worlds, all contribute to the economic well-being of a society as a result of the achievements of intellectually gifted.

As the high-level jobs in a society become more intellectually demanding, cognitive ability becomes more important in achieving economic success. One estimate (Herrnstein and Murray, 1994) is that the mean IQ of people entering such professions as law, medicine, science, mathematics, engineering, dentistry, college teaching, and architecture is 120. In 1900, 5 percent of the people in the upper 10 percent of intelligence range were in these occupations. At this time, 25 percent of the upper end of the intelligence range is in these professions. A similar conclusion is true for business executives. A much larger proportion of executives today have a graduate education than in times past. In sum, people with high intelligence are presently more concentrated in the professions and the upper echelons of the business community than they were in the past.

What explains the observed differences in human intelligence? The answer lies in unraveling the influences of nature and nurture and their complex interactions. This task is daunting in itself but becomes more difficult by the emotionally-laden ideological disputes that contaminate the empirical issues.

Ideology and the Nature-Nurture Controversy

The search for an understanding of intelligence, and other socially constructed concepts—mental health, racism, adjustment—returns us to the methodological issue of whether scientific investigations must reflect a value bias or if empirical truth can be pursued in a detached manner. In other words, should the effort to understand intelligence be directed by ideological or by scientific concerns? As with most distinctions a gray area divides the two, but in spite of the borderline ambiguity, the core differences are recognizable and significant. As noted previously, ideology can be considered a systematic doctrine that designates appropriate social goals; a vision about what should be, what is socially good and right (pp. 42–43). One subtle example of ideology is the combined opinion of two biologists and a psychologist that the "the ultimate tests [of a science] are always twofold: tests of truth and social function" (Lewontin, Rose, and Kamin, 1984, 33). Implied in their statement is the implication that science should be shaped by ideological goals. A contrasting orientation is that truth and social functions are independent concepts. Empirical truth is a statement that meets the epistemological demands of natural science while declarations about social function contain a moral judgment that is beyond the capacity of science to make.

To distinguish between scientific truth and social function, the neutral topic of suffrage can prove enlightening. The history of United States, since 1776, illustrates a continuous concern with deciding the democratic requirements for voting rights. Some answers have been "Solely landowners, only men, those who pay a poll tax, nonfelons above the age of 21, and so forth." Within a broader perspective, which of the following two statements reflects a true democracy? One, a democratic society is based upon a social contract between the elected government and those ruled, and therefore all those who are governed are entitled to voting rights. Two, a democratic society will only prevail when all who are qualified to vote meet demanding standards of citizenship. Which is correct, one or two? What empirical investigation can identify the appropriate standards for suffrage in a democracy? Although you may favor one moral criterion, you cannot logically demonstrate that natural science demands it.

Can a scientific investigator overcome moral judgments inconsistent with an area of scientific inquiry? Consider the case of Charles Darwin

(1809–1891) who was born to a well-to-do family and raised in a Christian household that required the study of the *Bible* with its creationist message. His early upbringing directed Darwin to prepare for the ministry at Cambridge University and a career in the Church of England (Desmond and Moore, 1992). But his life's course was redirected by the opportunity, at 22 years of age, to serve as a naturalist on the five-year voyage of the HMS Beagle. His zoological findings gradually but definitely forced him to abandon the belief in the special creation of each species in favor of the evolutionary principle that all life, including humankind, descended from a common ancestral origin. How is it possible that a creationist could become an evolutionist? How could Darwin overcome the ruling class ideology that dominated his life (Browne, 1995)? An obvious answer is that Darwin's observations, combined with an extraordinary intellect, forced him to perceive the biological world as it really is. God did not create species, nature did. Natural science methodology, free of value judgments aside from his commitment to interpret the empirical evidence, helped Darwin to become Darwin!

Admittedly, a single case is usually insufficient to undermine a strongly-held methodological position such as the inseparability of social function and natural science methodology. But the Darwinian example is offered not only to deny that values have a stranglehold on empirical observations, but also to force those who believe so to explain the obvious facts of scientific progress in the physical and biological sciences. If prevailing values, either social or theoretical, determine what is observed, then how can new conceptions, such as the Copernican model of the solar system, replace a previously-held conception like the Ptolemaic model of the planetary system that is based on a different value framework? The answer is that physical and biological "reality" forces scientists to ultimately adopt a "value orientation"–natural science methodology–that demands proposed explanations be consistent with empirical observations without abiding by any sociopolitical ideals. The important question for our present concern is whether a psychological reality exists that allows psychology to emulate the physical and biological sciences?

Nature and Nurture in Psychology

A subject that generates intense ideological fervor is the influence of environment and heredity on behavior. And when this topic focuses on intelligence, passions go unchecked, as the behavior geneticist, Robert Plomin, noted: "As soon as you mention intelligence or, God forbid, IQ, people go ballistic" (Mann, 1994). I have observed this reaction, not only on talk TV but also in professional discussions. Although this state of affairs encourages one to avoid the topic, it also mandates facing up to it. Although frankness will not guarantee agreement, it has the advantage of revealing the basic sources of disagreement.

A guiding principle of this book is that revealing sources of conflict is better than hiding them. This rule appears consistent with natural science methodology and political democracy, both of which promote freedom of individual expression and fairness in judging ideas and knowledge claims. And those who fear that certain kinds of facts are threatening should be reminded that the fact-value dichotomy acts as a barrier to employing facts alone to justify social policies. Facts are neutral in regard to value choices and this principle should be recognized in a democratic society. Facts are facts; they are not social policies nor do they demand any!

The Interdependence of Heredity and Environment

As already noted, heredity and environment interact from the moment the human sperm fertilizes the human egg. The genes control the development of the fetus, but that control can be modified by environmental influences. Two points need emphasis. First, genes do not directly control behavior. Genes control the development of the nervous system, including the brain, and other physiological structures that, in turn, influence behavior. Second, genetic influences always operate within an environmental setting and changes in that setting can affect genetic potential. Among songbirds, males are the ones that usually sing. The set of neurons in the male brain that controls singing is six times larger than the same area in females. If testosterone is blocked from entering this area during infancy, the male bird will never sing. But they will also never sing if during their infancy they fail to hear relatives sing. What causes males to sing? Hearing a song starts a process, involving testosterone, which shapes the brain to mediate singing (Blum, 1997). One can speculate, using this example, that Mozart probably would not have become an amazing musical genius if he had not been exposed to his early stimulating musical environment. At the same time, being exposed to such an environment would not automatically prepare a person to compose a symphony of the quality of Mozart's Symphony No. 41. Similarly the parietal lobe of Einstein's brain, the part responsible for visual thinking and spatial reasoning, was significantly larger than the average size brain (Roberts, 2006). One can guess this anatomical advantage helped Einstein formulate his theory of relativity.

If nature and nurture constantly interact, can their independent influences be disentangled? Consider the tragic case in the late 1950s of those women who took the sedative thalidomide during their early stage of pregnancy. Approximately 20 percent gave birth to babies with deformed limbs. Ten thousand such cases testify to the fact that genetically controlled developmental changes can be environmentally modified. Thalidomide overrode the genetic potential for normal limbs. This example suggests that for specific phenomena environmental and genetic influences can be separated. Two people, with a similar genetic liability to a major depression, will not necessarily experience the same outcome. The one that lives in an environment with significantly less stress will have less of a chance of succumbing to a major depression (K. S. Kendler and Prescott, 2006).

The major interest among behavior geneticists has been to investigate possible genetic influences on behavior. For example, by interbreeding groups of mice, it has been possible to develop pure strains that exhibit aggressive behavior or preference for alcohol (Barinaga, 1994). Such studies cannot be done with humans but nature provides a convenient alternative. Monozygotic twins—twins from the same fertilized egg—share the identical genetic endowment and by comparing their behavior with ordinary siblings it becomes possible to infer genetic influences on behavior.

Twin Studies. Hermann Siemens, a German dermatologist, published a study in 1924 (Mann, 1994) that employed a research design that was used later with many variations. The school transcripts of identical twins—offsprings of a single fertilized egg—were compared with those of fraternal twins—offsprings of two fertilized eggs—who are as genetically different as ordinary siblings. The grades and the teacher evaluations of the identical twins were more highly correlated than those of fraternal twins, suggesting that genetic factors play a role in academic achievement. But that conclusion can be challenged with the assumption that identical twins shared a more similar environment than fraternal twins. Because of their greater physical resemblance, people respond to them more alike than they do to fraternal twins. Perhaps Siemens' results were due primarily to environmental influences?

The effects of heredity are relatively easy to measure, while those of environment pose difficult problems. The reason for this discrepancy is that the genetic theory can make definitive estimates of hereditary influences, but little is known about environmental influences on such behaviors as cognitive ability. For example, in studying hereditary influences on IQ, quantitative principles of genetics postulate a coefficient of genetic relationships of 1.00 for identical twins and .50 for fraternal twins or ordinary siblings. This does not mean that one would expect the identical twins to behave exactly alike. The assumption that genes influence behavior does not deny the influence of environmental factors. Environmental differences between the identical twins could shape one to become a good student and the other an average or poor student. The major prediction from the assumption that genetic factors influence academic performance is that the behavior of identical twins would be more similar than that of fraternal twins. But, as already noted, such a demonstration as occurred in the Siemens' study is not sufficient to support a genetic influence unless it could be proved that environmental factors were not solely responsible for the results. Is that possible? Unlike laboratory studies, environmental influences cannot be completely controlled in studies with humans. Thus, if progress is to be made in unraveling hereditary from environmental influences of IQ, it becomes mandatory to develop methods of estimating environmental impacts.

ENVIRONMENTAL DETERMINISM VERSUS GENETIC INTERACTIONISM

The competing interpretations of human intelligence that are the center of controversy about human intelligence can be conveniently labeled as the *environmental determinist* view and the *genetic interactionist* position. The environmental determinist position is usually expressed as a denial of the role of genetic influences in IQ scores: "there exists no data which would lead a prudent man to accept the hypothesis that IQ scores are to any degree heritable" (Kamin, 1974, 1). The interactionist position states simply that genetic factors influence IQ, but at the same time acknowledges environmental impacts. A strong statement of this position is that for the American society as a whole "genetic factors are the single most important source of variation [in IQ scores]" (Bouchard, 1993, 83).

To evaluate these competing views one can judge them within a historical context (see pp. 17–18) and determine their relative merits and limitations (Lakatos, 1970a, 1970b). Of particular importance in this evaluation is the judgment as to whether the environmental determinism or genetic interactionist research program is progressive or degenerating. A progressive program is one in which the theoretical structure expands its knowledge base and explanatory capacity, while the degenerating program is relatively unproductive in generating new data, relying mainly on ad hoc assumptions to cope with inconsistent evidence. This progressive-degenerating frame of reference will be employed for analyzing the comparison of IQ scores of fraternal and identical twins.

In 1937, a study sought to identify environmental and genetic influences on intelligence test scores of identical and fraternal twins (Newman, Freeman, and Holzinger, 1937). To illustrate the significant role of genetic influence on IQs it was compared with the degree of resemblance in height, a highly heritable physical characteristic. Heritability is a statistical measure that estimates the relative contribution of genetic factors to some observed characteristic of an organism, such as height or intelligence. The coefficient of correlation for height was +.60 for like-sexed ordinary siblings, +.64 for like-sex fraternal twins, and +.93 for identical twins. The equivalent correlations for intelligence test scores were almost as large: +.53, +.63, and +.88. Knowing the greater similarity between the heights and IQ scores for identical twins as compared to fraternal twins and ordinary siblings, suggests the importance of genetic influences for height and intelligence. But an environmental determinist could question the significance of genetic influences in these data by noting that the correlation between the IQs of fraternal twins is higher than that for ordinary siblings (+.63 to +.53). Since there is no genetic reason for this, it can be attributed to the greater similarity in the environments in which the fraternal twins were raised. Perhaps the environmental argument could be extended to the relatively high correlations for IQs of identical twins. If the evidence implies that fraternal twins have more similar environments than ordinary siblings, can it be suggested that the environments of identical twins are more alike than those of fraternal twins? Because identical twins look alike, people, from their parents to their friends and teachers, are encouraged to treat them alike. Therefore the hypothesis that the greater similarity of the IQs of identical twins as compared to fraternal twins, is due to hereditary factors, must be reconsidered. The apparent genetic similarity may simply reflect environmental influences. This statement sets the stage for the battle between competing research programs that offer opposing interpretations—genetic versus environmental—of the greater similarity between the IQs of identical twins as compared to fraternal twins.

The battleground for the competing research programs were in studies examining the IQs of identical twins raised apart. If the similarity between the IQs of identical twins were primarily due to genetic factors, then raising identical twins in different families should have minimal effects on their IQs. If, however, similar environments were responsible for the resemblance in their IQs, raising them in different environments should reduce the IQ correspondence. Newman, Freeman, and Holzinger (1937), who had studied the similarity in heights and IQs of ordinary siblings, fraternal twins, and identical twins reported that the mean difference in IQs of identical twins reared apart was 8 points, only 2 more than the 6 points that separated the identical twins reared together. Similar findings that suggested that genetic factors played a significant role in the IQs of identical twins reared apart were reported by several studies done in Denmark (Juel-Nielsen, 1965, 1980; Shields, 1962), England (Burt, 1966), and the United States (Bouchard, Lykken, McGue, Segal, and Tellegen, 1990). A remarkable resemblance appears in all five studies, but for reasons that will be described later, the Burt study will be excluded from consideration. The remaining four studies reported correlations varying between +.69 to +.75 (Bouchard, Lykken, McGue, Segal, and Tellegen, 1990).

Nature-nurture research on IQ is bedeviled by difficulties in measuring environmental influences. As a consequence, environmental determinists always seem to have, according to genetic interactionists, an escape hatch that allows them to rescue their position from embarrassing evidence. Their major defense against the findings of studies of the IQs of identical twins raised apart is they all suffer from a *placement bias*. That is, the separated twins who had equivalent IQs were placed in adoptive homes that were similar to each other. How could you possibly conclude that hereditary factors were responsible for the corresponding IQs of identical twins who were raised separately in environments that were almost as similar as those of identical twins who were raised together?

The most effective defense of the placement bias hypothesis would be to test it directly by discovering environmental factors that influence IQ scores. Instead of doing such research, environmental-determinists (e.g., Farber, 1981; Taylor, 1980) fell back on reanalyzing data from studies of identical twins reared apart (Juel-Nielsen, 1965; Newman, Freeman, and Holzinger, 1937; Shields, 1962). Although reanalysis of available data is a legitimate scientific effort, cautious use of statistical procedures is imperative. One cannot pick and choose comparisons that appear favorable to one's hypothesis without violating statistical assumptions. Bouchard (1982, 1983) dismissed their reanalyses, as "pseudoanalysis" because of inappropriate data selection and unjustified statistical manipulations. But this reanalysis led to a slight backtracking from the environmental determinist position. Taylor (1980) cautiously concludes "Based on the reanalysis of the data from . . . studies of separated identical twins, it seems reasonable to suggest that the IQ correlation characterizing pairs of individuals with absolutely identical genes and absolutely uncorrelated environments would be extremely low" (pp. 100–101). An "extremely low" correlation is inconsistent with the environmental determinist position that genetics factors play no role. Equally revealing is the concept of "uncorrelated environments?" One twin going to school while the other is denied any schooling? The genetic paradigm for IQ assumes environmental influences and seeks to understand their influences. A large discrepancy between the IQs of a particular set of identical twins raised apart would not embarrass a genetic-interaction hypothesis if extreme environmental differences were identified. The problem would be similar to the previously mentioned example of the monozygotic twins that significantly differ in height because of a great difference in prenatal nourishment.

Progressive and Degenerating Research Programs

We will now return to a historical framework to judge the merits of the contrasting research programs of environmental determinism and a nature-nurture interactionism that stresses genetic factors to account for the similarity of IQs of identical twins reared apart. As just noted, the research program of extreme environmentalism–that assumes genes have no influence on cognitive behavior–is static, not initiating new research to prove its point, but instead reexamining studies reporting the importance of genetic factors. Such reexamination is not inherently wrong, but if the reinterpretation is unconvincing and fails to generate supportive evidence, then the environmental determinist research program can properly be diagnosed as degenerating. It adds more and more ad hoc assumptions without expanding its empirical range. Behavior geneticists could add an annoyance factor. They do all the research, including research designed to reveal environmental influences, while the environmental determinists, stand on the sideline and do little else but criticize.

The research program of the genetic interactionists, unlike that of the environmentalists, is self-propelling. Genetic theory lends itself to the scientific task of asking and answering empirical questions. It raises new questions from its rapidly expanding base in genetic theory; genetic mapping opens up new approaches to old questions. The dissection of the genetic bases of complex traits (e.g., personality, intelligence, temperament), previously an unapproachable task, is now entering the realm of the possible (Lander and Schork, 1994). Consider now, some of the theoretical and empirical spin-offs of the controversy generated by the similarity of the IQs of identical twins reared apart.

(1) Whereas the environmental determinists dismiss genetic factors as causal agents in IQ, contemporary hereditarians readily acknowledge environmental influences and deem them essential for comprehending genetic influences. Their effort to understand nurture has proceeded on several fronts, from treating the environment as a global entity (e.g., socioeconomic level), to considering specific influences (e.g., parents' educational levels), and viewing the environment in relation to genetic predispositions. Direct environmental influences, both general and specific, have been slight–such factors as parents' education; father's social economic status; cultural, scientific, intellectual facilities at home; and retrospective memories of upbringing proved to be of minor importance in explaining the intellectual similarities of identical twins reared apart (Bouchard, Lykken, McGue, Segal, and Tellegen, 1990).

A breakthrough occurred when researchers distinguished between the general environment in which a person lives and those features– *the effective environment*–that influence behavior. Although a town has a public library and a chess club, these would not necessarily entice all persons. Only those with a cognitive ability to profit from such sources of stimulation would be attracted to them. The concept of the effective environment has led to the measure of the genotype-environmental correlation (Plomin, DeFries, and Loehlin, 1977) that interprets environmental influences in terms of genetic predispositions. The effective environment can be analyzed into three components. A *passive* environmental influence would be one in which intellectually gifted parents would provide their offspring with an intellectually stimulating environment. A *reactive* environmental impact would occur when a bright child is selected to engage in special educational programs designed for the cognitively talented. An *active* influence would be the tendency of the bright child to gravitate toward environmental opportunities–a high school biology or literature club–that requires above average cognitive ability. The unit of environmental transmission is not the family as a whole, but instead a microenvironment in which individual children "evoke responses from others, actively select or ignore opportunities, and construct their own experiences" (Scarr, 1992, 14). In sum, children create their own environments and a powerful influence is their own genetic predispositions.

(2) With their shared heredity, one would expect that anthropomorphic measures of identical twins would be highly correlated and not markedly affected by being reared together or apart. The fingerprint ridge contours of identical twins are almost perfectly correlated and unaffected by separate rearing. The height and weight of identical twins are very similar with a slightly larger correlation for twins reared together than apart. Brain waves are markedly correlated with no effect of rearing differences. Measures of blood pressure and heart rate are significantly correlated for identical twins with slightly higher correlations for twins reared together. Should it be a source of wonderment that identical twins, with their common physiology, exhibit similar behavior? Behavior is not some mystical expression of a hidden soul but is, instead, a manifestation of underlying bodily processes. Thus it should come as no surprise that on measures of cognitive ability, personality, temperament, occupational and leisure-time interests, and social attitudes, identical twins reared apart are very similar, only

slightly less so than those of identical twins reared together (Bouchard, Lykken, McGue, Segal, and Tellegen, 1990).

(3) Would you expect the correlation of IQs of identical twins to remain constant, increase, or decrease with age? One popular intuition is that genetic factors should have their greatest impact during early life, but with increasing age, the wide range of possible experiences should increase environmental influences. McGue, Bouchard, Iacono, and Lykken (1993) report a slight increase in the correlation of IQs of identical twins in adulthood, with a concomitant drop for fraternal twins. This conclusion receives support from other studies (e.g., McCartney, Harris, and Bernieri, 1990; Pedersen, Plomin, Nesselroade, and McClearn, 1992) thus suggesting that genetic influences increase, or at least remain constant, but do not decrease with age. Recently (McClearn et al., 1997) have reported substantial genetic contributions on the cognitive abilities of identical twins 80 years of age or more. An interesting hypothesis to explain these results is that with age comes greater individual control over one's environmental experiences (Scarr and McCartney, 1983). Parents and teachers strongly influence the intellectual experiences of children and adolescents. This grip loosens in adulthood, when individuals are free to choose their own sources of intellectual expression. If this were true, then identical twins whose innate cognitive skills are more alike should drift closer together when outside restraints are minimized or disappear. However, when these restraints are removed for fraternal twins, or ordinary siblings, their IQs should diverge because their innate cognitive abilities differ.

(4) Initially, the nature-nurture controversy was concerned only with identifying environmental or genetic variables. The environmental determinist research program seemingly is still stuck at this early stage of research with its major emphasis disputing the evidence that suggests how genetic factors operate. The genetic-interactionism research program, in contrast, is progressing in its effort to add to its theoretical precision as well as to its empirical base. In this effort, quantitative principles of genetics, as already noted, facilitate the job. For example, in studying the genetic influence of familial resemblances in IQ, genetic theory postulates a coefficient of genetic relationship of 1.00 for identical twins, .50 for fraternal twins or ordinary siblings, .25 for half-siblings, and .00 for unrelated individuals. This model has been evaluated with data from 111 studies on familial resemblance in

measured intelligence (Bouchard and McGue, 1981). According to the model, identical twins reared in the same environment should have a correlation of +1.00. The weighted average correlation obtained for identical twins raised together is +.86 and when reared apart is +.72. With a polygenic model of intelligence that postulates that the genetic predisposition to intelligence involves many genes, the discrepancies between the theoretical and obtained correlations would be attributed to environmental influences: Presumed discrepancies in the environment of identical twins reared together and divergences in the different homes of twins reared apart. The correlations for fraternal twins and ordinary siblings are +.60 and +.47, respectively, suggesting the enhancement of the correlation of dizygotic twins for being raised together at the same time in the same place. Half siblings reared together have a correlation of +.31 and nonbiological siblings reared together by one biological parent of each child is +.29. Evidence suggesting that environmental restraints on cognitive performance are reduced with age is supported by the findings of studies with nonbiologically related children reared in the same household. During childhood their IQs correlated about +.25 but this figure is reduced to .00 when measurement of IQ took place in adulthood.

These findings and others reporting additional familial relationships can be summarized: "The higher the proportion of genes two family members have in common, the higher the average correlation between their IQs" and "the pattern of averaged correlations is remarkably consistent with polygenic theory" (Bouchard and McGue, 1981, 1055 and 1058). Such data raise many challenging questions for the environmental determinists. One returns us to the question of why the IQs of identical twins raised apart are so highly correlated? Behavior geneticists attribute the high correlation to the 100 percent overlap in the genes of identical twins. Environmental determinists argue that in spite of their separation they were raised in similar home environments. Therefore, how do the environmental determinists explain the correlation of +.72 for identical twins raised in *different family environments* with the correlation of .00 for nonbiological siblings in adulthood who shared the *same family environment* during childhood?

The data reported largely occur in families of a socioeconomic level above poverty. In rare instances when poor families adopt children of well-to-do parents, the adoptee's IQs are significantly lower than when they are adopted in households of a socioeconomic level equivalent to their previous one. In a similar fashion, when children from a poverty level are adopted by well-off parents, a modest increase in their IQs occur (Kirp, 2006, Turkheimer, et al., 2003). Such data point to the importance of a society providing, through education and social services, as much intellectual stimulation as possible to help the children elevate their IQs to the highest positive levels. The child and society will both benefit.

(5) Some intelligence tests consist of several subtests. This has enabled some psychologists and statisticians to discover the genetic influence of specific cognitive skills. Vandenberg (1968) reported that for one test battery *verbal, word fluency,* and *spatial tests* were more heritable than *number, reasoning,* and *memory* subtests. Other studies reported that the difference between monozygotic (identical) and dizygotic (fraternal) twins is greater, and hence more heritable, for measures of *verbal comprehension* and *spatial visualization* than for *numerical ability* and *memory* (Nichols, 1978; Osborne, 1980). Specific genetic contributions have been revealed in *verbal comprehension, spatial,* and *word fluency* subtests (Martin and Eaves, 1977). The genetic approach has reached the point of formulating specific models (Eaves, Eysenck, and Martin, 1989) of genetic-environmental interactions. Data can then be analyzed to determine which particular model best represents the obtained evidence. These successful models can subsequently be exploited to discover the molecular bases of the genetic correlates of behavioral phenomena. Ultimately, such information can be utilized in preparing effective educational programs for all children.

(6) The expectation from an environmental determinist viewpoint is that the IQs of adopted children should resemble their adopted parents, with whom they share a common environment more than their biological mother, to whom they are genetically related. A summary statement of the findings is:

> The most important modern studies—the Texas, Colorado, and Minnesota studies—all have large samples and indicate at least for older children and young adults, that adopted children tend to have IQs that are more highly correlated with the characteristics of their biological mothers than with the characteristics of their adoptive parents. (Brody, 1992, 145)

Shared genetic background is much more important than shared family environment in determining a person's IQ (Plomin and Thompson, 1987; Scarr, 1992).

Genes influence the biological makeup of humans. If heredity influences cognitive ability, should not IQ be correlated with biological measures? Recent research has reported that nerve conductance velocity, brain electrical activity, brain metabolism, and myopia are correlated with IQ (Jensen, 1998). The first step in revealing the genetic basis for cognitive ability has also been made. New genetic scanning techniques reveal that a particular variant of a certain gene is twice as common among children with IQs above 160 as those with average scores (Chorney et al., 1998). Although the difference is not great, the finding is important because many genes and their interactions influence intelligence.

The beginning of the search for biological correlates of IQ highlights two important points. First, in order to discover biological correlates of cognitive behavior, a method of measuring intelligence was necessary. IQ tests, in spite of limitations, have effectively served that function. Second, the search for links between biology and IQ illustrate the progressive nature of the genetic interactionism research program.

(8) A final progressive contribution of the behavior genetics research program is controversial both in regard to the nature of the data and its interpretation. The data approaches the bizarre and for some represents an overdramatic attempt to convince others about the power of genetic determination. A number of curious similarities have shown up in reunions of monozygotic twins who had been reared apart. One of the less dramatic reports is that of a pair of identical twins "who at their first adult reunion discovered that they both used Vandemecum toothpaste, Canoe shaving lotion, Vitalis hair tonic, and Lucky Strike cigarettes (Lykken, McGue, Tellegen, and Bouchard, 1992). Since their sensory system was programmed by the same genes it does not appear too surprising that they would select products with the same sensory attributes. But what about more unusual behavioral similarities of identical twins reared apart: the phobic tendencies of two women who always entered the water backwards only up to their knees, two women who wore seven rings, two who had been married five times, two who left little love notes around the house for their wives, and two twins who designed and constructed circumarboreal benches in their backyards before they knew of the other's existence

(Lykken, 1982)?

Are these chance coincidences or do they reflect some genetic linkages? This question cannot be answered unequivocally, one reason being that they may not result from the same set of genetic variables. A genetic link in selecting similar sensory experiences may appear more reasonable than planning and building a bench around a tree. When considering these unusual similarities, Lykken (1982) concludes they must be based on a special sort of polygenic transmission. The common polygenic transmission for a trait, such as physical height, is thought to result from the additive effect of a number of genes. Lykken suggests that the strong influence of genetic transmission on such behaviors already reviewed–aptitudes, personality traits, psychophysiological measures, and possibly these unusual similarities–are "emergenic." That is "they are determined by the interaction–rather than the sum–of genetic influences" (Lykken, 1982, 361).

Lykken carries over the idea of a configurational genetic pattern to the occurrence of unexpected geniuses. Although all geniuses are unusual, some like Johann Sebastian Bach and Charles Darwin are not unexpected in the sense that members of their family had previously exhibited similar talents, but to a lesser degree. But the mathematical genius of Karl Frederich Gauss was completely unexpected because he was a product of a union of a peasant woman and a bricklayer and, unlike Bach and Darwin, none of Gauss's descendants inherited his special talents. Emergenic traits, according to Lykken, although genetic in origin, tend not to run in families because of the unlikely possibility that the complete genetic configuration responsible for the exceptional behavior will be passed on to offsprings.

Regardless of what the future holds for emergenic theory, it represents, along with the other efforts generated by the genetic-interactionism research program, a definite progressive direction. In sharp contrast is the degenerating direction of the environmental determinists. The reason for being stuck in the rut is not because of a lack of importance of environmental influences in cognitive and other forms of behavior. Rather the sterility of the approach stems from the refusal to recognize that nurture interacts with nature. Why the opaqueness? Ideology, as the next chapter will show.

Chapter 3

IDEOLOGY AND IQ

The environmental determinists' interpretation of cognitive ability is untenable but not unpopular. Recent years have seen an explosion of research in behavior genetics that has demonstrated that in a wide variety of behaviors, in addition to intelligence, genetic influences are powerful. Why then, in the face of mounting evidence that genetic factors play a significant role in intelligence, does the belief remain that with appropriate environmental interventions practically all people can achieve an equal level of cognitive ability?

A powerful factor, referred to previously, is the natural-law principle contained in the influential 1776 Declaration of Independence: "We hold these truths to be self evident, that all men are created equal, that they are endowed by their Creator with certain unalienable Rights, that among these are Life, Liberty, and the Pursuit of Happiness." This idea was anticipated in the writings of both John Locke (1632–1704) and Jean Jacques Rousseau (1712–1778), both of whom extolled the unity of humankind, an idea that was antithetical to the belief that aristocrats were innately superior to the common herd of humanity. The philosophical ideal of *human equality* pervaded the American scene and attracted waves of European immigrants. A dominant ideal, expressed by Horatio Alger (1834–1899) in his more than 100 books for boys, was that if they received an education and became dedicated workers, they could overcome adversity and poverty to achieve honor and wealth.

But there is another component of environmental determinism that is not naïvely starry-eyed in pursuit of human equality. Instead, a deliberate effort was made to implement a visionary world view, an ideology based on the malleability of human nature that assumed that

76

environmental factors alone determine the cognitive ability of humans. This ideological position is expressed in a quotation, already mentioned (p. 65), in a book by Leon Kamin (1974), entitled *The Science and Politics of IQ:* ". . . there exists no data which would lead a prudent man to accept the hypothesis that IQ scores are in any degree heritable" (1). The assumption of a zero impact of heredity was repeated in a book entitled *Not in Our Genes* (Lewontin, Rose, and Kamin, 1984). The accusation that genes are unrelated to cognitive behavior is coupled with the accusation that IQ tests have served as instruments to oppress the poor by attributing their economic deprivation to "fixed biological causes" (Kamin, 1974, 2). Kamin confesses that the purpose in writing his book "is not only to contribute to scientific knowledge, but also to influence policymakers and, perhaps, some scientists who do not recognize that their science and their politics are not clearly separable" (3). For Kamin politics infiltrate scientific results. An opposed thesis, enunciated in this book, is that ideology can corrupt evidence but need not if natural science standards are met.

THE BURT AFFAIR

Kamin was instrumental in diverting attention from the empirical and theoretical features of intelligence testing to its political aspects. At that time, a general naïveté prevailed about whether these two different perspectives–science and politics–could be treated in isolation or whether they were inextricably intertwined. The Burt Affair offers an answer by dramatically illustrating how politics can obfuscate the question of whether genetic factors are involved in human intelligence.

Kamin created a ruckus when he implied that Sir Cyril Burt (1883–1971) might have fudged evidence in his study of twins reared apart to support his belief that intelligence was strongly influenced by heredity. Burt was considered, at that time, to be one of the leading British psychologists. In addition to his studies on IQ, he had developed important factor analytic techniques as well as conducting significant research in the areas of educational psychology. His achievements led him to being knighted in 1946.

After his death at the age of 88, a series of events, worthy of a bizarre TV soap opera, destroyed Burt's reputation. A journalist,

(Gillie, 1976), influenced by Kamin (1976), went one step further and explicitly accused Burt of fraud. A biography followed by Hearnshaw (1979), a psychologist who had eulogized Burt at his memorial service. In preparing to write an official biography, Hearnshaw was given access to Burt's unpublished correspondence and diaries, which ultimately convinced him that Burt had actually indulged in fraudulent representation of data. The attacks by Gillie and Hearnshaw damaged Burt's reputation both in the general public and professional circles. For those who were suspicious of intelligence tests "Burt's deceptions" delivered a *coup de grace.* Intelligence testing was considered to be an outgrowth of Nazis' racial views and eugenicists' efforts to sterilize the poor.

The Burt affair would not end. More or less by chance, Robert Joynson, another psychologist got involved in the dispute. Joynson never knew Burt, nor was he professionally involved in the nature-nurture controversy. He had suddenly shifted his professional interest to the history of psychology and came across Hearnshaw's biography of Burt. He was struck by certain inconsistencies and began to suspect the accusation of "deceptions" was ill-founded. He became convinced that Burt had suffered a grave injustice and felt compelled to express these views (Joynson, 1989) in fairness to Burt and to the history of psychology. He concluded that Burt had not been guilty of any deliberate falsifications, while admitting that Burt suffered from "weakness of character" (vii). A similar conclusion was drawn by Ronald Fletcher (1991), a sociologist who investigated independently of Joynson, the so-called Cyril Burt Scandal.

Joynson, however, was not willing to rest his case with the conclusion that Burt was essentially innocent. Why was Burt being attacked? Joynson accused Burt's accusers of carrying on a vendetta against Burt because of their ideological commitments to a "genetic equalitarianism" (Rushton, 2000) that rejects the idea that genetics could possibly influence intelligence. The effort to depict Burt as an ideological elitist and reactionary who ignored the problem of educational inequalities in the slums of London is denied, Joynson believed, in Burt's own words:

> To conclude off-hand that in each individual case poverty is the main cause of dullness or incompetence would be neither just nor logical. A bare smattering of biography is sufficient to refute that simple induction

. . . Faraday, the blacksmith's son . . . Abraham Lincoln . . . the son of a carpenter–these and many like them have risen to the loftiest intellectual eminence from the lowliest social spheres. The poorest tenements of London contain many youthful geniuses–more of whom merit but fail to win–a free place or scholarship at a secondary school or college. (Burt 1937/1961, 105)

The next chapter in this saga was a book entitled *Cyril Burt/Fraud or Framed?* (Mackintosh, 1995) that viewed the controversy from several perspectives. Several conclusions are possible. One charitable interpretation is that Burt did not cheat; he made sloppy mistakes but they could be attributed to his old age and enormous productivity. After retiring at the age of 68, he published more than 200 papers, working continuously to the time of his death at 88. A more cautious judgment is that the case of fraud against Burt deserves the Scottish verdict, *Not Proven*. A more critical call is that Burt deceived his audience, thus invalidating all the evidence that suggested the influence of heredity on intelligence.

If one switches from the politics to science the Burt Affair loses its steam. This is not to suggest that scientific fraud is not a serious scientific and social matter. Faking data, whether Burt did or did not, damages science and society. But the final protection against fraud in science is empirical replication. And from this perspective it should be noted that Burt's finding of a correlation of +.77 in IQs of identical twins reared apart is consistent with four other independent studies, mentioned previously (p. 67), that reported positive correlations of .69, .71, .75, and .75 (Bouchard, 1993). Basic data in science is replicated data.

THE ROLE OF SCIENCE IN SOCIETY

Lewontin, Rose, and Kamin, wrote a book, previously mentioned, entitled *Not in Our Genes* (1984) that attacked so-called biological determinism, a synonym for behavior genetics. They questioned the ethical justification of this field, but refreshingly, revealed the source of their discontent. Their suspicion of behavior genetics stems from their Marxist bias: "We share a commitment to the prospects of a creation of a more socially just–a socialist–society" (ix). All facts, for them, are embedded in a social context from which the data cannot be extricat-

ed. This assumption encourages them to believe that positive findings
in the field of behavior genetics, such as the genetic involvement in
cognitive ability and even schizophrenia, would be used to attribute
the social and economic inequities of capitalism to genetic differences
among people. As a result of their ideological commitment, they seek
to discredit research that supports a strong genetic component in
behavior. In the case of schizophrenia, after a long history of sterile
attempts to assign environmental influences as the sole factor, the evidence now is clearly overwhelmingly in favor of hereditary factors
being involved in its etiology (e.g., Riley and K. S. Kendler, 2006).
Today, the research problem in schizophrenia is to identify the genetic mode of transmission as well as its genetic-environmental interactions.

At the root of Lewontin, Rose, and Kamin's resistance (1984) to
"biological determinism" is the murky holistic Marxist assumption of
"the power based on human consciousness in both interpreting and
changing the world, a power based on understanding of the essential
dialectical unity of the biological and social, not as two distinct
spheres, or separable components of actions, but as ontologically
coterminous" (p. 76). They cite Mao Zedong (1893–1976) as one of the
proponents of this idea but understandably ignore the role such ideology has played in the Cultural Revolution in China and other Marxist
tragedies involving the death of millions.

Lewontin (1987) offers a deeper insight into his resistance to acknowledging the importance of hereditary factors in cognitive ability
in an article addressed, not to the academic community, but instead to
his fellow "leftists." In a brief comment in the journal *Science for the
People* under the title "The Irrelevance of Heritability: Resisting the
Hereditarian Agenda," Lewontin responds to the criticism that he has
been too concerned with arguing that genetic factors play no role in
cognitive ability:

> As . . . [the critic] quite correctly points out, this would be a mistaken
> tack, both because it accepts the basic erroneous claim of hereditarians
> that the value of heritability is a critical issue for social policy, and
> because if the heritability of IQ should turn out, in fact, to be high, the
> left critics would have defeated themselves. I am chagrined that we
> have so consistently given the impression that the value of heritability
> of IQ is important and that the critics of biological determinism believe

that the heritability is zero. Let me explicitly reject both these claims. I do not know how heritable IQ is in various populations. I doubt that it can be truly zero, and I reject that the true value of heritability in any population is of the slightest importance to social action. (Lewontin, 1987, 23)

At first glance, the admission that the empirical evidence of heritability (the estimate of the relative importance of genetic factors for a given trait in a given population) has no relevance for social policy might seem to suggest that Lewontin accepts David Hume's fact/value dichotomy. Not at all! He freely admits that leftists, such as himself, have accused the hereditarians (behavior geneticists) of "ideological bias and motivation" while possibly giving the impression that he is wholly objective. He proudly denies this, acknowledging that he is also ideologically motivated but vigorously rejects the idea that "symmetry" prevails between his ideological bias and those of the behavior geneticists. His bias is justified but theirs is not because his encourages social change while they support the "inevitability of things as they are." Why do the hereditarians waste their time, asks Lewontin, in investigating heritability when they should be studying how society can be changed? The reason they do not do what Lewontin prescribes is because "the answer would come out in the wrong direction" (p. 32); it would reveal that environmental influences can achieve the changes that we all should desire. Lewontin's final conclusion is that the fundamental difference between the "hereditarian and antihereditarian" research programs is that "the two ideologies have very different stakes in finding out the truth about human flexibility" (p. 32).

Lewontin's argument seems to have its roots in old-time Marxist ideology that saw capitalistic societies as battlegrounds between the environmentally-oriented good guys struggling to gain their freedom and dignity from the repressive, powerful, nasty hereditarians. Recent history has destroyed much of the meaning of Lewontin's argument. The disasters of environmentally-oriented Marxism and hereditarian-Nazism coupled with the revolutionary breakthroughs in the science of genetics, should have laid to rest the impoverished and distorted views of the eternal battle between nature and nurture. If it had not been for these ideological passions and the misrepresentations they produce, the nature-nurture problem would have remained a productive research area instead of being the site of political warfare.

Within the context of natural science methodology "human flexibility"–malleability–is something to be discovered not proclaimed. With the potentialities of genetic counseling, genetic therapy, and genetic engineering, the possible successes of genetic interventions for some behaviors may exceed those of environmental modifications. However, a broader outlook will not pit nature against nurture but, instead, employ them in a joint enterprise to fully understand human behavior and its potentialities (e.g., K. S. Kendler and Prescott, 2006).

Lewontin's view of the conflict between hereditarians and environmentalists being fundamentally ideological in nature challenges the ideal of reliable empirical knowledge. A detached search for empirical truth is unattainable because ideological commitments infiltrate empirical evidence, thus precluding agreement about basic facts. History repeatedly supports this grim contention. The Inquisition in 1636 forced Galileo to deny the earth revolves around the sun. A few years ago the supreme religious authority of Saudi Arabia issued a fatwa, an interpretation of the Koran, that the earth is flat, with the added proviso that anyone who argues otherwise is an atheist deserving of punishment (Ibrahim, 1995). These empirical absurdities are not restricted to religion. The Nazi's labeled Einstein's theory of relativity as false because its author was Jewish, and Lysenkoism, the agronomical theory of the inheritance of acquired characteristics, was declared true by Stalin who assumed, consistent with Marxism, that environmental influences are all powerful. Although ideological commitments can contaminate "empirical truth," they need not, as was noted in the truth-seeking achievements of Darwin. Consistent with Darwin's success in discovering truth can be cited the Roman Catholic Church's reversal, in 1992, of its condemnation of Galileo. Einstein's theory now reigns in Germany and Lysenkoism has been discarded in Russia.

But where exactly do Lewontin and Kamin stand in regard to the belief in objective truth? Do they deny that it can ever exist or only that socially relevant data cannot be isolated from ideology? Lewontin claims, "Nothing we can know about the genetics of human behavior can have any implications for human society" (Wade, 1976, 115). One can suggest that Lewontin's own work in quantitative genetics and Kamin's research in conditioning were designed to reveal empirical relationships independent of Marxist ideology. If true, then empirical evidence can be isolated from ideology. Empirical data can stand alone even for ideologically committed researchers! If, however,

Lewontin is arguing that empirical evidence becomes contaminated only when used to influence social policy, then an apparent inconsistency is created. It would be possible for a detached researcher to discover empirical truth when investigating a phenomenon free of social implications (e.g., sexual selection in birds) but later, when the finding becomes relevant for humans, the data lose their truth status. Is not this position contradictory because it assumes that objective truth is possible except when ideology is involved?

BOOSTING IQ

One could easily assume that genetic interactionism, with its emphasis on genetic influences, would postulate a ceiling effect beyond which a person's IQ could not be raised by special educational programs. The basic assumption would be that genetic endowment creates a cognitive limit that environmental influences could not exceed. But careful thought would reveal that the genetic-interaction model is moot about the potential limits of possible environmental influences. An infinite number of interventions are possible, including science-fiction type biological procedures. All that can be done presently in evaluating the ability to boost IQs is to look critically at some widely publicized efforts.

Perhaps the greatest hope for a major breakthrough in exceeding modest gains in IQ scores (p. 58) was the heralded Project Head Start that began during the "War on Poverty" during President Lyndon Johnson's administration. This program was designed to provide slum children with an intellectually enriched preschool environment that would increase their cognitive performance and prepare them to cope with public school education. The mean benefit at the conclusion of the Head Start program was an increase in IQ of 7.42 points. Three or four years later this difference between the experimental and control groups decreased to 3.04 points. After seven to ten years the difference evaporated, suggesting that intellectual-enrichment programs had no lasting effect on the children's IQ (Brody, 1992). Head Start is still being supported because of beneficial social influences on children who participate.

Another effort to boost IQs was the Milwaukee Project that received wide publicity for its reported success in raising the cognitive ability of slum children. Twenty experimental children received a program of intensive cognitive stimulation and their IQs were compared with 20 control subjects from the same neighborhood. The study claimed "a remarkable acceleration of intellectual development on the part of [children] . . . exposed to the infant stimulation program" so that "the discrepancy between Experimental and Control [children] . . . varies from a minimum of 25 IQ points at 24 months to 30 points at 66 months" (Heber et al., 1972, 50). Such evidence was widely heralded as proving that the low IQ of children in slum areas was a result of their unstimulating environment. The cognitive training of the experimental children presumably raised their intellectual ability well beyond what would be expected by their genetic endowment.

One important factor was overlooked in publicizing this educational "magic bullet." The research was never described in detail nor subjected to peer review. And it certainly was not replicated, an important requirement, as has been repeatedly noted, for any scientific evidence. A brief progress report was released in 1971 with a more detailed description a year later (Heber et al., 1972) that promised a comprehensive final report in 1974 that never materialized. Fourteen years later more information was published (Garber, 1988) but the evidence cited fell far short of demonstrating "a remarkable acceleration of intellectual development." Although the experimental children, in their early teens, had IQ scores that were 10 points higher than control subjects, the two groups did not differ in academic performance. By the time they reached the fourth grade both groups were one to two years below average in both mathematics and reading skills. Perhaps the 10 IQ point advantage that the experimental children exhibited during their teens resulted from the repeated testing and familiarization with the content of intelligence tests (Jensen, 1989) and not from a boost in their cognitive skills, or perhaps the advantage had some basis in fact. As noted previously (Gray and Klaus, 1965; Kirp, 2006; Smith, 1942), modest increases in IQs have been reported when children from an intellectually deprived environment are exposed to a more stimulating one. Such an effect would be socially important because it would increase the capacity of such children to cope more effectively with the demands of society.

Another effort to boost cognitive ability of children with a high-risk for mental retardation was the Abecedarian Project at the University of North Carolina (Ramey, MacPhee, and Yeates, 1982; Ramey, 1992).

One month after the children were born, the experimental subjects began an intensive cognitive enrichment program. At the end of the third year the experimental children outscored the controls by 14.7 IQ points. At the age of four and one-half years the experimental children had a mean IQ of 101.4, 8.7 points higher than the control subjects. At eight years the difference dropped to five points. It would seem that the difference between the IQs of the experimental and control subjects were gradually fading out as they had done in the Head Start Program. But data obtained at 12 years of age presents a more favorable picture. The experimental group was doing better than the controls in that fewer (28% to 55%) had repeated a school grade and fewer (13% to 44%) had IQs below 88. The charge has been made (Spitz, 1992) that the two groups were not comparable at the beginning of the study; the experimental subjects had outscored the controls in a cognitive performance test at one year of age. Therefore, any difference in performance on cognitive tests may not be a function of intensive intellectual stimulation but, instead, to the superior aptitude of the experimental group. Ramey (1992), the lead investigator of the Abecedarian Project, acknowledges this possibility but believes it is unlikely.

What can be made of these three studies? The most important point is that the ability to boost IQ scores by intensive cognitive stimulation is *presently* limited. Interpreting the data of the Milwaukee and Abecedarian Projects in their most favorable light, while ignoring their methodological deficiencies, would suggest that the intensive cognitive stimulation led to a 5 to 10 point IQ gain. One reviewer of the Abecedarian Project (Neisser, 1997) estimates the gain to be "five IQ points." Locurto (1990) concludes that when children are adopted in a home environment that is superior to the one offered by their biological parents their IQs are elevated about 6 IQ points. These estimates of enhanced cognitive ability of 5 to 10 IQ points are individually and socially important. But such increases do not justify the conclusion that cognitive ability is completely malleable as a consequence of cognitively stimulating environments.

The second point to note is the manner in which these studies have been publicized. Caution was thrown to the wind in the case of the Milwaukee Project. The hyperbole–"a remarkable acceleration of intellectual development"–was particularly unfitting considering the tentative nature of the results. When the positive findings dissipated with time it became incumbent upon those who publicized them, researchers and the press, to inform the public that the dramatic claims of radically elevating cognitive ability were unjustified. But that did not happen. Instead the deception was swept under the rug and many who learned about the success of the Milwaukee Project never heard about its failure.

Was it simply exaggeration that was behind the overselling of the Milwaukee and Abecedarian Projects or was some underlying political effort being made to minimize the importance of genetic factors in cognitive behavior? Hillary Clinton (1996) cited the results of the Abecedarian Projects as being in opposition to the pro-heredity views of the "The Bell Curve" (Hernstein and Murray, 1994). The fact that hereditary factors influence cognitive behavior in no way denies the possibility that appropriate training techniques can elevate intellectual performance. The important question is how much IQ upgrading can be achieved? By refusing to consider genetic factors one can easily adopt a naïvely optimistic view that with the right training, anybody can learn anything and everything. Such a view encourages the idea that everybody will profit from going to college and will have the potential to graduate. But psychological evidence fails to support such a fantasy, assuming that demanding academic standards are to be maintained in higher education. Training techniques are effective only with those who have the necessary aptitudes to acquire the skills that are being taught. For effective educational planning neither nature nor nurture should be ignored. One can suggest that the democratic spirit encourages the policy that every effort should be made to develop educational programs that will allow all to achieve their potential (Wickelgren, 1999). But such a goal cannot be achieved by ignoring genetic influences on cognitive behavior.

Finally, an important methodological point must be made. When ideology drives science, empirical truth will be sacrificed for political goals. To achieve a balanced view of a research area, such as boosting children's IQ, all relevant research should be considered, not only the evidence that appears to be consistent with ideological commitments.

THE PERSISTENCE OF A RADICAL ENVIRONMENTALISM

Why does radical environmentalism with its implication of a genetic equality for all forms of behavior persist? I am reluctant to cope with such a complicated question but believe that an attempt is demanded. To do so requires my return to an early part of my life (Kendler, 2002). An event of enormous social impact was the Great Depression that began with the stock market crash of 1929. I have been unsuccessful in conveying to my children and grandchildren the pain and helplessness that the Depression generated. Even the necessities of life–food, clothing, shelter–were threatened. A quarter of the working force was unemployed and the gross national product fell by almost 50 percent from 1929 to 1933. Such objective indices convey the nature of the disaster but not the debilitating experience of poverty that a large segment of the population was forced to endure. In contrast, many people spent the Depression years in affluence thus encouraging civil strife between the "haves" and "have nots." The social devastation raised the question, "Isn't there a better way?" An immediate solution was available in the form of Marxism. Presumably based on rigid laws of history, one could easily be seduced into believing its promises of full employment without exploitation, equality of humankind, communitarian values such as "from each according to his abilities to each according to his needs," and other utopian goodies. The ideals of Marxism and the realities of capitalism persuaded many that a "better way" was the Marxist way. An ideal environment, based on Marxist principles, would lead to an ideal society.

The appeal of Marxism is not difficult to understand, but its persistence is. As the information increased about communism's political horrors and economic failures, disenchantment grew until finally adherence to its principles was left only to those true believers whose ideological commitments were beyond falsification. Ad hoc rationalizations of its failures were numerous, the most common being that communism in the USSR was kidnapped by the ruthlessly paranoid Joseph Stalin. The portrait of Lenin as a humane leader had crumbled under the weight of historical evidence that showed him sharing the malevolence of his successor (R. Pipes, 1990, 1993; Volkogonov, 1994). And more importantly, history replicated the Soviet disaster with other leaders–Mao Zedong, Pol Pot, Castro, Kim Il Sung, Kim Jong-Il–and now it seems that tyrants did not destroy communism but, instead, communism bred tyrants.

The aim of discussing the failures of communism is not to serve as a cheerleader for capitalistic democracies with their free market economies. Although having troubling social and economic ills, capitalistic democracies have the virtues of being open societies (Popper, 1945) accessible to the ideas and opinions of others, even their severest critics. And when open societies clashed with closed ones, the former seem preferable to most people. Attempts to blend certain Marxist economic ideas with political democracy have occurred in Scandinavia in so-called welfare states. Norman Thomas (1884–1968), who ran for President in the United States six times, embraced democratic socialism and believed Franklin Roosevelt's New Deal was heading in that direction.

My purpose is not to reflect about social philosophy but, instead, to analyze the corrupting influence that ideological warfare can have on scientific efforts. The environmental determinists' actions in the nature-nurture controversy about IQ represent a sequence of political maneuvers, not a systematic scientific analysis: (1) a political attack on the investigation of genetic influences on intelligence, (2) the accusation that "hereditarian" researchers are biological determinists who ignore environmental influences in their devious attempt to blame the working class for the social ills of capitalism, (3) the denial of genetic influences (heritability of IQ is zero), (4) the subsequent admission that heredity probably plays a role in intelligence, (5) the assertion that all scientists indulge in ideological warfare to generate evidence in support of their dogma, (6) the conclusion that ideological biases in science are not symmetrical because ideology in favor of change is good while ideology in favor of the status quo is bad. What a mockery of science! My dismay does not stem from a naïve conception that scientific inquiry can be guided by simple rules that preclude ideological and theoretical contamination of empirical efforts. Separating empirical issues from conceptual pollution can be messy and difficult in scientific research, especially in the social sciences. But if one desires to seek a detached view of the world, the *will* will create the way. And with the cooperation of other scientists who share a tough-minded, problem-solving, empirical orientation, the goal of reliable scientific evidence can be achieved.

Good intentions alone, however, will not provide society with reliable knowledge that can guide the formulation of effective social policy. The reason is that a counterforce operates that defines psychology and the social sciences not as disciplines designed to reveal empirical truth, but instead, as an adjunct weapon to achieve political and social goals (e.g., Fox, 1993). Many reasons are offered to justify these anti-scientific methodological orientations, varying from the denial that natural science methodology can be applied to the so-called human sciences to the complete rejection of the idea of empirical truth (Fishman, 1999). Thus the conflict between natural-science psychology and these competing methodological orientations cannot be reconciled and the differences cannot be ignored. As a result, society faces an overwhelming problem in determining the epistemological criteria that should be used in evaluating socially relevant evidence. For the present, the issue will simply be acknowledged. The problem that society faces in separating the empirical wheat from the political chaff will be addressed later.

ETHICAL IMPLICATIONS OF GENETIC INFLUENCES ON INTELLIGENCE

Although individual differences in intelligence are recognized, the idea that it has a hereditary component is resisted in spite of the overwhelming evidence supporting the relationship. Why?

The Talmud, the collection of Jewish law, warns against the dangers of hereditary differences:

> Why did creation begin with a single human being? For the sake of the righteous and the wicked, that none might ascribe their differing characters to hereditary differences. And lest families boast of their high lineage. This they do nonetheless how much worse it would be if all were not descended from a single source.

History has revealed a constant struggle against the idea of a natural aristocracy, a family group that is born to rule because of its innate superiority. Since we are all descended from the same source, according to the Talmud, one family group cannot declare its own superiority. Whereas the quotation from the Talmud allows it to be interpreted as attributing human behavioral differences to nurture, not nature, John B. Watson, the famous behaviorist, leaves no doubt about his views.

> Give me a dozen healthy infants, well formed, and my own specified world to bring them up in, and I'll guarantee to take any at random and

train him to become any type of specialist I might select—a doctor, lawyer, artist, merchant chief, and yes even beggar-man and thief, regardless of his talents and penchants, tendencies, abilities, vocations and race of his ancestors. (Watson, 1926, 10)

Both anti-hereditary comments, the Talmud and Watson's, are not as unyielding as they initially appear. The Talmud's deontological principle of equality based upon a single genetic origin was formulated prior to Darwin's evolutionary theory of natural selection and the science of genetics. In spite of a common ancestry, humans differ in their genetic heritage. Large numbers of breeding populations survived in widely divergent environments. Natural selection of the traits conducive to survival in contrasting environments—hunting and fishing, agriculture, commercial—results in genetic differences among various groups. Variations in physiology of different breeding populations would probably be accompanied by variations in behavior. But the Talmud's misguided genetics does not negate the vaguely stated moral value of social equality.

Watson's extreme environmentalism was an exaggeration and he realized it. He acknowledged genetic influences when admitting that certain kinds of physical structures combined with appropriate training *slanted* a person toward exceptional skills in sports. He also admitted overstating his boast about his exceptional training skills, "I'm going beyond my facts and I admit it, but so have the advocates to the contrary, but they have been doing it for many thousands of years." By implication an extreme environmentalism was as phony as an extreme hereditarianism. In sum, Watson extolled the virtues of education while grudgingly admitting some genetic influences. One of the driving forces behind Watson's environmentalism was that he was basically a social engineer, and in those days education was the only practical method for modifying behavior. It is interesting to speculate whether Watson would have been such a devout environmentalist if in his time genetic engineering had its present-day potential.

What ethical issues are raised by the distribution of intellectual talent? Let us try to answer this question in the most innocuous manner possible in hope of avoiding the many emotional pitfalls with which history has burdened us. To dampen the emotionality, three points should be made clear. First, no matter what the facts are about individual differences, they do not dictate, as the fact/value dichotomy maintains, that empirical evidence demands a particular social policy. Second, whatever genetic differences are found, their consequences may not be fixed or unmodifiable. For example, phenylketonuria, a disorder of protein metabolism, which is transmitted as a simple recessive hereditary characteristic, can be alleviated by an appropriate diet during infancy, thereby avoiding severe intellectual retardation in later life. Third, the fact that hereditary influences can sometimes be diminished or overcome does not justify the claim that individual differences based on a genetic component can always be eliminated. In fact, the empirical evidence suggests otherwise. Thus society in shaping social policy is constantly confronted with a choice between *what is* and *what can be,* between hard facts and comforting hopes.

Consider an oversimplified example of an ethnically homogeneous society in which the members vary in intelligence test scores, a description consistent with an enormous amount of evidence that indicates that people with a common ethnicity vary in their cognitive ability. This is also true for the members of the same family. How are the children and young people to be assigned to educational programs that lead to different vocations and professions that vary in their economic rewards and social prestige? Should everybody have an opportunity to start in an educational track that terminates at the highest educational goals and then redirect those who do not succeed into paths more consistent with their talents, or should students be initially assigned to educational routes appropriate to their cognitive aptitudes as potential radio operators were in the Navy during World War II? Is either policy more ethical than the other? Moral arguments can be offered to support both alternatives but neither can be independently judged as being ethically valid. The justification for the use of an effective aptitude test is in its consequences; it promotes efficiency and effectiveness. An intelligence test in society can identify students who have the potential to acquire a range of important cognitive skills that contribute to the economic wealth and health of a nation. It also can identify those students who have a small chance of succeeding in certain educational programs and thereby avoid the failures that such attempts would bring.

Although effective in predicting future academic success, IQ scores need not rigidly assign a child to a given educational track. A sensitive and flexible educational system should be able to recognize misdirections that the test might encourage so that an error can be remedied.

Also, an effective system should be able to identify students whose achievements are below expectations, not because the estimate of the student's ability was erroneous, but because nonacademic variables (e.g., personality disorders, sensory deficits) are downgrading the student's performance. In conclusion, the intelligence test is not a perfect predictor of future cognitive ability, but its accuracy far exceeds that of other measures. And if the past reflects the future, the predictive capacity of intelligence tests and other aptitude tests will improve.

The moral issues in employing the radio code aptitude test were minimal because of the social agreement that prevailed in the military and in society that any personnel selection procedure that would improve military effectiveness was ethically justified. But the use of intelligence tests in an ethnically homogeneous society raises moral issues that go beyond the effectiveness of the tests to their social impact upon the entire society. Consider the problems of individuals who earned IQ scores below 68 during World War II. They were rejected for military service because of their inability to acquire necessary military skills. What are society's moral obligations to those who are inadequate for military service and those whose economic value is low or even nonexistent? This brings us to the moral issue of the distribution of wealth among the members of our homogeneous society. How does a society in general cope with the relationship between economic rewards and intellectual ability? Although financial rewards are not simply a function of a person's IQ, a person's intelligence is nevertheless a fairly good predictor of economic success.

How should society deal with the talent differential among the members of an ethnically homogeneous society? One can suggest that those who won the genetic lottery for intelligence "deserve" exceptional rewards because their ingenuity and creativity are root causes for the economic success of their society. But is not some social intervention required to balance out the inequities of the distribution of talent to prevent those with lesser amounts from suffering excessive deprivation? Such action cannot only be justified by humane concerns, but also by the self-interests of the upper socioeconomic group. Social turmoil is frequently generated by *relative deprivation* (Gurr, 1970), a discrepancy between what people think they deserve and what they actually have. The greater the gap between the lifestyles of the wealthy and the poor, the greater the dissimilarity between what people think they should have and actually have, can trigger resentment and civil strife.

Societies seem to employ a moral guidance system to help select social policies. In authoritarian societies the control of the system is in the hands of the dictators. In a democracy the system is more complex because many conflicting forces control it. According to what may be called *democratic instrumentalism,* the adopted governmental policy achieves moral justification, not because it is right or true or that everybody favors it, but because it is authorized by democratic processes, and can be changed by the same mechanism that created it. Instrumentalism can be likened to a car's overdrive that enhances functioning. By receiving information about the consequences of proposed policies, the electorate and their representatives are in a better position to make an informed judgment in choosing among social policies. Science and psychology, in principle, can play a crucial role in providing reliable information about the outcomes of competing policies.

Government policies in a political democracy will strongly influence the distribution of economic rewards. Disagreements will inevitably occur about the existing policy and suggested changes. Although the financial community can argue that a wage policy that produces the greatest economic productivity should be adopted, and labor can favor a high wage program, and other interest groups can favor plans that benefit their social agenda, no group can logically argue that their proposal is for the common good. The concept of common good is not an empirical event but a moral judgment. One can argue that humanistic values or a religious ethic or business efficiency or communitarian values are the fundamental ethic that should govern a democratic society, but it should now be apparent that such views do not carry the weight of moral truth.

A summary statement about democratic instrumentalism is now in order. The system does not provide any absolute judgment about social policies or the political structure of democracies. The entire approach can be judged as pragmatic, not idealistic. Means, not goals, are emphasized. Both democratic procedures and adopted social policies are likened to ongoing experiments designed to produce consequences that achieve greater social approval. Thus, when the problem of economic rewards in an ethnically homogeneous society is raised, we will be forced to acknowledge that no recipe is available, only an orientation that emphasizes social experimentation and democratic choice. Admittedly this combination contains many loopholes in which the intent of democratic instrumentalism can be compromised by poor science or a corrupted democracy. But a vigilant and sophisticated citizenry can counteract such threats. If we translate the problems of individual differences in intelligence into the framework of democratic instrumentalism, then the social problem becomes one of making choices about the selection and education of all people, and whether knowledge about cognitive difference should be exploited or ignored.

Chapter 4

RACIAL DIFFERENCES:
FACTS AND SPECULATIONS

The United States has, for several decades, been in the grip of racial and ethnic strife that generates political conflict and social turmoil. My aim is not to offer an explanation of, or a solution to, this crisis. Instead, these social problems will be utilized as a backdrop to discuss and analyze the moral issues and their scientific and psychological counterparts. Rather than wade into the center of the conflicts, the central issues will be approached tangentially in an effort to focus on fundamental epistemological problems.

RACE, INTELLIGENCE, AND SOCIAL POLICY

The combination of three concepts–*race, intelligence,* and *social policy*–can be likened to a witch's brew that will poison those who consume it. But perhaps the stew can prove nourishing for those who dare devour it. With this hope in mind, each concept will be discussed separately.

Race

For the person on the street the meaning of race is like a popular view of pornography; one can't define it, but one can recognize it. The concept of *race* dates back to the ancient Egyptians who distinguished, although imprecisely, in the appearance of Egyptians, Asiatics, Libyans, and Nubians. This classification, as well as others throughout history, can be criticized because of the fuzziness of the borders that makes impossible a clear-cut racial assignment of some individuals, especially those of "interracial" matings. Consequently, the charge has been made that the concept of race is too ill-defined to serve any social or scientific function (e.g., Zuckerman, 1990). From this perspective, an attempt has made to bar the concept of race from scientific discourse. An extreme and erroneous position is the conclusion that race is purely a social concept without any biological basis. In other words, one cannot distinguish among humans on the basis of only biological differences.

Rejecting the concept of race because of its ambiguity is scientifically unjustified. Ambiguous definitions are not necessarily useless. A clear dividing line does not exist between night and day or between life and death, yet such distinctions serve a purpose. Race is a shorthand way of describing, with limited precision, genetic differences among people. One fivefold classification are groups that were native to Europe, East Asia, Africa, America, and Australasia, the major races of traditional anthropology (Leroi, 2005). We can distinguish among many people with this fivefold division even though some humans do not fit into the classification. There are biological reasons for the ambiguity of the concept of race. Humans from all parts of the world are interfertile, and throughout the course of history interbreeding has occurred among previously isolated breeding populations. Yet race can have a reliable meaning if it is understood that races are essentially breeding populations with distinctive patterns of genetic characteristics. Within this context races can be defined in terms of the frequency of certain selected genes in a population, not in the individual. For example, although the Basques, an early Caucasoid race, has a relatively high incidence of the genotype responsible for Rh-negative type blood, this same genotype is practically absent among East Asians. Yet there are many Basques who do not possess this genotype and some East Asians who do.

As suggested, the gene is the unit of inheritance. The formulation, as well as the use of a particular system, is dictated by the purpose to which the classification is placed. Classifications of breeding populations have been useful in medicine in identifying the genetic bases of particular diseases. Single-gene medical disorders show striking variations in frequency among different breeding populations and ethnic groups. Sickle cell anemia is primarily confined to blacks, especially to those of west African descent. Cystic fibrosis is much more prevalent in whites as compared to blacks. Tay-Sachs disease occurs at a rate one hundred times higher among Ashkenazi Jews than among any other ethnic group. The risk of multiple sclerosis among white Americans is twice as great than among African Americans. In contrast, the incidence of hypertensive heart disease or prostate cancer is much greater among African Americans. Some drugs that are effective in treating the heart conditions of whites are ineffective or harmful in the care of blacks. Genetic differences, based upon racial classifications, are due to play an increasing role in medical care.

Should the searchlight of racial comparisons be directed toward black/white psychological differences? Could it serve any useful social or scientific function? Such a question should immediately be recognized as a value judgment. It is beyond dispute that such inquiries could be misused to justify differential–unequal and unfair–treatment of blacks, repeating the racism that prevailed in the United States during periods of slavery before the Civil War and Jim Crow after. The phony idea of racial superiority has scarred history, most notably by the Nazis who proclaimed the "racial" superiority of the "Nordic" over other "races," particularly Jews and Gypsies. With junk science they proved to themselves their own "racial superiority" and instituted a "eugenics" program in the form of the Holocaust designed to enhance the quality of Europeans by eliminating "inferior" elements.

The horrible consequences of the Nazi's actions have cast terrible suspicion on any scientist who dares to research racial differences. Not only are they perceived as racists who aspire to deny civil rights to members of certain racial or ethnic groups, but they are automatically seen as proponents of a eugenic program designed to elevate the "quality" of the human race by controlling the reproductive behavior of "undesirables."

Such interpretations are gratuitous for three reasons. First, it is based on faulty logic. The study of racial differences by Nazis does not mean that those who study such differences are motivated by Nazi values. Investigating sickle-cell anemia in blacks is a case in point. Carriers of the sickle-cell gene are resistant to malaria. If two carriers of the disease have children, one in four of their children will have the disease, which has no known cure and until recently proved fatal in childhood. Although mortality is still high among young sickle cell children under 5, improved techniques of treatment enable some victims to live to adulthood and some can have children. But the problems that face the victims of sickle cell anemia, as well as their parents, are overwhelming and, therefore, the common medical recommendation is for a couple with a strong genetic potential of bearing a sickle cell child to undergo genetic counseling. Tests can also be performed during early pregnancy to determine whether the fetus will develop into a sickle cell anemic child. This is only one of many examples that demonstrate an involvement with racial differences need not be driven by racist attitudes that are designed to justify unjust treatment.

The second objection to employing the pejorative term *racist* to identify scientists who study racial differences is that the epithet attacks the freedom of inquiry that is fundamental to both science and democracy. No one knows for sure where scientists will be driven by empirical evidence and, in respect for their pursuit of knowledge, no unreasonable obstacle should be placed in their path. To understand the course of human evolution or physiological processes or distribution of diseases or disproportionate behavioral achievements may require some examination of the differences among breeding populations.

The third reason to reject the notion that studying racial differences is intrinsically evil, in the sense that it resembles the efforts of the Nazis, is that empirical data are intrinsically neutral. *They do not logically generate any social policy.* Society need not adopt any legislation that prevents parents from making their own decision about their genetic potential to have a sickle-cell anemic or Tay-Sachs or cystic fibrosis offspring. They can choose to receive genetic counseling for family planning or, if pregnancy results, they can request tests to reveal the fetus's potential, and if it proves susceptible to the disorder, the parents can choose abortion or birth. One cannot logically insist that one outcome is morally preferable to others unless one is committed to some ethical system, such as a religion that prescribes or proscribes certain actions. But a democratic society can adopt a hands-off policy to allow the parents to make the final decision about inherited maladies of their offspring. Or society can intervene and establish policies that are designed to reduce births of incapacitated offsprings. What must be understood is that such policies emerge from the value system of the society, not from the facts of genetic disabilities.

Intelligence

The concept of *intelligence* outstrips the concept of *race* in generating disagreements about its meaning, as well as reservations about its social value. At one extreme is the judgment that *intelligence tests* are scientifically useless and socially dangerous. The test neither measures true intelligence nor does it recognize that cognitive ability is culturally bound. A reasonable response to such an unreasonable argument is:

> . . . no serious scholar claims either that IQ tests measure nothing important or that they measure everything important. At the very least they do tap certain abilities that are relevant to success in school and do so with remarkably consistency. (Neisser, 1997, 440)

One can accept this evaluation but still have reservations about using IQ tests in measuring racial differences. Many scientists of good will believe that studying racial difference in intelligence is intemperate and dangerous, like removing a land mine with inadequate tools. Their position is understandable and perhaps even justifiable if one is willing to admit that some knowledge is best unknown, that ignorance can be bliss. The atomic bomb is a case in point. But a veil of ignorance cannot resist being lifted. Science and democracy encourage a free rein for curiosity, especially when a popular belief is that all racial, ethnic, and gender groups have equal aptitude for all forms of behavior. And when such an assumption is used to justify a controversial policy, such as affirmative action (Chapter 6), the testing of the conjecture about behavioral equality becomes inevitable.

Social Policy

The *fact/value dichotomy* (pp. 26–27) has served as a core methodological point in many previous discussions. Nowhere is it more important than when examining ethical implications of racial difference in behavior. If abortions, for argument sake, produce greater harm or good measured in terms of the psychological health of the aborted mother, such evidence cannot logically lead to the moral justification of a pro- or antiabortion policy. Such a conclusion is difficult to swallow for a person who views abortion within a moral framework. Finding that abortions produce irreparable psychological disturbances to pregnant women would confirm to the antiabortion activist that his or her position has been validated. Similarly, if denying abortions to women who desire them produces greater psychological damage than permitting them, the evidence would justify the conclusion of pro-abortion activists that they occupy the high moral ground. But such moral self-approval should dissipate when it is recognized that the moral argument results, not from the evidence, but from a priori ethical commitment. If the evidence were negative to their position they would not abandon their pro-choice or pro-life views. Their moral position, if it is an ethical imperative, is impervious to evidence. In other words, reliable empirical evidence is incapable of logically rejecting moral principles. But reliable empirical evidence can be persuasive for those who believe that social policies should be shaped by practical considerations.

Racial Differences in Intelligence
Test Scores: Possible or Impossible?

I recall sitting next to a distinguished social psychologist during a colloquium back in the 1950s that touched upon racial differences in intelligence. She leaned over to me saying, "I think all racial groups have equal intelligence, don't you?" I was initially tempted to agree but the complexity of the problem flashed through my mind and I cautiously responded, "I don't know." I was not knowledgeable about the origins of Homo sapiens at that time but entertained the possibility that there might have been differences among early breeding populations. Although the popular current assumption is that Homo sapiens emerged from Africa, a multiregional interpretation has not been abandoned (Penniski, 1999). But even if one accepts the African assumption, different migration patterns from Africa to other continents (Fischman, 1996) could have resulted in different breeding populations being exposed to contrasting environments. Perhaps interbreeding occurred between Neanderthals (with their smaller brains) and modern humans. Could that influence the cognitive ability of certain breeding populations?

When writing an introductory psychology text (Kendler, 1963) my thoughts about racial differences in cognitive ability was focused on the course of human evolution through approximately 200,000 years. I speculated about environmental and cultural differences that could influence the reproductive rate of individuals with different cognitive abilities. If survival in cold climates is more difficult than in warm climates would the reproductive rate of the more cognitively gifted be higher in the colder climate (Rushton, 2000)? Would all societies—

hunters, hunter-gatherers, agricultural, industrial-commercial–place equal cognitive demands on their members? Would societies with a written language make greater cognitive demands than those that are limited to oral communication? Is orally rooted and textually mediated thought different? What would be the influence of religions with bibles whose members would be encouraged to read and interpret them, as contrasted with belief systems that one is simply forced to obey submissively? Throughout the current world one can point to some breeding populations that fail to compete effectively with their neighbors.

If differences occur in the outward structure of humans could not similar differences occur in internal organs, including the brain? When discussing physical differences among humans in an introductory psychology class, a young lady remarked, "I thought all our brains are alike!" How could she reach such a conclusion when marked physical differences are so obvious? Isn't the brain a physical property of a person just as height, weight, or facial features? The brain case of indigenous Australians is massive with the thickness of the bones of the cranial vault twice as great as most other races. The capacity of the brain case is relatively small, averaging about 84 percent of the capacity of the skulls of the Anglo-Saxons who invaded Great Britain about the fifth century (Baker, 1974). The fact that one race has a larger brain case than another does not prove that it is cognitively superior, nor do the previous speculations about the influence of cultural differences on the natural selection of the more cognitively gifted *prove* anything about racial differences in intelligence. These speculations are offered only to evaluate the hypothesis that so many people are willing to accept: All breeding populations are equal in their potential to develop cognitive skills. At the same time, a discrepancy occurs among the Caucasoid, Mongoloid, and Negroid races in their physical build, physiological function (Rushton, 2000), and in their apparent athletic and artistic skills. In sum, it would appear unlikely that evolutionary processes, within a tremendous range of environments, would have bequeathed all breeding populations with equal cognitive potential, and parity among other abilities as well.

Two dominant themes in American society resist the notion of racial differences. One is the belief in the natural equality of human beings and the other is the effectiveness of a democratic society to improve people's lives. These themes combine to generate an optimism that environmental interventions can overcome presumed differences that "hereditarians" suggest exist among various breeding populations. From an ethical point of view this extreme environmentalism–or *environmental determinism*–provides support for a communitarian spirit that favors a social responsibility for everybody's well-being. Society should provide educational opportunities for everybody to achieve equality. Although this social sensitivity can be applauded, the methodological implications of the environmentally-based optimism should not be ignored. Its claims are impossible to reject! If behavioral equality cannot be achieved by one method, others should be tried. An infinite number of environmental interventions are possible thereby making it impossible to deny the idea that some environmental intervention program will be able to achieve psychological equality.

The difficulty of rejecting an extreme environmental hypothesis is illustrated by the mean height difference of more than a foot between the African Pygmies and Watusis (Jensen, 1973). The two groups live in markedly different environments and consume different diets. The presumption is that genetic factors are responsible for the height discrepancy because of two reasons: the magnitude of the difference relative to the variations within each group and the fact that human height has been demonstrated to be a physical trait with high heritability. But this presumption is not a final "proof" because an environmental determinist could maintain that some unexplored factor is responsible for the discrepancy. When an environmental determinist takes this extreme position he is essentially protecting his assumption from possible falsification. And the question can be raised in anticipation of subsequent discussion of behavior genetics: Do environmental determinists assume an impregnable position?

Another comparison will throw light on an important methodological problem involved in the investigation of differences between contrasting breeding populations. IQ differences were investigated between two kinds of Jews–descendents of Askenazim and Sephardim–living in the same neighborhood in Brooklyn, New York. Ashkenazi Jews lived in various communities with a distinctive culture in Eastern Europe while Sephardic Jews are descendents of Jews who were expelled from Spain in 1492 and dispersed themselves mainly throughout the Mediterranean basin. Gross (1967) reported a significant difference between the mean IQs of Brooklyn-born boys in favor of the descendents of the Ashkenazim as compared to the Sephardim. The family environments of the two groups were examined to discover the possible reason for this discrepancy. One significant factor was the stronger academic motivation instilled in Ashkenazi boys. Sephardic mothers stressed the value of becoming "wealthy" while Ashkenazi mothers emphasized more the importance of education without regard to future wealth. These findings were interpreted by Havighurst (1970) to illustrate the importance of rewards in the education of socially disadvantaged children. The greater emphasis on education per se without concern for financial rewards was assumed by Havighurst to be responsible for the higher IQ of the Ashkenazi boys.

Havighurst's emphasis on the beneficial effects of increasing academic motivation for socially disadvantaged children appears reasonable, but his explanation of the superior IQ of Ashkenazi children is open to challenge. He automatically adopts an environmental-determinist position that IQ differences must exclusively be due to environmental factors. Such a preconception allows the identification of any environmental difference to explain the IQ discrepancy between groups. Such reasoning suffers from two major faults. First the possibility that genetic factors could have played a role is ignored. Descendents of Ashkenazim have exhibited enormous intellectual achievement as indicated by being awarded Nobel Prizes in the sciences well beyond their proportion in the population. One can also suggest that the two Jewish subpopulations differ genetically to some extent, as indicated by the susceptibility of the Ashkenazim to Tay-Sachs and several other genetic disorders. Presumably these defects resulted from genetic bottlenecks in small Ashkenazi communities (shtetles) that dotted Eastern Europe between 800 to 1500 A.D. Closely related persons (e.g., cousins) married thus making their offsprings more susceptible to genetic abnormalities. At the same time, scholarship was so highly valued that the more cognitively talented may have had a higher reproductive rate. Although these speculations are not offered as a genetic explanation of cognitive differences between Ashkenazi and Sephardic Jews, they are proposed to highlight the point that when interpreting behavioral differences, genetic factors should not automatically be ignored and environmental influences should not automatically be assumed. Should it not be incumbent upon those who advance ad hoc conjectures to ask themselves, "What evidence is

available and what study can be done to support my contention?"
Should not environmental determinists, such as Havighurst, be
encouraged to obtain independent evidence to justify their hypothesis? Could it be demonstrated that parental attitudes favoring financial
over educational rewards significantly influence IQ scores in school
children? These demands for evidence should extend to genetic
hypotheses as well. Last but not least, a replication is needed (Cohen,
1994) to justify any conclusion about the IQ scores of Ashkenazi and
Sephardic school children. Meeting demanding standards of empirical
evidence is particularly important when dealing with emotional social
issues.

A final point will bring to the surface the inordinate social pressures
that prevent discussing racial differences because of the risk of being
labeled a racist, if not an outright Nazi. A few years ago a candidate
for the presidency of a university was chastised for suggesting that
blacks may have a greater genetic aptitude for sports than whites. That
comment was judged to be fascist presumably because acknowledging
the fact that one race, in regard to particular skills, could be, on average, superior to others. If the implications of the candidate's remarks
were restricted to basketball, football, and track, could it not be defended with the widely used procedure of identifying disproportionate
representation in various jobs as significant evidence that some selection process is operating? Is it beyond reason to suggest a possible
genetic link? In this case blacks are grossly overrepresented, about 80
percent, among professional basketball players, while constituting
about 13 percent of the general population (Schoenfeld, 1995). Were
whites being discriminated against or were blacks, on average, more
skillful?

In explaining the dominance of blacks in basketball many people
reject the possibility that genetic factors could be responsible. For
them, environmental influences are sufficient. Blacks, they argue, are
powerfully motivated to excel in basketball and urban playgrounds
provide them a unique opportunity to sharpen their skills. In addition,
basketball, like football and sprints races in track, two other sports in
which blacks are disproportionately represented, afford an opportunity for blacks to escape from the financial squalor of the ghetto. Such
an environmental explanation overlooks three factors. First, the conclusion may drastically underestimate the motivation of white youths

in America to succeed in all sports, including basketball. Second, the requirement of urban playground experiences seems to be bypassed by many blacks, as well as whites, who develop in rural areas. More importantly, in recent years several blacks have become NBA stars without any early training in basketball. Hakeem Olajuwon, the most valuable player in the NBA season of 1993–1994, played little basketball in his native Nigeria. An athletic scholarship to the University of Houston started him on a career in basketball that led to his NBA stardom. Dikembe Mutombo, born in Zaire, now the Democratic Republic of the Congo, played basketball at Georgetown, and then became a star player in the NBA. Several active players in the NBA were born and raised in Africa. The third reason for dispelling the simple environmental explanation comes from a careful scrutiny of the athletic skills of black and white professionals.

Larry Bird and Steve Nash, famous white basketball players both garnered the Most Valuable Player Award on several occasions, were not as fast as most black professional players nor could they match their vertical leaping ability. Their shooting and passing skills and their leadership qualities, were of the highest level, making both exceptional players. But the skills of Michael Jordan, of the past, and Kobe Bryant and Dwayne Wade of the present, with their quickness, speed, coordination, and jumping, equaled by other black players, were well beyond the capacity of practically all white players. The exceptional whites played basketball on the ground while the exceptional blacks played basketball in the air. The common cliché "white men can't jump" is not a racial slur but a statement with some truth value. Such an opinion gains credence from an apparent advantage that blacks have in basketball of leaping high, providing them with the invaluable gift of an option to make one of several choices—which shot to take or to whom to pass-off—before returning to earth. One six-foot eleven-inch white NBA basketball player acknowledges the racial differences, "I think I'm athletic, but I'm not nearly as athletic as some of the [black] guys who can play the game. I can dunk, but I don't dunk like some of these guys do (Schoenfeld, 1995, 37). Another white player agrees, "white people can't jump as high. That's a fact. And it's a fact that white people don't have much rhythm. We are stiff" (Schoenfeld, 1995, 37). These differences, it must be noted, represent average differences with some overlap between the skills of the two groups. Some whites are faster or quicker than some blacks but, on average, the two groups differ. The most pronounced difference occurs among the tallest basketball players with the agility and coordination of blacks being unmatched by whites.

The emphasis on the disproportionate representation of blacks in professional basketball and their speed, quickness, and extraordinary leaping ability, as well as the apparently large hands and relatively long arms of some, is not offered as a "reasonable explanation" of a genetic difference between blacks and whites. Reasonableness by itself, as noted, is not sufficient to validate an empirical relationship. I have heard rumors about physiological research in skeletal and muscular differences but have not been able to track them down. Perhaps it is not politically correct to report such evidence. A stranglehold presently operates in many parts of our society, including Academe, to suffocate the idea that racial, or even gender, differences, in behavior can occur. The methodological, empirical, and ethical aspects of this problem will now be analyzed in relation to the volatile topic of black/white differences in intelligence.

Black/White Differences in Intelligence

The effort at analyzing black/white differences in intelligence will be conducted in two steps. First, the meaning of intelligence will be briefly returned to and evaluated both within a scientific and social framework. Second, black/white differences in intelligence will be reviewed to set the stage for the examination of their implications.

The justification for intelligence tests as a scientific construct has been made in Chapter 3, but in spite of their pragmatic usefulness, they encounter strong criticism including efforts to bar their use. Why does not society adopt intelligence tests with the same willingness that the Navy in World War II used the radio code aptitude test? Both tests have the capacity to predict important behavior. But practical value obviously is not the only criterion for evaluating aptitude tests. Political and social implications become important especially when raw-nerve issues are involved. To some extent, this conflict between the scientific and the political arises from the misconception that they cannot be separated, as is prescribed by the fact/value dichotomy. Do racial differences in behavior have rigid implications for social policy or can they be melded with a variety of ethical orientations to yield different public policy implications?

Facts and Speculations

The discussion of black/white differences in intelligence raises questions about the bases of the differentiation. As already noted the borderline between races is not sharp, although most major racial classifications distinguish between whites and blacks (Caucasoid and Negroid). The problem of distinguishing the two groups in the United States presents special problems. Except for recent black immigrants from Africa, few if any American blacks are exclusively of African stock. Twenty percent of the black-American gene pool has been estimated to be Caucasian. But even if a black person's white ancestry is higher, that person usually identifies himself or herself as black while others might try to "pass" into the Caucasian population. In other countries offsprings of black and white parents readily accept the designation of mulatto or some other mixed-race characterization, but in the United States a person with both white and black parents usually will choose one of the two racial classifications. Senator Barack Obama of Illinois, whose mother was white and father black, is generally considered to be an African American. In light of this reluctance to employ mixed-race designations, some would prefer to use *ethnic group* instead of race, although the two, in this case, would be correlated. For the most part, the subjects in the studies reporting black/white differences in IQ identified the ethnic group to which they belonged. This procedure of self-identification is consistent with past governmental guidelines in the census and social programs that require racial or ethnic identification.

What are the facts about differences in cognitive ability between blacks and whites? The results of 156 studies conducted between 1918 and 1990 (Herrnstein and Murray, 1994), employing a variety of tests of cognitive ability and a wide range of samples from different parts of the country, report a consistent pattern of superior average performance by whites. Not unexpectedly, the exact average difference between the two groups varies from study to study with the mean difference approximating 15 points (e.g., Hartigan and Wigdor, 1989; Osborne and McGurk, 1982; Shuey, 1966). This difference represents one standard deviation unit, meaning that the mean IQ of whites is equivalent to the 84 percentile score of blacks. In other words, the IQ of the median white, the fiftieth percentile score, is higher than approximately 84 percent of blacks. But that also means that 16 percent of blacks have higher IQs than the average white. In addition, and most importantly, the IQs of blacks are distributed throughout the broad range of IQ scores.

This overview essentially represents the major finding about black/white racial differences in IQ, not the entire detailed picture. Two major explanations have been proposed to account for this IQ difference.

IQ Tests are Culturally Biased. A major criticism of intelligence tests is that they are culturally biased. They were designed for the white American subculture, but are inappropriately used for members of the black subculture. How can you expect a child, raised in a distinctive subculture, to be tested fairly by an examination designed for middle-America? Suppose a test of cognitive ability consisted of items limited to black ghetto language, like Ebonics? Blacks would do better than whites, thus confirming the hypothesis that cultural factors can influence test performance while simultaneously denying the possibility of fairly testing, with a single test, the cognitive ability of two ethnic groups in widely divergent environments. To truly test cognitive ability of different ethnic groups, cultural factors must be controlled. Hence, the 15-point black/white difference in traditional intelligence tests reflects cultural factors, not genetic influences.

Racism. A black columnist of the *New York Times* painfully and passionately responded to the data reported in *The Bell Curve* (Herrnstein and Murray, 1994) by attributing the IQ difference to the pernicious effects of racism; the differential social treatment, past and present, accorded to blacks and whites:

> The book shows that, on average, blacks score about 15 points lower than whites on intelligence tests, a point that was widely known and has not been in dispute. Mr. Murray and I (and many, many others) differ on the reasons for the disparity. I would argue that a group that was enslaved until little more than a century ago; that has long been subjected to the most brutal, often murderous, oppression; that has been deprived of competent, sympathetic political representation; that has most often had to live in the hideous physical conditions that are the hallmark of abject poverty; that has tried its best to survive with little or no prenatal care, and with inadequate health care and nutrition; that has been segregated and ghettoized in communities that were then red-

lined by banks and insurance companies and otherwise shunned by business and industry; that has been systematically frozen out of the job market; that has in large measure been deprived of a reasonably decent education; that has been forced to cope with the humiliation of being treated always as inferior, even by imbeciles–I would argue that these are factors that just might contribute to a certain amount of social pathology and to a slippage in intelligence scores.

Mr. Murray says no. His book strongly suggests that the disparity is inherent, genetic, and there is little to be done about it . . . A great deal of damage has been done. The conclusions so disingenuously trumpeted by Mr. Murray were just what millions of people wanted to hear. It was just the message needed to enable whites to distance themselves still further from any responsibility for the profound negative effect that white racism continues to have on all blacks. (Herbert, 1994)

Evaluation of Criticisms

The two criticisms–*culturally biased IQ tests* and *racism* (social or environmental disadvantage hypothesis)–are persuasive arguments to many because they are intuitively appealing. They seem obviously true. But one must recognize that intuitive understanding does not qualify as empirical truth. To judge these two criticisms of the reported 15-point discrepancy within a scientific framework demands a critical look at the evidence.

Cultural Bias. The claim that intelligence tests are culturally biased appears to automatically invalidate the use of any measure of cognitive ability for individuals whose ethnicity is different from the culture in which the test was constructed. This claim is contradicted by evidence that the tests predict academic and job performance of blacks and whites with equal validity (e.g., Hartigan and Wigdor, 1989; Gottfredson, 1994; Hunter and Schmidt, 1990; Sackett and Wilk, 1994; Schmidt, 1988). The intelligence tests would be culturally biased if they predicted that blacks would do worse than they actually do or predict that whites would do better than they actually do. A particular score on the test, regardless of whether the testee is white or black, has the same predictive value. Thus the attempt to dismiss tests of cognitive ability as biased because they underestimate the future performance of blacks or other minorities, is without empirical support. Consistent with this conclusion are the previously reported findings (page 46) on the ability of numerous aptitude tests to predict success in graduate schools and postgraduate careers (Kuncel and Hezlett, 2007). These tests, like intelligence tests, are not biased against racial or ethnic groups. Any given test score is correlated with the same level of future performance, independent of group membership.

Racism. In evaluating the environmental disadvantage hypothesis from the viewpoint of empirical evidence two conflicting sets of data can be invoked but neither one can support an unqualified conclusion about the cause of the black/white discrepancy of 15 IQ points. The available evidence, reviewed in the previous chapter, clearly indicates that genetic factors play a significant role in cognitive ability as measured by intelligence tests. Any denial of this fact properly belongs to junk science in which such conceptions as *Lysenkoism,* and *the earth is flat* inhabit. But the fact that genetic factors influence the IQs of blacks and whites does not necessarily indicate that the total mean difference between the two is a consequence of heredity. Nor does it mean that genetic factors play no role. A realm of uncertainty prevails that precludes a final decision.

One can argue that "The only valid conclusion that can be drawn from the evidence is a negative one, namely, there is no direct proof that the obtained difference between the average black IQ and the average white IQ are due to genetic factors" (Kendler, 1974, 507), a conclusion that was generally considered fair in 1963 when the first edition of my introductory textbook, *Basic Psychology,* was published. The same conclusion was judged by some to be racist in the third edition in 1974, because it allowed for the possibility that genetic factors could, to some extent, be responsible for the difference.

One can suggest that the evidence at this writing, although incapable of completely refuting the environmental deprivation hypothesis, is nevertheless acquiring greater consistency with a model that emphasizes strong genetic influences on the cognitive ability of different breeding populations. Four reasons can be cited. The first two were reviewed in the previous chapter. One of these is that the evidence in support of the genetic loading of IQ is becoming overwhelming. The other reason is that environmental techniques to enhance IQ by a large number, such as 15 points, have not been reliably demonstrated (Spitz, 1986).

The third reason for considering racial and ethnic differences in cognitive ability is their prevalence. Why should the prejudgment be made that environmental influences are the causal factor to the complete exclusion of genetic factors. Several studies have been reported (Herrnstein and Murray, 1994; Rushton, 2000) suggesting that the mean IQs of Japanese, Chinese, and Koreans are higher than their white counterparts. These East Asian suffered poverty environments when they immigrated to the United States. A current explanation of the IQ advantage of East Asians in North America results from their higher socioeconomic status (Stevenson et al., 1985). But it can be argued that IQ scores determine socioeconomic level, not the other way around. There are substantial differences in the average IQ of members of different social classes (e.g., Burt, 1961; Jencks et al., 1972; Terman, 1916). This evidence has been cited to demonstrate that IQ tests favor the upper classes. But social mobility is correlated with IQ. Sons with higher IQs than their fathers are more likely to move up the social ladder by capturing higher status jobs while offsprings with lower IQs are more likely to descend (Mascie-Taylor and Gibson, 1978; Waller, 1971). The history of the United States is filled with examples of poor immigrant groups overcoming low social status and discrimination to ascend the socioeconomic ladder. Another factor, usually ignored when comparing the cognitive abilities of various sub-populations, is that the disparities can be specific rather than general. East Asians appear to have higher-level skills in spatial relations and mathematical skills than in verbal ability. Such evidence is consistent with the exceptional achievement of the East Asian students in the biological and natural sciences relative to other scholarly pursuits (Vernon, 1982). A comparison of Jewish and Scandinavian children in Minneapolis (Brown, 1944) revealed that Jewish children were superior on tests of verbal comprehension and information, whereas the Scandinavian children excelled in tests requiring spatial orientation and sensorimotor coordination.

The fourth reason is that a variety of research methodologies have generated data suggestive of a genetic involvement in black/white differences in IQ scores. Environment determinists proposed a crucial test case: "The only way to answer the question of genetic differences in IQ between groups would be to study adoption across racial and class boundaries" (Lewontin, Rose, and Kamin, 1984, 127). A major study involved black infants and preschoolers who were adopted by middle-class white parents (Scarr and Weinberg, 1976; Weinberg, Scarr, and Waldman, 1992). At the age of seven, the black children had IQs of approximately 106, well beyond the national average of their group. But over the years that level of performance gradually declined reaching a score of 89 during adolescence. At that age-level the average IQ of the biological children of the adopting parents was 109 and 106 for the white adopted children. Thus in spite of "adoption across racial and class boundaries" the typical black/white difference in IQ persisted.

The analysis of college graduation rates suggests that academic aptitude, not racial discrimination, is responsible for the difference in the college graduation rates of whites and blacks. Although they vary for different colleges the graduation rate of blacks, on average, is below that of whites. When IQ scores are equated, the difference between the two groups evaporates (Herrnstein and Murray, 1994). A similar finding was obtained for income. While the average income of whites exceeded those of blacks the difference disappears for a person of average age with an average IQ of 100 (Herrnstein and Murray, 1994). Some data sets suggest that the brain size of whites slightly exceeds that of blacks (Rushton, 2000) and brain size has a low correlation with IQ (Jensen and Sinha, 1993). Size, however, is not the whole story. A prevailing assumption until recently has been that the human brain, except for size and organization, was not anatomically different from chimpanzees and lower apes. Recent research (Balter, 2007) suggests that the level of human cognitive ability is due, to some extent, to anatomical differences in some of the neurons of human brains as contrasted with those of chimpanzees, other primates, and lower animals. The total pattern of results is consistent with the idea that genetic factors play a role in the anatomical structure of the brain and the resulting cognitive ability.

The topic of genetic differences in cognitive ability has indirectly become a central issue in President George W. Bush's educational policy of No Child Left Behind (NCLB). This program was initiated in Texas when Bush was the governor and its presumed success was advertised as a positive achievement of Bush's leadership. One target of NCLB program was to have every child be able to read at a level appropriate to the third grade. Although no one expected *every* child in Texas to achieve this level of competency, the plan was to elevate the average performance of all children including blacks and Hispanics. When initially reporting the results, the claim was made that the NCLB had been a success for all students, including the minorities. It took some time to discover that grave errors had been made in reporting the data. Students, more commonly members of the minorities, who dropped out of school were not counted, thereby elevating the average performance of the group. A similar effect resulted from not promoting poor students, thereby eliminating their impact on determining the average performance of their age group. A wide variety of similar errors were made in encouraging the impression that NCLB was a great success when, in fact, the method of reporting the data under the control of the individual schools led to inflated performance levels. These distorted results encouraged the idea that the racial IQ gap could be eliminated.

Newspapers are filled with stories about the achievement gap between minorities and other groups. One tale (Gootman, 2006) recounts the effort of New York City to prepare black and Hispanic students for the difficult test of gaining admission to three elite high schools that offer top-notch educational experiences. In spite of their special training, the number of minority students gaining admission declined! Why? A number of answers are possible, considering that the program was not a carefully designed investigation. One possibility is that the achievement gap is real. Different breeding populations can differ in their cognitive ability. Consistent with this explanation was the increased enrollment of East Asian students. Those who challenge these results question the use of a single test for gaining admission to the prestigious schools. They maintain the use of a single test is an expression of institutional racism that is designed to maintain color-blind standards at the expense of racial diversity. Some argue the admission gap results, in part or completely, from the hiring of private tutors by middle-class parents to give their children an advantage in "getting ahead." A weighty argument is that the quality of teachers in minority schools is below those in middle-class schools.

A similar divisive issue has been brought to the fore by a study (Glater, 2006) suggesting the paucity of minority partners in large law firms is due to their inferior grades to whites in law school. This conclusion has been challenged because numerous other factors operate in the selection of law firm partners, e.g., contacts with potential clients, talent to work with others, special gift of knowing a foreign language necessary for important clients, and so on. When interpreting natural occurring events such as the selection of students for elite high schools or partners in prestigious law firms, one must recognize the evidence is not the product of a controlled investigation such as a laboratory experiment in which the number of relevant variables has been reduced to a minimum. Instead, a sizable number of potential factors operate, precluding the identification of the exact cause of the finding.

In spite of all evidence cited some argue that the existence of cognitive inequalities has not been proven beyond a shadow of a doubt. Will this argument ever be resolved? Emotional issues never appear to be. Darwinian evolution, which most scientists accept as a valid theory, still has not achieved unanimous acceptance over the idea of "intelligent design" that fails to meet the standard of falsifiability (p. 16). The criteria for scientific confirmation and public acceptance obviously differ!

Scientists will persist in their efforts to nail down the racial IQ differences. Relevant to this issue is the recent disagreement about whether the racial IQ gap between blacks and whites, which has been estimated to be close to 15 points, can be reduced and, perhaps, ultimately eliminated. Dickens and Flynn (2006) suggest "that blacks gained 4 to 7 IQ points on non-Hispanic whites between 1972 and 2002 (913), while Rushton and Jensen (2006) insist the black/white IQ differences of 15 to 18 points have been stabilized for almost 100 years. They also buttress their argument by noting that the average IQ of East Asians is 106 and sub-Saharan Africans is 70. Perhaps more agreement will be attained if the molecular-genetic basis of intelligence (Sabeti et al., 2006) is identified even though complete agreement will never be achieved. The crucial question is what social policy should to be adopted about racial differences in cognitive ability. One must remember, as has been repeatedly noted, facts cannot dictate what policy *should* be adopted.

RACIAL SUPERIORITY: EMPIRICAL
CONCEPT OR VALUE JUDGMENT

The topic of racial differences in intelligence immediately evokes the concept of *racial superiority*. Yet there is no logical relationship between the two because the concept of racial superiority, the overall supremacy of one race over another, has no independent basis in fact. And the same can be said about ideas of ethnic or gender superiority;

they too are creations of value judgments, not of empirical evidence. The conclusion that one group–racial, ethnic, gender–can be proven to be generally superior to others can only be accomplished by deceptive logic.

Consider the multi-event track-and-field contest known as the decathlon, where points are awarded in a series of independent events according to a formula. The participant who wins the decathlon is judged to be the "best" all-around athlete, the most superior. Can a cultural decathlon be arranged to discover the superiority of competing racial, ethnic, and gender groups? What events–literature, music, religion, art, philosophy, science, dance, athletics, humor, eroticism, social sciences, etc.–should be included? What forms, for example, of the dance would be listed: ballet, Native American ghost dance, Greek choral dance, Japanese Geisha dance, Polish polonaise, Spanish flamenco, Scottish highland fling, Italian tarantella, Irish jig, Argentinean tango, Brazilian samba, American tap dancing, hip-hop, ballroom dancing, modern dance, interpretive dance? Should the various forms be given equal weight, or do some deserve more points because of the greater skill involved? Questions of this sort can go on forever. But they need not before one realizes that the project of constructing a cultural decathlon will inevitably fail because of the inability to achieve agreement about the value assigned to different cultural efforts and achievements. No ethnic group values opera as much as Italians or ballroom dancing as much as the English or Jewish jokes as much as New York Jews. Although conclusions have probably been drawn about the superiority of every racial, ethnic, and gender group such judgments cannot be supported by any universally accepted criterion. In other words, the general superiority of one group over others can be claimed, but it has no meaning independent of the value judgments of those making the assertion.

In spite of the indemonstrable nature of group superiority one must frankly acknowledge the fears that are generated by evidence of racial and ethnic as well as gender differences. Such differences can be exploited to justify some groups being judged superior to others, thus raising the specter of past crimes committed under such a guise. In addition, the bogus underpinnings of a general racial, ethnic, or gender superiority does not shield individuals from feelings of inferiority because of their group identity. One should not minimize the personal impact and consequences of such feelings, as for example, that occurring among some blacks because of evidence linking their racial group to below-average IQ. Such feelings although painfully disturbing should be placed in proper perspective. First, a person's cognitive ability is reflected in the person's score not the group to which he or she belongs. The individual IQs of blacks are distributed over the broad range of scores and, therefore, the feeling of personally being below average is not necessarily justified. It also should be recognized that the sense of intellectual inadequacy is practically a universal experience. Regardless of our IQ, all of us experience the frustration of being confronted with problems that are beyond our intellectual capabilities. Even Einstein failed in his attempt to formulate a unified field theory in physics. Second, in evaluating mean differences in IQ scores one should also recognize that all groups cannot be above average. Whereas one group may be below in one talent, the same group can be above average in another talent. Therefore, feelings of inferiority demand the cooperation of the victim of such a belief. The third issue to confront is the consequence of the unequal distribution of talent among different groups. Must it be as socially divisive as some believe? For argument sake, let us assume that some future research demonstrates that there is a neurological basis to the average superiority of Chinese, Japanese, and Koreans in certain mathematical and scientific skills. If persons of East Asian ancestry have a disproportionate employment in universities, research institutes, and business that require such skills, will resentment be an inevitable consequence, or will society be pleased to benefit from their talents? At this writing, basketball is catching up to soccer as the world's most popular sport. And the blacks are generally recognized as the most talented players with admiration, not resentment. More importantly, from a cultural perspective, the disproportionate contributions of blacks to jazz and related performing arts are admired throughout the world. Why cannot individual excellence be the fundamental measuring rod for all talents, not group achievements?

POLICY IMPLICATIONS OF RACIAL
DIFFERENCES IN IQ SCORES

As repeatedly stated, empirical data do not logically dictate the adoption of any particular policy: Social "policy is determined in the light of facts, but is not deduced from them" (Passmore, 1953, 675). School segregation of blacks and whites in southern states was justified by the assumption that whites were superior to blacks in cognitive ability. The 15 IQ point discrepancy, it was argued, supported separate educational programs for blacks and whites. The IQ comparison only indicates that the average white is cognitively ahead of the average black, but that many blacks exceed the cognitive ability of many whites. If educational programs are geared to cognitive ability, then school integration not segregation should be the empirically justified policy.

A current controversy surrounds the issue of school segregation that involves contradictory testimony by psychologists in the famous *Brown vs. Board of Education* case that outlawed school segregation. One distinguished psychologist, Henry E. Garrett, a former President of the American Psychological Association (1946), testified that the cognitive talents of blacks and whites differ both qualitatively and quantitatively. This led to the recommendation that it would be best for both groups to be educated in the style that characterizes their talents. At the same time, a black psychologist rejects the notion that assimilation and desegregation are the only answers, or necessarily the best, in dealing with all problems confronting blacks in a dominantly white society. The promotion of race consciousness can have merit and black schools can "provide black students a more affirming psychological environment and produce equal educational results" (Scott, 1997, 129). This conclusion goes counter to the results of a survey of opinions of anthropologists, sociologists, and psychologists (Deutscher and Chein, 1948) about the psychological consequences of enforced segregation. Ninety percent of those who responded to the poll concluded that segregation of the races had a detrimental effect on black children even if the separate educational facilities were truly equal to those of white children. A slightly smaller percentage, 83 percent, judged that school segregation had detrimental effects on white children.

Instead of offering an ideological reaction to segregation, social scientists could have conducted an objective empirical inquiry into the effects on enforced segregation on the education and personal adjustment of children, both black and white. Why offer dubious evidence when rigorous scientific standards should have been sought? Is it not the responsibility of the scientists to offer unbiased evidence? If psy-

chology is to play a significant role in evaluating the empirical consequences of different social policies, and thereby assist political institutions in executing their responsibilities, then its evidence must be trusted. Unless that confidence is earned, it will not be forthcoming, and
the potential value of psychology to society will have been lost.

Chapter 5

AFFIRMATIVE ACTION: COMMON GROUND OR ETERNAL CONFLICT?

The driving force behind affirmative action in education was the need to overcome the negative effects of past social discrimination against blacks. Later, other groups who were victims of discrimination such as women and Hispanics were judged to be candidates for affirmative action. The manner in which affirmative action was to be implemented took many forms, from informal programs to strict legal requirements. The simplest and least controversial is to discover those members of minorities and women whose talents go unrecognized. For example, a black high school student whose academic aptitudes were ignored or overlooked would be awarded a scholarship to college. Women with high mathematical and scientific aptitudes would be given incentives to counteract social prejudice or personal reluctance to pursue a science or engineering career. The basic assumption of this form of affirmative action is that minority and female students, whose talents match those of successful candidates, are denied equal opportunity. Affirmative action is designed to rectify those discriminatory policies, but does it?

Critics of modest affirmative action programs that merely identify overlooked talent contend that the plan ignores the task of eradicating the corroding effects of discrimination on *all* victims. It merely searches for a select few while overlooking the many whose cognitive skills were stunted by a destructive ghetto environment or anti-women attitudes. An affirmative action program is needed for all who were deprived of the chance to achieve their potential, or in the popular parlance of the day, affirmative action is needed "to level the playing field." Another popular metaphor is that of a footrace in which the victims of past discrimination had to be given a head start to make the contest fair. Preferential treatment, the argument went, achieved the equality that was denied by past unequal treatment.

Various forms of preferential treatment were used, such as lowering admission requirements for those who were presumably discriminated against. To implement these programs a measure of the impact of previous racism, ethnic bias, or sexism was needed. One informal method was to give preferential treatment to those applicants who seem to need it. But such a method can be criticized on two counts. It is too subjective and it fails to effectively counteract the destructive effects of past discrimination for all victims. To answer such criticisms a formal program of preferential treatment was proposed, to compensate for the negative effects of past discrimination. If a minority group is under-represented in a college population or in a particular job, a preferential treatment program should balance its representation in proportion to the total population. For example, if blacks represented 8 percent of college students and 13 percent of the population of people of college age, then the conclusion was drawn that racism prevented the remaining 5 percent of blacks from achieving college training. Similarly, if women constituted only 20 percent of an entering class in engineering school, then sexism was assumed to have operated to deny 30 percent of women the opportunity to study engineering. In sum, the failure to be proportionally represented was taken as prima facie evidence of social discrimination. This formal model–*statistical proportionality*–had the virtue of having clear empirical implications. While not explicitly arguing so, the statistical proportionality assumption embraced an environmental determinist premise that cognitive aptitude for science and engineering training is solely a function of environmental variables.

AFFIRMATIVE ACTION AND THE LAW

Affirmative action programs grew out of the civil rights movement. Proponents of affirmative action argue that minorities and women who suffered social discrimination, require preferential treatment to overcome the obstacles imposed by their past victimization. Critics reject this argument insisting that affirmative action is basically an attack on the democratic principle of *individual rights* that functioned as the goal of the civil rights movement. The conflict revolves around the meaning of civil rights; the governmental protection of persons against discriminatory treatment. But how should *discrimination* be defined and estimated? Understanding the legal, ethical, and psychological aspects of discrimination will prove useful in appreciating the social consequences of affirmative action.

Constitutional Cases and Civil Rights Laws

The history of the United States reflects a persistent struggle to achieve the goals of individual rights and equality of opportunity. During the early stages of American history these social ideals were denied to many, most notably blacks and women, but also to many ethnic minorities. The highlights of the effort to expand individual rights were the Thirteenth, Fourteenth, and Fifteenth Amendments that terminated slavery and gave civil rights to blacks, including voting rights to black men. The Nineteenth Amendment afforded voting rights to women. But these constitutional changes were only steps in the direction of procuring full individual rights for blacks and women; social prejudice and exclusionary customs prevented them from having opportunities that were available to white men.

One particular constitutional case in 1896, *Plessy vs. Ferguson,* had pivotal significance in the ongoing conflict about the meaning of civil rights. Homer Plessy was one-eighth black, who under Louisiana laws in 1896 was required to sit in the separate "colored" section of railroad trains. To test the constitutionality of the law, Plessy bought a first-class ticket and refused to sit in the segregated area. He was arrested and with the financial assistance of some railroad companies brought a case against racial segregation in public transportation. The Supreme Court ruled 8 to 1 that the Fourteenth Amendment's protection of a person's civil rights was not intended to abolish racial distinctions that were natural and reasonable. However, Justice John Marshall Harlan (1833–1911), whose grandson also became a Supreme Court Justice, vigorously dissented, arguing that racial distinctions of any kind infringe upon a person's civil rights. In other words, according to Justice Harlan the United States should be a colorblind society.

The problem of racial segregation was returned to in 1954 in the case of *Brown vs. Board of Education* of Topeka, Kansas in which Thurgood Marshall, the plaintiff's attorney, argued that the Constitution denies "the state any power to make any racial classification in any governmental field" (Bolick, 1996, 71). The Supreme Court unanimously overruled the "separate but equal doctrine" of the *Plessy vs. Feguson* decision, charging that segregation assigned a badge of inferiority to minority children regardless of the quality of their academic facilities. Racial segregation from that time on was deemed to be unconstitutional in public schools. The Supreme Court, however, did not embrace the goal of a color-blind society although at that time many white and black leaders did, including Martin Luther King.

The legal basis of many affirmative action programs was the Civil Rights Act of 1964 that, among other provisions, forbade discrimination on the basis of color, race, religion, national origin, and gender. In support of the bill President Lyndon Johnson declared "We seek not just . . . equality as a right and theory, but equality as a fact and equality as a result." That proved to be an opening wedge in a soon-to-be strident debate about whether racial classifications would be permissible if they led to racial equality as a "fact" and "result." Senator Hubert Humphrey, a leading liberal who was a major driving force behind the law's passage, had insisted that the Act did not condone the use of racial preferences for any reason. Thus the political implications of this law were ambiguous wavering between the extremes of forbidding all racial classification for any purpose to encouraging racial preferences in the effort to overcome the effects of past discrimination.

Although the idea of racial preferences was controversial, it initially did not generate significant opposition when the racial discrimination was so flagrant that any effort to rectify matters was accepted. For example, the Philadelphia Plan that enjoyed the support of President Richard Nixon, a conservative Republican, called for racial quotas in the building trades in Philadelphia because blacks had been excluded from being hired. The idea that these quotas might be a form of reverse discrimination–discriminating against whites–did not receive serious consideration because the punishment inflicted on the white population–preferential treatment for blacks–seemed to fit the crime.

The struggle to bring blacks into the mainstream of American society via preferential treatment programs had a dampening effect on the ethical ideal of a color-blind society. A shift occurred from the general proposition that a color-blind society is a virtue to the specific principle that the application of racial distinctions can be put to good use. Thurgood Marshall, for example, who had initially argued before the

Supreme Court that the Constitution advocated a color-blind society later switched to the position that racial classifications were legal and socially beneficial. This distinction led to two opposed interpretations of equality: individual versus group. Individual equality occurs in a group-blind society where people are judged as individuals regardless of their race, ethnicity, or gender. Individual equality demands that all persons are treated equally; nobody is forced to go to the back of the bus. Group equality requires some degree of parity among racial, ethnic, and gender groups throughout all employment segments of society. In contrast to the ideal of a color- and gender-blind society, the group-based ideal of equality requires that society distinguish among members of different groups. As Reverend Jesse Jackson said, "to ignore race and gender is racist and sexist" (cited in Bolick, 1996, p. 39).

The civil rights struggle that initially strove to achieve individual equality, split into two competing factions: One that persisted in its original intent while the other shifted to the ideal of group equality. The individual equality principle was generally perceived as being more consistent with constitutional tradition. However, the question was raised as to whether that ideal could be achieved without first employing preferential treatment to approach the goal of group equality. The proponents of individual equality rejected that suggestion, warning that once preferential treatment was instituted group equality would become a permanent goal. For many proponents of affirmative action group equality is presently considered a civil right.

This political and legal debate about the meaning of equality inevitably brought into play psychological tests and the perennial question about whether their results could be attributed to environmental or hereditary influences. In 1971, the Supreme Court decision of *Griggs vs. Duke Power, Inc.* pitted affirmative action programs against psychological tests. Stripped of its legalisms and political overtones, the question was raised as to whether general ability tests, such as intelligence tests, were used as forms of illegal discrimination against blacks. Duke Power Company in North Carolina had decided to upgrade the quality of their personnel by demanding a high school diploma and a particular level of performance on a general ability test. A smaller proportion of blacks than whites met these criteria. Was Duke Power really trying to upgrade their personnel or were they practicing a subtle form of racial discrimination? The Supreme Court ruled that they were discriminating because the criteria utilized were not directly related to job performance. Essentially the Supreme Court was arguing that if a company, for example, desires to hire machinists they must use a selection test that is designed to test the skills of a machinist, otherwise their test can be judged as a surreptitious attempt to avoid anti-discrimination laws. This legal ruling implied that effective tests for personnel selection must be tailored to individual jobs; no general ability was needed for most if not all jobs. But empirical evidence indicates that general ability and aptitude tests, such as intelligence tests, are correlated with job performance in an enormous range of occupations (Ree, 1992; Schmidt, Ones and Hunter, 1992). From farm workers, bricklayers, machinists, shipping clerks, secretaries, and executives, cognitive ability enhances job performance. The United States military organizations used general tests of intelligence with great effectiveness by assigning personnel to military jobs in which they would likely succeed.

The legal status of affirmative action programs became more confused in the famous Bakke case. The Medical School of the University of California, Davis initiated an affirmative action program by setting aside 16 of the 100 places in the first year class for "disadvantaged students" defined in terms of racial and ethnic membership. These 16 students received preferential treatment by not requiring them to meet the admission standards for other students. Allen Bakke, a white applicant was rejected both in 1973 and 1974, even though he would have been admitted on the strength of his qualifications had he been black. Bakke had scored in the 90th percentile in the medical school admission test, while the mean of the minority students was below the 50th percentile.

The California Supreme Court ruled that this special admission plan violated the equal protection clause of the Fourteenth Amendment; no state should "deny to any person within its jurisdiction the equal protection of the laws." The California Court's ruling was not against special admission policies for minorities but against racial criteria. The Court held that if minority status were defined in economic terms, the preferential treatment would be judged legal. But an economic definition of disadvantaged would not serve the purpose of the University's affirmative action program that was designed to achieve increased representation of blacks in medical school. An economic measure of disadvantaged would sometimes result in the substitution of less affluent whites in medical school for more affluent whites. Consequently, the University of California appealed its case to the United States Supreme Court in its effort to increase the number of black medical students.

Since the time of the Bakke Case numerous other affirmative action cases have been ruled on. One case in particular reveals the lack of agreement about the meaning of the crucial and widely used term *discrimination.* In 1996, the people of California voted in favor of Proposition 209, the California Civil Rights Initiative, prohibiting preferential treatment for access to state universities, jobs or contracts for reasons of race, ethnicity, or gender. A Federal judge initially blocked the enforcement of this proposition because it threatened the equal protection clause of the Fourteenth Amendment of the Constitution. This was a shocking ruling for proponents of Propositions 209, who maintained their Initiative was needed to uphold the equal protection clause. How could two opposed policies–preferential treatment vs. no preferential treatment–be justified by the same legal principle that prohibits discrimination? Simply by employing different meanings of discrimination! The equal treatment that the California Civil Rights Initiative, according to "affirmative-actioneers," endorsed discrimination against minorities and women by disregarding past and present acts of discrimination against them. But proponents of Proposition 209 argued that their Initiative could not be considered a violation of the Fourteenth Amendment because the Fourteenth Amendment prohibits discrimination by race, ethnicity, and gender. In sum, should discrimination be defined by individual or group criteria? And perhaps more importantly, should this controversy be limited to legal issues or should it be expanded to studying the empirical consequences of defining discrimination in these two different ways? The answers to these questions can be clarified by examining the historical events that produced affirmative action programs.

AFFIRMATIVE ACTION: PAST AND PRESENT

A strong current in American politics since the days of the presidency of Franklin D. Roosevelt was to initiate programs that would improve the lives of blacks so that they could achieve "racial equality." A major obstacle to that goal was racial segregation, most notably in

schools in the South. The effort to overcome racial segregation pre-
ceded the attempt to initiate affirmative action, but the two policies are
historically related both psychologically and morally.

School Desegregation

Racial segregation, unlike affirmative action, was considered more
of a moral issue than a question of social policy. The fundamental
democratic mandate of equality seemed to be denied by racial segregation. In contrast, affirmative action is not an ethical imperative but,
instead, a governmental policy that was created to solve a serious and
recalcitrant social problem stemming from the disadvantaged status of
a large minority group. The difference in the degree of moral involvement in the policies of racial segregation and affirmative action is
reflected in their Constitutional implication. Although it took a long
time for the Supreme Court to reject the inequalities imposed by slavery, segregation, and the denial of voting rights to women, in retrospect it seems that the historical course toward justice could not be
stopped. In contrast, the Supreme Court has been unable to formulate
a compelling legal principle to convert affirmative action into a moral
prescription equivalent in force to the Supreme Court's ruling in 1954
against school segregation. The difficulty of meshing the principle of
affirmative action with the Constitution, as contrasted with the 9 to 0
ruling in the famous *Brown vs. Board of Education* case, illustrates the
differences between implementing social policies that are based on
constitutionally mandated moral imperatives as compared to those
that are designed to achieve politically inspired goals.

According to the *Brown vs. Board of Education* decision, a policy of
enforced school segregation is morally wrong in a society dedicated to
the principle of equality before the law. The legal interpretation meant
that blacks barred from schools with whites are denied equal protection of the law as guaranteed by the Fourteenth Amendment. The 9 to
0 decision rejected previous rulings that separate but equal facilities
were possible on the grounds that segregation in public schools is
"inherently unequal."

The abstract nature of legal principles–*school desegregation* and *affirmative action*–allows for a variety of implementations. A constant problem is retaining the "spirit" of the principle in its legal form. The task
of executing the desegregation ruling opened a hornet's nest of prob-

lems, many of which were carried over to conflicts about affirmative action.

The Supreme Court, although ruling against school segregation, failed to offer much direction to the Federal district courts that they ordered to proceed with integration "with all deliberate speed." Those southern states with segregation laws resisted mandated integration with obstructive political maneuverings. And in many locations in the north white and black neighborhood patterns resulted in segregated schools that blacks sued to eliminate. A turning point occurred in 1964 when President Lyndon Johnson persuaded Congress to pass a civil rights law that gave the Federal government special power to promote desegregation. Federal funds would be withdrawn if school programs continued to practice segregation. In 1964, only two southern states had more than two percent of blacks students enrolled in integrated schools, but the financial threat increased the percentage to six the following year.

Blacks gradually became disenchanted with the progress of desegregation and sought to act on their own. Stokley Carmichael preached "black power" and became leader of the Student Nonviolent Coordinating Committee that initially accepted white members, but then excluded them. In the early 1970s, busing students to nonadjacent neighborhoods was initiated to achieve racial balance. These efforts often backfired by encouraging whites to flee to the suburbs, leaving the inner city schools all black. In 1972 a higher percentage of black students in the south, as contrasted to the north, went to a predominantly white primary school.

Numerous efforts were made to achieve more racially balanced schools, but a sizable segment of the white population did everything possible to remain in, or to move to, school districts that were predominantly white. One showcase effort to encourage integration occurred in Kansas City (Greenhouse, 1995). Lower Federal courts had ordered the State of Missouri to help pay for a state-of-the-art magnet school in Kansas City in hopes of attracting white students from the surrounding suburbs. One reason that the Federal District Court ruled that the State should continue to pay half the costs of the magnet school was that its students continually failed to meet the national norms on standardized tests. This failure was interpreted by the Federal District Court to mean that Missouri was delinquent in meeting its responsibilities to its students; otherwise their performance would have been higher. The majority view of the Supreme Court dismissed this suggestion, arguing that other factors besides educational effectiveness of the magnet school might be responsible for the relatively poor performance of its students. The Supreme Court further questioned the lower court decree that required the State, after seven years, to continue to spend almost 200 million dollars yearly in support of the magnet school in an apparently doomed effort to create an acceptable degree of racial balance. The majority of the Justices of the Supreme Court judged the decree of the Federal District Court to be unconstitutional.

In a concurring opinion, Justice Clarence Thomas, a black Supreme Court Justice with a strong conservative bent, raised a point about desegregation that had generally been overlooked. Thomas suggested that the effort to achieve desegregation by arranging school populations that proportionally represent blacks and whites in the entire population was insulting to blacks. The *New York Times* account of Thomas's views reads as follows:

> "It never seems to amaze me that the courts are so willing to assume that anything that is predominantly black must be inferior," Justice Thomas said. The theory that "segregation injures blacks because blacks, when left on their own, cannot achieve" is the result of "a jurisprudence based upon a theory of black inferiority," he said, adding "The point of the Equal Protection Clause is not to enforce strict race mixing, but to insure that blacks and whites are treated by the state without regard to their skin color." (Greenhouse, 1995, A9)

Replacing segregation with desegregation following the Brown decision was more difficult than anticipated. Many southern states and city governments resisted a radically new social order with every available political trick including token integration–the scattering of a few whites in predominantly black schools and vice versa. Federal law enforcement combined with financial inducements to attack the remnants of segregation failed to slow white flight to the suburbs. The effort to achieve racially balanced schools continued with the assistance of busing, but this effort brought storms of opposition. Some students, both white and black, were required to travel great distances to achieve the desired amount of integration. Their parents, some of whom favored integration, argued that the burden of the excessive time spent on the bus was too great a price for students to pay to attain racially balanced integration. And the lower courts were, for the most part, reluctant to extend integration policy between urban and suburban districts. The Kansas City effort, described above, finally collapsed in 1999 after billions of dollars had been spent without improving educational performance.

In examining desegregation in retrospect, certain features stand out. First is the conflation of issues. Desegregation is conflated with "racially balanced" classrooms. The fundamental aim of school desegregation was to eliminate legally enforced segregation; blacks should not be barred from going to schools with whites. A corollary of this goal is that educational facilities should be essentially equal among schools regardless of their racial balance. Thus, it does not logically follow that "true" desegregation demands classes in which blacks and whites are proportionally balanced. The concept of discrimination also has been conflated with voluntary racial and ethnic associations. We should not simply attribute ethnocentric behavior to discrimination against outsiders. We must recognize the strength of ethnic and racial identity and shared experience as factors in the formation of neighborhoods. Catholic parents who send their children to parochial schools may choose a Catholic neighborhood over a Jewish one, not because of presumed anti-Semitism but, instead, because of the greater opportunity provided for their children to mesh their school and social, including church, lives together. Are black students who voluntarily separate themselves into segregated dormitories victims or practitioners of discrimination? Discrimination as a psychological concept must not be conceived as a one-way street in which the negative attitudes toward "victims" are judged to be the only factor that operates. Sociobiologists who study evolutionary influences on behavior have speculated that ethnocentrism has a biological base in the effort of genetically similar people to propagate their own genes (van der Dennen, 1987). This point is not raised to deny or excuse discrimination against ethnic groups but, instead, to clarify the complex nature of discrimination so that social policies can be based on reality not ideology.

A host of fundamental questions are raised by Thomas's conclusion. According to Thomas there is nothing intrinsically wrong, legally and morally, for an integration policy to permit schools and classrooms to be predominantly black, not racially balanced as espoused by many leaders of the civil rights movement. Thomas was essentially denying that a significant presence of whites in a classroom was needed to improve the educational achievements of blacks. Morally rejecting racial segregation does not automatically imply a preference for classes that are racially balanced or those that have a broad range of racial mixing.

Affirmative Action and Social Discrimination

As already noted, one reason affirmative action programs generated so much legal action and political debate is that the exact meaning of social discrimination was never clearly stated or fully shared. Affirmative action was proposed, and is still being defended, as a plan to discover qualified members of minorities, or women, who could benefit from educational opportunities otherwise unavailable to them. From an effort to establish equality of opportunity, affirmative action programs were gradually transformed into a policy designed to achieve equality of results. Preferential treatment was the means by which this goal would be attained. And the principle by which "equality of results" would be applied became a source of disagreement and confusion. At one extreme there was the goal of proportional representation, set-asides or quotas, of all minorities and women. The justification for this policy was that discrimination could only be wiped out by guaranteeing equality of representation to those who had been discriminated against. At the other extreme was the less strident idea that exact quotas were not being sought but, instead, only goals that would make universities, businesses, and the professions reflect "the face of America." In spite of differences in emphasis and public appeal, an attempt was made to replace the concept of individual equality with group equality while making the concept more palatable by keeping its meaning out of focus.

Facts, and more facts, have justified affirmative action programs. No one can deny the incontrovertible evidence of past discrimination to which blacks have been subjected: slavery, laws, social bigotry, economic bias. However, one need not deny the facts of past abuse to argue against preferential treatment for blacks. One can fault racial preferences on moral grounds. If racism—the differential treatment of members of different races—is bad then racial preferences are bad. And a possible side effect of racial preferences should be considered; society runs the risk of increasing, not reducing, racial and ethnic and gender antagonisms. And, finally, one can rebut the claim that racial preferences are needed to make the "playing field level" for blacks. The playing field in some areas of life is already level. Applicants for admissions into colleges and professional schools, without affirmative action programs, are judged fairly, in a colorblind fashion. They are selected on the basis of aptitude scores and nonracial criteria. Such aptitude tests predict with equal effectiveness the academic performance of blacks and whites. Qualified blacks are treated in the same manner as qualified whites and hence do not need preferential treatment. And it might be noted that other minorities that have been discriminated against in the past, like Jews, Irish Catholics, and East Asians, have coped effectively with their past mistreatment without the assistance of preferential treatment programs.

Arguments about affirmative action can go on interminably, and have, with rare mention of the fact/value dichotomy. Even if accepted, the dichotomy can easily be ignored because of the intuitive feeling that facts can settle all controversies. One automatically assumes that if the environmental deprivation hypothesis is correct then preferential treatment for black applicants into medical school is justified because their lower aptitude scores reflect the effects of past discrimination. On the other hand, if genetic factors are involved in black-white IQ differences, then disproportionate rates of acceptance are acceptable because they are not a product of discrimination. But neither of these empirical justifications for social policies is logically demanded. They appear to be because they are perceived within a common moral framework that emphasizes fair treatment. Hence, preferential treatment is condoned when it rights past wrongs, but condemned when it treats individuals unequally. If one adopts communitarian values in preference to an individual-rights morality, then the black-white IQ evidence can be viewed differently. A person who equates an ideal multicultural society with one that has approximately proportional representation of races throughout society would endorse affirmative action. One can also argue that the position of African Americans in American society is unique, demanding special dispensations:

> I do not want the question of the admission of blacks to selective institutions determined by the stark application of color blind principle today, because I think the radical reduction of blacks in selective insti-

tutions of higher education would be a terrible blow to their prospects in American society, and because it would reduce sharply the degree to which they can participate at the highest levels in our society. (Glazer, 1998, 31)

In a similar fashion one can propose that affirmative action programs have been responsible for creating a backbone of a black middle-class that serves the needs of the entire society (Bowen and Bok, 1998).

Instead of perceiving preferential treatment programs not from the perspective of communitarian values but by other criteria, such as economic productivity or technological effectiveness, then one might oppose affirmative action programs because they would not guarantee the assignment of the most productive person to each job.

Of course, this effort to clarify the relationship between facts and values represents an oversimplification of the moral and empirical issues involved in the controversial social policy of affirmative action. But in spite of this, the discussion should reveal the dead-end quality of debates that are limited to moral arguments and presumed empirical evidence. They suffer from three severe limitations. First, the dispute is conceptualized solely as a moral conflict instead of a disagreement between competing social policies. Second, the controversy tends to be frozen between two extreme positions that are basically irreconcilable. The disagreement is carried out on global level, thus hiding from view component issues that may be less controversial than are the primary ones. Third, the evidence that is typically cited aims at political persuasion, not empirical accuracy.

A SCIENTIFIC-PSYCHOLOGICAL ANALYSIS OF AFFIRMATIVE ACTION

Can such an emotional topic as affirmative action be analyzed in a detached scientific manner? I think so. Certainly we can try.

Basic Methodological Problems

Three fundamental methodological problems surround a scientific-psychological analysis of affirmative action. The first two involve empirical problems that can be revealed by two penetrating questions:

What do you mean? How do you know? (Feigl, 1949). The initial query seeks to pinpoint the meaning of the major concepts under discussion. Before judging affirmative action, knowledge of its meaning is obviously demanded. The second question seeks to identify the empirical consequences of affirmative action programs. The remaining questions: *Is affirmative action socially justified? Is affirmative action effective?* These are more complex questions because the answer will be determined by value judgments that differ among those who are actively engaged in the controversy.

The Meaning of Affirmative Action

Although affirmative action has been defined and defended in many different ways, the controversy that surrounds the policy is primarily about preferential treatment. Nobody appears to object to nondiscriminatory affirmative action programs that seek to assist everybody to fully realize their potential. Preferential treatment is another matter! This concept emerged from Johnson's promise to "seek not just . . . equality as a right and theory, but equality as a fact and equality as a result." This promise was transformed into policies during the tenures of Presidents Johnson and Nixon, requiring governmental agencies to report the degree to which minorities and women are included in the labor force. Underrepresentation of these groups was seen as evidence of bias, thereby encouraging remedial action to increase their representation in different jobs and professions. Preferential treatment in hiring was instituted to decrease or eliminate the underrepresentation of those groups who presumably were discriminated against.

The Consequences of Affirmative Action

Evaluating the consequences of affirmative action is best approached by analyzing the problem into its major components. Consider the history of a preferential-treatment type of affirmative action program of the Birmingham, Alabama Fire Department (Bragg, 1995). At one time, when Jim Crow prevailed in the Old South, blacks were excluded from employment in the fire department. The first black firefighter was hired in 1968 and the second eight years later. An affirmative action program began in 1981 when the first black mayor, Richard Arrington, signed into law a consent decree that initiated a rigid one-to-one hiring and promotion policy for blacks and whites.

Half of the new firefighters had to be black, as did those who were promoted. In 1983, 95 whites and 19 blacks took an examination for promotion to the rank of lieutenant. Eighty-nine whites and 9 blacks received passing grades. The operating schedule required that the five promotions be distributed among three blacks and two whites. The city promoted the two whites who ranked first and second in the examination and then passed over 76 others to select the next three highest black candidates.

To prepare for the subsequent analysis of affirmative action it will prove useful to identify four core features in the Birmingham example. First, is the preferential treatment. Both in hiring and promotion tests blacks were not required to meet the same standards as whites. If they had, the distribution of white and black firefighters would not have been equal, as demanded by the consent decree. In addition, if test results were the only criterion for selection, the proportion of blacks hired would be less than their representation in the population but more than occurred during the days of Jim Crow.

Second, is the nature of the psychological tests used. Were they relevant to the purpose for which they were designed? In other words, did they predict job performance of firefighters or did they operate merely as obstacles to reduce minority representation among firefighters? If the selection test has predictive validity–could predict job performance–then the test is justified. If the test does not predict job performance then the question of its purpose can be raised. Whereas the use of popular assessment measures, such as intelligence tests, is justified because test scores are positively correlated to job performance (Schmidt, Ones, and Hunter, 1992), the hiring and promotion tests used by the Birmingham Fire Department can only be defended by their face validity. The test evaluated the candidate's knowledge of the rules and regulations of firefighting that are presumably demanded for effective job performance. Typically tests for renewal of a driver's license have face validity in that knowledge of traffic laws is presumed to be required for obeying them. Similarly, the assumption is that firefighters can only be effective if they know the rules and regulations of firefighting. A critic of the test, however, could argue that face validity is insufficient in situations where racially unbalanced hiring policies result. A selection test to prove its worth must exhibit predictive validity, the ability to estimate on-the-job performance. A defender of the testing program of the Birmingham Fire Department could respond by suggesting that a person's knowledge of firefighting rules is most likely correlated with tests of general ability (intelligence) that have predictive ability for all kinds of jobs.

Third, what are the consequences of affirmative action programs? To answer this question, it must be narrowed down. The number of possible outcomes of affirmative action programs is limited only by the imagination of their proponents and critics. If attention is focused on the case of the Birmingham Fire Department, certain outcomes appear fundamental. Was the affirmative action successful? Although some blacks expressed criticism of the details of the affirmative action program, they agreed that it was effective in creating group-based equality of blacks. Did the affirmative action program influence the effectiveness of the Fire Department? There is no hard evidence to answer this essential question. If the selection tests used were to be trusted, then one would expect some deterioration of service. One white firefighter, however, denied that the preferential treatment of blacks resulted in lowered firefighter efficiency. How did affirmative action affect race relations? Because racial attitudes before and after affirmative action were not measured, a definitive answer cannot be offered. Although the firefighters believed that their colleagues, white or black, would protect them during firefighting, their social interactions were decidedly cool. During coffee breaks practically no fraternizing between blacks and whites occurred. Several white firefighters felt the affirmative action program destroyed their careers. They expected that their superior performance on promotion examinations would guarantee them high-level positions, a hope that was dashed by the preferential treatment given to blacks. Blacks ignored the gripes of their white colleagues because for them the preferential arrangement for hiring and promotions compensated for the past wrongs to them and their race.

The fourth and final core question about an affirmative action program is its legal status. The Birmingham Fire Department's program was ruled unconstitutional by a United States Appeal Court, 13 years after it was initiated, because it violated the 1964 Civil Rights Act and the due-process clause of the Constitution. The Supreme Court sustained this ruling. The Appeal Court wrote:

> We can imagine nothing less conducive to eliminating the vestiges of past discrimination than a government separating its employees into

two categories, black and non-black, and allocating a rigid, inflexible number of promotions to each group, year in and year out. (Bragg, 1995, A8)

If nothing else, the Birmingham Case illustrates the complexities of judging affirmative action programs. Many different outcomes can be measured, but their relative importance represents a value judgment. From the viewpoint of many blacks, affirmative action opened up social and economic opportunities that were previously denied. From the viewpoint of many whites, affirmative action denied whites and members of others minorities opportunities they deserve. From the viewpoint of an entire society, affirmative action programs generated political conflicts that created racial and ethnic tensions but not as great as those occurring during the Jim Crow era. Even the legal system, as revealed by the ambiguities of the Bakke decision (pp. 124–125), seemed incapable of producing a clear-cut and decisive constitutional ruling on the legality of group-based preferential treatment programs.

Psychological Research on Affirmative Action

The social impact of affirmative action proved to be a fertile research field for behavior scientists to investigate. An ideal arrangement would have been one in which a systematic research program could have been designed and executed that would reveal the major social consequences of affirmative action. With such information, a policy based on objective evidence instead of gut reactions could be shaped. To be specific, instead of intuitively guessing at the influence of preferential treatment on racial attitudes or the psychological effects of past discrimination on blacks or the on-job performance of medical students given preferential treatment or the post-college careers of students who majored in ethnic studies, a well-designed research program could offer quantitative indices of the influences of these and other outcomes. But broad-based research programs designed to meet the needs of a democratic society are not easy to plan, execute, or fund. Disagreements would inevitably arise as to what variables are to be investigated, what behavioral measures are to be used, who should conduct the research, and how the findings should be interpreted. Such apparent difficulties may be small in comparison to resistance to the notion that such research is possible.

For many, value-free or neutral research is a fantasy. Their thesis is that all social science research has political goals, either to maintain a prevailing social power structure or to achieve specific partisan ends. Consequently, all research programs are designed to obtain evidence in favor of affirmative action or against it, not to offer a detached description of its consequences. Opposed to such a view, and one that is consistent with the history of the physical and biological science, is that value free research, such as the theory of relativity and evolutionary theory, or the effects of aspirin on heart attacks or the psychological consequences of abortion, is possible. A socio-psychological "reality" exists and well-designed and well-executed research can provide information that would help estimate the consequences of social policies such as affirmative action. Admittedly, this is easier said than done because such efforts can easily be contaminated by preconceptions that shape research findings to fit a desired mold. Several examples of research degradation of this sort will now be described.

Equating a Social Policy with a Moral Imperative. Although favoring or opposing affirmative action need not result in a research bias, it can often lead to that. A case in point is Harrington and Miller's (1992) view of affirmative action as a moral imperative. Like many psychologists who believe that they are competent to make valid moral judgments, Harrington and Miller offer an unqualified endorsement of affirmative action:

> We, the authors, wish to establish a continuing case for affirmative action and describe how social psychological theory and research can contribute to strategies for its success in industry. The values on which we premise our support of affirmative action are redressing past injustices, protecting against contemporary prejudice, and enlightening self-interest for the long-term peace and prosperity of society. (Harrington and Miller, 1992, 121)

One must distinguish between Harrington and Miller's desire to contribute to the success of affirmative action from their moral and scientific justification of it. Psychologists, like everyone else, have the right to speak out in favor of social programs that they endorse. But partisan convictions are not scientific conclusions and, therefore, they mislead the public by suggesting, without proof, that scientific data support the judgment that affirmative action will atone for past injustices, reduce bias, and contribute to better race relations and economic prosperity. One can suggest that the authors' failure to distinguish sharply between moral judgment and empirical data encourages them to conflate the two.

The possible contaminating influence of viewing affirmative action as an ethical imperative is revealed in Beer's (1992) evaluation that completely opposes Harrington and Miller's conclusions. Instead of redressing past injustices, protecting minorities against contemporary prejudice and encouraging long-term interracial peace and economic prosperity, Beer concludes that affirmative action creates new injustices, increases prejudice against minorities, and augments racial and ethnic strife. Do these conflicting judgments–Harrington and Miller's versus Beer's–merely reflect different moral judgments about affirmative action? Beer's caustic comment appears to justify such a conclusion:

> . . . affirmative action was never seriously intended to serve as a policy to ameliorate the conditions of black Americans. It is primarily a gesture of expiation made by white liberals to assuage their guilt over past wrongs suffered by blacks and a form of emotional extortion employed by some black leaders to advance their own agendas. As other minority groups have climbed onto the affirmative action bandwagon, their dynamics have been the same. (Beer, 1992, 137)

This strong conclusion seems at odds with Beer's (1992) admission that "There is little empirical research on which the effects of affirmative action can be evaluated" (p. 146). Although he fails to offer a compelling justification for his conclusion he does offer a smattering of data that suggests that affirmative action programs can increase racial animosity of whites toward blacks because of perceived injustices of reverse discrimination. In addition, receiving preferential treatment in university admission or job hiring is accomplished at a price of lost self-respect for some blacks. In sum "affirmative action is a social policy without a scientific base" (Beer, 1992, 146).

The Opprobrium of Racism. The confusion generated by the failure to isolate moral judgments from empirical evidence is no more clearly exhibited than in the use of the term *racism.* The meaning of the term has evolved from a simple moral criticism designed to identify unequal treatment, to a political weapon to achieve partisan goals. Jim

Crow laws forced differential treatment of blacks originally exemplified as racist behavior. Denying blacks the opportunity to apply for a job or be admitted into a restaurant was a sign of racism and American society finally rejected these undemocratic laws and conventions during the civil rights era. Today, however, a person is designated a racist for a variety of actions, including taking political stands in opposition to those proposed by leaders of black organizations. The epithet "racist" was directed at some who disagreed with the O. J. Simpson verdict in 1995.

The charge of racism cuts off rational discussions of a social policy by automatically rejecting it as immoral. The concept of symbolic racism (Kinder and Sears, 1981) adds to the ease with which reasonable exchange about policy matters can be stifled by racist accusations. The idea behind symbolic racism is that political opposition to social policies, such as busing or affirmative action, is a more valid index of racial attitudes than are fundamental ethical views about treatment for all members of society. Symbolic racism leaves no room for those who oppose busing and affirmative action to escape the accusation of racial prejudice. The expansion of the meaning of racism carries with it the threat of increasing racial friction and prevents a detached analysis of the black-white problems in the United States. In sum, viewing opposition to affirmative action as racism is not only unfair, but it is unproductive for cooperative social planning.

Excluding Variables from Consideration. Harrington and Miller (1992) exhibit another shortcoming of a partisan approach to the policy of affirmative action. It can block serious consideration of potentially important variables. They raise the question of whether all ethnic and racial groups are behaviorally equal, but refuse to seriously consider the evidence. Unencumbered by any distracting information, they feel free to assume that science and morality is on their side: ". . . if one examines results and finds inequality [in employment], then how does one know if it is because of discrimination or instead, if there are actual group level differences in ability, motivation, education, interest, etc.? We suggest that many, if not all, existing differences are due to the legacy of systematic exclusion" (Harrington and Miller, 1992, 123). By uncritically accepting the assumption that all ethnic and racial groups share the same level and range of human competencies as well as past efforts and present motivations, a conclusion is easily reached that is consistent with the social policy that is being advocated. If disproportionate representation of an ethnic or racial group occurs, then discrimination must be the cause! Would Harrington and Miller dare apply that principle to the various contests at the Olympics?

The Fallacy of Inferred Past Discrimination. Affirmative action is based on the assumption that the underrepresentation of an ethnic group, such as blacks, in some social slot, such as professors in universities, is a result of past discrimination. The leap from fact to theory, from underrepresentation to past discrimination causing the underrepresentation, is labeled by Beer (1992) the fallacy of inferred past discrimination because it lacks empirical validation. If lowered social achievement is a result of past discrimination then Beer asks why three of the four most prosperous groups in the United States–Jewish Americans, Chinese Americans, Japanese Americans–suffered much more discrimination than other ethnic groups like Anglo-Saxons and yet achieved a higher level of economic and educational success?

Beer's argument does not rule out the possibility that the plight of the blacks in the United States is a result of the unique pattern of intense deprivation and discrimination, far more powerful than was suffered by the three successful minorities. Quite obviously such debates cannot be resolved unless past discrimination and deprivation can be quantified. For the present, Beer's point raises the issue as to whether it is wise for a society to automatically buy into the idea that preferential treatment programs are required to compensate for past injustices. Perhaps other programs of compensation can better offset the effects of past maltreatment.

Japanese American citizens who were interned during World War II were given financial payments to offset the injustice they suffered, not sufficient to erase the anguish, but enough to close the book on the entire painful episode. Should cash payments be a way of compensating for past wrongs or should each group receive special consideration that reflects the degree of their victimization, or should a principle be adopted that past inequities are beyond redemption and only present wrongs can be rectified, as was the case for the Japanese Americans who were interned? Focusing on the past may distract society from correcting current problems. Is preferential treatment the most effective procedure to help blacks and other minorities cope with their immediate difficulties? Is it wise to encourage some minority students to apply to universities where their chances of succeeding are much less, than to other colleges where the probability of graduating is much greater? Can another remedy be less divisive and more effective? Preferential treatment became a social policy more by political happenstance than by careful design. Resorting to social planning on the basis of reason and evidence may be a better alternative.

The Moral Justification of Affirmative Action

It should be apparent by now that the moral justification or condemnation of affirmative action involving preferential treatment can take many forms. On the simplest level the conflict is cast in two opposing moralities. One is the traditional value, not adhered to during most years of American history, that people should have the equal protection of the law and, therefore, should be judged as individuals, not as members of any racial, ethnic, or gender group. Or in the immortal words of Martin Luther King describing his dream "that my four little children will one day live in a nation where they will not be judged by the color of their skin, but by the content of their character." The competing moral principle, expressed in the language of torts, is that the breach of any duty entitles the injured party to compensatory damages. In the case of the Birmingham Fire Department, the first moral principle was directly pitted against the second: the rights of whites to be treated as individuals, not as a member of a racial group, in the hiring and promotion of firefighters versus the rights of blacks to receive compensatory damages for their exclusion from past hiring.

Two fundamental modes of coping with this moral conflict seem possible: political and judicial. Government-inspired affirmative action programs were initiated to overcome the presumed effects of past societal discrimination. By allocating jobs or granting admissions into universities, the expectation was that minorities and women would improve their socioeconomic conditions. Various aspects of these programs met resistance, but with time, the opposition became more focused on the incompatibility of preferential treatment with individual rights. If left to a political resolution, the resulting policy would reflect the strength of competing forces. However, a "moral authority" in the form of judicial processes would shape this political struggle by imposing constitutional restraints. When the Constitution was invoked, as in the case of the Birmingham Fire Department, it clearly assigned more moral value to individual rights than to compensation for past injuries to blacks. But one cannot presently envision a clear end game with a declared winner in the political struggle about affirmative action. The Constitution is sufficiently ambiguous to allow it to be interpreted in a variety of ways, and possibly reinterpreted later. Added to the difficulty of estimating the possible future of preferential treatment programs are the interactions occurring among the judicial, executive, and legislative branches of government. Although presumably independent, each branch can subtly influence the actions of the others.

The point of identifying the complexities of democratic procedures dealing with affirmative action and preferential treatment is not to deride the political process. If anything, the review of the political intricacies can be considered a virtue in that a wide variety of inputs operate in designing important social policies. If left to the decision of one or a few politicians, the chances of arbitrary and inflexible policies being adopted become greater. At the same time, however, a gigantic gap appears in the effort to fashion an effective policy. Without any clear idea about the consequences of affirmative action programs, legal and moral analyses by themselves will prove ineffective, at best, and destructive, at worst. The disadvantages of limiting policymaking to legal and moral issues are twofold. One is the consequences of the proposed policies are ignored. The other is that focusing on one policy overlooks other possibilities that may be more effective in coping with the underlying social problem.

A Summary: A Blueprint for a
Scientific-Psychological Appraisal

Affirmative action has been analyzed from ethical, scientific, and psychological perspectives. Within each view one can focus on different issues, as well as interactions among them, thus creating an endless number of problem areas to scrutinize. Although it would be reassuring to know which issues are the most important, one should recognize that their significance depends upon the social criteria employed. The following therefore represents a subjective estimate about the critical issues affirmative action has bequeathed to American society.

Preferential Treatment is the Core
Social Issue in Affirmative Action

The meaning of affirmative action must be frozen to be evaluated.

No sizable opposition to affirmative action occurs when the policy means the identification of talented minority members who have been overlooked. Nor is there any resistance to special training programs designed to compensate for the environmental deprivation of minority children and women of all ethnic groups. The only demand is that such programs should be evaluated, not in terms of their purpose, but in terms of their results.

The core issue of affirmative action is preferential treatment. Preferential treatment has usually involved blacks as the favored group, but because of the resulting racial polarization, other criteria have been suggested, such as socioeconomic level. Although the social consequences of using nonracial or nonethnic criteria may reduce opposition to preferential treatment it should be noted that regardless of the recipients chosen, preferential treatment selects those who have a lower probability of succeeding than candidates who are bypassed. Such a conclusion depends on selection procedures that are effective in predicting subsequent job performance, as was the case for the choice of the radio code operators in the Navy during World War II (pp. 44–47). Thus, society is confronted with a decision as to whether the benefits from preferential treatment are greater than the costs. In this comparison, "costs" and "benefits" are difficult to define because they are embedded in ethical commitments not shared by all. In addition, the words *costs* and *benefits* imply plural consequences that demand a complex calculus for forming a personal judgment about whether the total good resulting from preferential treatment exceeds the total bad.

Consequences of Preferential Treatment in Medical School Education

To concretize the task of judging the consequences of preferential treatment, a study that assesses the outcome of affirmative action in medical schools for the class of 1975 will now be reviewed (Keith, Bell, and Williams, 1987). The study is cited, not because it offers the final word on preferential treatment in medical school education, but instead, because it highlights fundamental issues. The study compared majority medical students with minority medical students (blacks, Mexican Americans, mainland Puerto Ricans, and Native American Indians). A summary statement of the report offers the following evaluation:

Although affirmative action in medical education has reached certain important goals, there is no question of its overall success. Our analysis demonstrated achievement of multiple objectives. Although some of these objectives compete, the success of affirmative action can be appreciated by all its advocates. (Keith, Bell, and Williams, vi)

The major goal was to increase the entry of minorities into medical schools and their subsequent graduation. The doubling of black physicians and the larger gain for other minorities testifies to the effectiveness of affirmative action. Ancillary achievements can also be cited in support of preferential treatment:

(1) making the racial/ethnic mix of medical school classes approach that of the general population; (2) improving the upward social mobility of disadvantaged minority individuals by improving access to a prestigious profession; (3) eliminating racial barriers within the medical profession; (4) increasing the number of physicians who choose to care for minority populations specifically, and the poor more generally; (5) increasing the number of physicians choosing to practice the primary care specialties; and (6) rectifying the perceived geographic maldistribution of physicians. (Keith, Bell, and Williams, 1987)

In light of such evidence, how can one criticize affirmative action? Two ways. First, regardless of its consequences, preferential treatment is basically unethical because of its denial of individual rights. Second, the conclusion that "the success of affirmative action can be appreciated by all its advocates" immediately raises the question about the response of critics. Keith, Bell, and Williams (1987) frankly acknowledge that their results are not all positive. If attention is shifted from the social advantages that accrue to minorities to the quality of medical care for patients, the total picture becomes murky. Did minority members perform less well in medical school or is such a question a veiled expression of symbolic racism that is used to oppose affirmative action? The fact is that "affirmative action students in medical school had demonstrably inferior records" (p. 139). Is this surprising considering that the preadmission performance of minority students, based on undergraduate science courses and the Medical School Admission Test, was far below that of nonminority students? "Approximately two-thirds of minority graduates had performance indexes that would rank in the bottom 7 percent for all nonminorities" (Keith, Bell, and

Williams, 8).

How do the two groups perform in medical practice? What criterion should be used? Physicians and their professional organizations, unlike athletic coaches, are not willing to test on-the-job performance, thus making necessary the use of indirect performance measures. The one selected was the incidence of certification by specialty board examination, tests that evaluate essential knowledge for the practice of medical specialties:

> Increasingly, board certification is being seen in the health care community as a measure of a physician's qualifications, particularly for recent graduates. There is a small but growing body of literature that suggests board certified physicians provide higher quality of care. (Keith, Bell, and Williams, 1987, 33)

Keith, Bell, and Williams (1987), who favor affirmative action, readily acknowledge that the "most troubling aspect of the data . . . is the low certification for minority graduates" (p. 35). Forty-eight percent of minority physicians in this study attained board certification, while the comparable figure for nonminority physicians was 80 percent. For all board certifications the percent of minority to nonminority board-certified physicians ranged from 46 (obstetrics/gynecology), to 72 (family/general practice) percent. Particularly striking were the certification rates of the graduates of Howard University and Meharry Medical Schools who, in the 1975 sample under consideration, had only black graduates. These schools, prior to affirmative action, graduated the vast majority of black physicians. In this study Meharry had only 21 percent certified physicians while the rate for Howard was 43 percent.

Although generally favoring preferential treatment for medical education, Keith, Bell, and Williams (1987) fully recognize the problems created by the apparently lower average quality of minority as compared to nonminority physicians.

> The lower rate of specialty board certification among minorities should be a matter of concern. The lower rate can be explained in substantial part by the minority graduates' premedical school characteristics and by the patient population they serve. However, there is no escaping concern even with the most favorable interpretation of either of these findings. Although lower premedical school achievement among minorities would be expected to result in lower certification rates, it is

troublesome that affirmative action programs have not succeeded in raising their rates, at least to those of comparable nonminorities. Although minorities may be less predisposed to become board certified because that credential is not very important to the patient population they serve, one must be at least somewhat concerned that quality of patient care may suffer when certification standards are not met by those who serve the poor. (Keith, Bell, and Williams, 1987, 43–44)

Although generally favoring preferential treatment for medical education, Keith, Bell, and Williams (1987) fully recognize the problems created by the apparently lower average quality of minority as compared to nonminority physicians. The research findings of the entire project can be used to highlight the moral, empirical, and political aspects of preferential treatment.

Moral Aspects of Preferential Treatment. A simple way of judging preferential treatment is to consider only its ethical implications, whether it is morally right or wrong. A strong moral commitment can lead to a clear judgment, but the decision will be determined by the ethical principle employed, not by the moral issue itself. If one is committed to the ideal of individual rights, then preferential treatment is morally wrong. Not only is the person who receives the undeserved benefits being corrupted, but also the person who is deprived of the goal sought is being cheated. In contrast, the ethical idealist who views ethics from a communal perspective could conclude that preferential treatment is morally valid because it contributes to the welfare of the entire society by alleviating the deprived conditions of the least fortunate (Rawls, 1971).

Moral systems need not provide clear answers to social policy issues especially when legal processes intrude. An ethical traditionalist could view affirmative action in a detached manner as a troublesome legal problem that will wind its way to some solution. But one should not be deceived into believing that the law is insulated from outside influences. Courts have already offered a variety of rulings that have sometimes affirmed or denied the legality of preferential treatment programs while, at other times, have obfuscated the legal issues. This is not surprising because the interpretation of the Constitution is not simply a matter of logic and reason. The Constitution is not expressed in logical form and ordinary language is intrinsically ambiguous. According to Oliver Wendell Holmes, "The life of the law has not been logic: It has been experience." Thus, too many unknown factors operate before legal decisions are reached and even then they can be overturned or put aside by constitutional amendments. Although the fight about preferential treatment may appear to be in the Courts, extra-legal forces will probably influence the final verdict. For the time being it is possible to empathize with blacks, like the Birmingham fire-fighters, who felt that preferential treatment is an appropriate compensation for past wrongs, while simultaneously concluding that past injustices cannot be rectified by present injustices. The ambivalence toward affirmative action is caught in the conclusion of a review of affirmative action, "a policy can be a bad idea in theory and a good one in practice" (Wolfe, 1998, 115). An alternative summation appears equally compelling for some; "preferential treatment is a policy that is a good idea in theory, but a bad one in practice."

Empirical Aspects of Preferential Treatment. The initial argument in favor of preferential treatment was that it was justified because racism prevents blacks from competing fairly and equally with other groups. If racism were eliminated, the performance, for example, of black medical students and physicians would not diverge from other groups. The underlying rationale for preferential treatment is psychological equalitarianism, the assumption that all races, ethnic, and gender groups have abilities that are essentially equal. The implication of this assumption is that statistical proportionality should, in principle, reign in universities and prestigious occupations and any marked deviation from distribution is a consequence of social bias.

For a variety of reasons, other than bias, groups (racial, ethnic, gender) in various countries do not distribute themselves proportionally among the various economic and professional niches (Sowell, 1990). Minorities, for example, who are not in a position to discriminate against others—Chinese in Malaysia, southerners in Nigeria, Tamils in Sri Lanka—are overrepresented in universities. Some groups in the history of the United Stated have been strikingly overrepresented in certain businesses, such as Irish politicians, Jewish clothiers, German piano manufacturers, Japanese farmers, East-Asian computer scientists, and so forth. And, finally there is the irony of blacks being overrepresented in professional basketball in the United States, at a level that is unmatched in any other pursuit. Imagine how ludicrous it would appear if the claim was advanced that the underrepresentation of whites or East Asians was a function of past discrimination in the form of their being excluded from ghetto basketball courts, where many black players hone their skills. Imagine how foolish it would be to deny the possibility that genetic factors play a role in those sports that demand a high level of speed, quickness, and coordination, where blacks have excelled.

The arguments that past discrimination is solely responsible for social disparities challenges credulity. It is a convenient hypothesis in search of supporting evidence. No universal explanation of statistical disparities is possible because the causes vary. Complex interactions among a host of variables—genetic, cultural traditions, personal experiences, and others including chance factors—determine career choices. The reasons for the overrepresentation of Italian tenors, men in firefighting, women in psychology, and blacks in jazz may vary for each group. Is it better for society to strive to achieve a goal of a proportional representation of all groups in universities or to allow nature and nurture to take their course with the strong proviso that unjust forms of discrimination be rooted out and eliminated, while optimal conditions for education are available to all?

Proponents of affirmative action would argue that preferential treatment is the only sure procedure to prevent discrimination. But such a rationale is based on the false premise that all groups have equal potentialities. Take the case of women who, in the past, have been deprived of educational opportunities because of gender bias. This issue moved to the center stage when Lawrence H. Summers (2005), then president of Harvard University, spoke at a conference focused on the problem of diversifying the science and engineering workforce. Summers suggested possible reasons for the disparities between men and women in high-level jobs in these areas. One hypothesis suggested the female underrepresentation in prestigious academic positions resulted from their reluctance to pursue a career track, which required competing at that level. This factor operated in a study of equally mathematically talented adolescent boys and girls whose aptitude scores were in the upper 1 percent (Benbow, Lubinski, Shea, and Eftekhari-Sanjani, 2000). When in their early thirties, the men and women exhibited a marked difference in career choices. Whereas men were predominantly in the physical sciences and engineering, women's major participation was in biological sciences, social sciences, arts, and the humanities. Career success was more important for men, while women sought more "balanced lives" in regard to career, family, and friends (Benbow, Lubinski, Shea, and Eftekhari-Sanjani, 2000). Nevertheless a social change appears to be occurring. Women in 1966 earned only 4.5 percent of the doctoral degrees in the physical sciences in the United States. In 2000 the proportion rose to 42 percent (Linn, 2007).

The second speculation about the lower representation of women in science and technology is that men and women may differ in their capacity to exhibit extraordinary aptitude. To flesh out Summers' point, reference to research on mathematical talent, an essential aptitude for success in the sciences and technology, will prove enlightening. Among the mathematically precocious from preschoolers to adolescents, boys significantly outnumber girls (Robinson, Abbott, Berninger, and Busse, 1997). When children are exposed to a mathematical enrichment program, boys gained more than girls (Robinson, Abbott, Berninger, Busse, and Mukhopadhyah, 1996). The ratio of males to females who achieve Scholastic Aptitude Test (SAT) mathematical scores of above 700 is 13:1 (Benbow, 1988). In recent years this ratio has fallen to 2.8:1, still a significant difference (Linn, 2007). Another example comes from the life sciences, where "over a 30-year period show that women faculty members patent about 40 percent of the rate of men" (Ding, Murray, and Stuart, 2006). On the other side of the balance sheet in the "gender conflicts" are a variety of findings that suggest women have a genetic advantage in verbal skills.

Summers' explanation of the possible causes of the underrepresentation of women in science and technology and the conflict it generated in Harvard's faculty, contributed to his decision to resign as president of Harvard. Many assumed, quite wrongly, that he suggested men are more intelligent than women. Actually, Summers was simply suggesting two possible explanations–social influences and slightly different cognitive aptitudes–to account for the gender discrepancy. Although the ultimate explanation of the differential may have to await a neurological explanation, the Summers' socialization and cognitive hypotheses appear reasonable to many. He simply suggested social factors operated to produce a higher ratio of men succeeding in science and technology, not that women can't succeed in these fields. His cognitive differential could be interpreted as an evolutionary hypothesis that natural selection would operate to encourage males to cope effectively with environmental challenges, while women acquire management skills needed for family and social problems.

Summers was not necessarily satisfied with the present distribution of men and women in science and technology. He did not deny that if the playing field became "more level" a higher proportion of women would be represented. In fact, Summers helped develop a program to identify women who had the aptitude to become scientists and engineers.

Not surprisingly, some psychologists question whether an innate gender difference exists in mathematical talent. This topic is controversial both scientifically and ideologically and it is difficult to separate their respective influences. Spelke (2005) argues in favor of the assumption "that mathematical and scientific reasoning develop from a set of biologically-based cognitive capacities that males and females share. These capacities lead men and women to develop equal talent for mathematics and science" (p. 950). Males have no "advantage in learning advanced mathematics" (p. 956). Although convincing herself, Spelke recognizes the complexity of the issue and admits that the future may prove her wrong. Within the spirit of her attitude hard data may prove her correct.

Psychological equalitarianism is such an attractive hypothesis to some that it is beyond disproof. Proponents of preferential treatment for certain minorities in university admissions argue that environmental deprivation resulting from racism is the cause of their lower average scores on college admission tests. Can such a statement be empirically verified, demonstrated to be true or false? In principle, yes; in practice, unlikely. Racism is a vague word for the investigator who seeks to identify and measure it. And, if a researcher tried to eliminate racism from a real-world study, he or she would soon discover that the task is impossible in the eyes of those who are environmental determinists. When studies show a genetic influence on the IQ of black children who were adopted into white households (e.g., Weinberg, Scarr, and Waldman, 1992) the argument is offered that being black in American society itself produces such profound negative consequences in schools and everyday society that environmental disadvantages cannot possibly be overcome. And some who support preferential treatment would go one step further. Psychological assessments tests— IQ, medical aptitude, medical certification—are culturally biased, resulting in the underperformance of blacks. To test blacks fairly demands examinations that reflect black culture.

These arguments essentially remove the environmental disadvantage hypothesis from empirical evaluation. According to Popper's principle of falsifiability (pp. 16–17), the conjecture that racism handicaps the performance of blacks in medical education and practice fails to qualify as a reasonable explanation. If a scientific hypothesis cannot, in principle, be falsified, it cannot, according to Popper, be supported. Would not a democracy benefit from a realistic appraisal of empirical issues involved in policy questions such as affirmative action and preferential treatment? We demand truth in advertising. Why not make the same demand for empirical arguments in favor of social policies that are at the heart of society?

The popular belief that environmental influences are the sole determiners of cognitive ability can presently be assigned to the realm of the absurd. Brody (1992), who favors affirmative action policies, writes:

> In 1974, Kamin wrote a book suggesting that there was little or no evidence that intelligence was a heritable trait. I believe he was able to maintain this position by a distorted and convoluted approach to the literature. It is inconceivable to me that any responsible scholar could write a book taking this position in 1990. In several respects our understanding of the behavior genetics of intelligence has been significantly enhanced in the last 15 years. We have new data on separated twins, large new data sets on twins reared together, better adoption studies, the emergence of developmental behavior genetics and longitudinal data sets permitting an investigation of developmental changes in genetic and environmental influence on intelligence, and the development of new and sophisticated methods of analysis of behavior genetic data. These developments provide deeper insights into the ways in which genes and the environment influence intelligence. (Brody, 1992, 167)

The evidence that is consistent with the idea of racial difference in cognitive ability and other behaviors raises, for some, the specter of racial superiority and all its tragic consequences. But this is an overreaction triggered by the mistaken notion that racial superiority is an empirical concept instead of a value judgment (p. 52). Persecution is not an automatic consequence of racial differences. Knowledge of differences can be beneficial in the field of medicine and should be for the entire society. It is worth noting that in the world of facts the concept of racial superiority is contradicted by the fact that no racial or ethnic group is above average in all behaviors and not below in some.

And, finally, cognitive ability is not equivalent to human excellence. Many other traits are typically involved when judging individuals.

The ideologue, who is committed to individual rights independent of any group affiliation, looks with great suspicion on rationalizations that seek to convert all psychological differences into a homogenized similarity. Individual rights demand distinguishing between the democratic ideal that every person and every group should have the opportunity to achieve their full potential from the psychological fiction that every person and every group are equal in all behavioral predispositions. Preferential treatment is a direct attack on equal rights because it denies every person the right to be judged as an individual. Not only is the practice of equal rights for individuals a moral and legal virtue, but it also has a pragmatic advantage. It is more simply administered than complex preferential treatment programs that constantly struggle with a rational justification for the degree of preference to be assigned to various groups seeking special advantages. And what group should qualify as a group? Should children of an interracial marriage between a white and black be considered biracial, black, or white? Should persons of Cuban ancestry be identified as Hispanic along with those of Mexican extraction?

The conflict between group rights and individual rights inevitably produces racial, ethnic, and gender strife. Does the comment of a self-identified liberal ring true? "Before affirmative action I would not hesitate to see a black physician, but now I might be proved foolish. That does not make me a racist, only a practitioner of probability theory." What is the implication of such a comment for the black physician who rose through the ranks of medicine without any push from preferential treatment?

Other factors being equal, preferential treatment diminishes the quality of medical care. In light of the available psychological test results, the most practical social policy to pursue is to select the best-qualified candidates for medical training to obtain physicians with the highest possible level of skills. More important to the patient who seeks the best medical care is the skill of the physician, not whether the population of physicians resembles the "face of America."

Political Aspects of Preferential Treatment. A common misconception is that the socioeconomic conditions of black Americans began to improve in the 1960s as a result of civil rights legislation and affirmative action programs. In actual fact, tremendous social and economic strides were made during the 1940s and 1950s.

> These huge gains by black Americans occurred in a time of buoyant economic expansion and spreading affluence, which felt all the more remarkable following on the heels of the worst economic catastrophe in American history. Blacks shared not only the rising prosperity of the war and the immediate postwar years; they advanced more rapidly than whites. In the 1940s and 1950s, the economic gap between the races narrowed with greater speed than in any comparable short span of years since then. The number of African Americans living in poverty plunged. It is not an overstatement to say that no ethnic group in American history has ever improved its position so dramatically in so short a period though it must be said in the same breadth that no other group had so far to go. (Thernstrom and Thernstrom, 1997, 70)

Spurred on by the victory over fascist ideology, American society sought to achieve the ideals of a democratic ethic. Breakthroughs by Marian Anderson and Jackie Robinson encouraged talent searches that were rewarded by discoveries that projected minority members into the front rank of their respective fields. The later successes of Jesseye Norman and Tiger Woods did not result from preferential treatment but from the willing acceptance of exceptional talent independent of racial and ethnic considerations. Thus in the evaluation of preferential treatment programs one must distinguish between progress achieved from historical changes from those imposed by preferential treatment.

Consider the effects of preferential treatment programs in universities. What criteria should be used to evaluate their effects? For some, simply increasing black representation in higher education is sufficient justification for preferential admission policies. The argument has been advanced that such programs have to continue until proportional representation of all minorities has been achieved. Limiting the effects of preferential treatment programs to the diversity of the student population leaves basic educational issues unaddressed. How well do students perform after preferential admissions? Do they do as well as students who meet prevailing SAT requirements? Critics of the SAT argue that the test overlooks minority students who could succeed in college if given an opportunity. A perceptive evaluation of individual black applicants, the argument goes, will enable the identification of minority students whose academic success will go well beyond their "SAT potential." If true, then minority students afforded preferential admissions should do as well as those majority students who are required to meet certain SAT standards.

The educational effectiveness of preferential treatment programs can be judged by comparing the graduation rates of blacks and whites (Thernstrom and Thernstrom, 1997). Blacks admitted to Harvard in 1992 had an average SAT of 1305, 95 points below their white classmates. Five percent of blacks dropped out before graduating, while only three percent of whites did. These results suggest that the impact of preferential treatment was relatively slight, both in regard to the amount of preference afforded and the deleterious impact on black graduation rate. This conclusion, however, is limited to Harvard where the SAT requirement for blacks was higher than the average SAT score demanded at such elite colleges as Chicago, Cornell, and Pennsylvania. An entirely different picture emerges from the University of California, Berkeley, a public institution, where the racial gap between the average SAT score of blacks and whites was 288 points, with the mean black score being 947, 358 points lower than those obtained by blacks admitted to Harvard. At Berkeley 16 percent of whites and 42 percent of blacks failed to graduate. In the case of Berkeley, preferential admission policies markedly depress the graduation rates of blacks as compared to whites. Surprisingly, the school that produces an equal rate of graduates for both blacks and whites is the University of Mississippi, where during the 1984 to 1987 period, graduated 49 percent white students and 48 percent blacks. The school sets a "minimum" SAT for admissions that "is high enough to bar students likely to experience severe academic difficulties" (Thernstrom and Thernstrom, 1997, 412).

The effects of preferential admissions policies on minority graduation rates appear to be a joint function of the level of academic standard required for college admission and the amount of deviation from that standard that is afforded to minority applicants. The greater the amount of deviation (preference), the larger will be the ratio of minority to majority student dropouts. One can argue that focus of attention should be on the successful black students who, with the benefit of preferential treatment, graduated from selective colleges leading to socioeconomic successes that would have been beyond reach but for the helping hand (Bowen and Bok, 1998). But does not such a view callously disregard those "beneficiaries" of preferential treatment who fail to graduate? The evidence suggests that if these minority students had attended less prestigious universities with lower SAT requirements they would have done better than the "elite drop outs."

> In 1986, 14 years after leaving high school, black college dropouts were earning one-quarter less than their counterparts who went to less selective schools in the first place but managed to graduate. When colleges attempt to display their social commitments by admitting "high risk" students from minority groups . . . it is the student that suffers when the risks don't pan out. The schools may feel better, having demonstrated the racial virtue, but many of their beneficiaries end up worse off. (Thernstrom and Thernstrom, 1997, 411)

Limiting an evaluation of preferential treatment to recipients who succeed or fail to graduate ignores other significant consequences of affirmative action programs. At the forefront of social issues is the racial animosity generated by racial double standards. The denial of access to distinguished educational institutions in spite of superior qualifications to those selected is a bitter pill for victims and their families to swallow. The offense is exacerbated by politicians' double-talk. In a press conference of December 16, 1997, President Clinton embraced the principle that "best qualified people ought to get what they are best qualified for," while simultaneously agreeing with the rule "that people who had a hard time ought to have a hand up" (*New York Times,* December 12, 1997, A16). Thus, preferential treatment was simultaneously rejected and endorsed. But Clinton's comments hint at a possible consistency between the two maxims. Preferential treatment is antithetical to the first principle that proposes that the most qualified should be selected for university admissions. The second principle–a hand up should be given to those who have suffered a hard time–need not be interpreted as supporting preferential treatment in college admissions but, instead, as a commitment to eliminate environmental inequalities that deny people the opportunity to achieve their full potential. One of the most important obligations of society is to provide the best possible education for all, not only to fulfill its responsibilities to develop children's cognitive skills to their fullest, but also to serve the needs of the entire nation. The different interpretation of a "hand up"–preferential treatment for college admissions versus educational enhancement through kindergarten to high school–represent not only a policy difference, but starkly contrasting views about the morality of preferential treatment and the psychology of group differences.

Some Final Reflections on Preferential Treatment

The enthusiastic support of the principle of individual rights with the concomitant rejection of preferential treatment can easily produce blind spots that allow social injustices. For example, everybody can resonate to the idea of training a group of physicians that has the greatest chance of succeeding and providing the highest level of medical care. But at the same time, one should recognize that such a goal does not automatically produce an equitable distribution of medical care. One of the successes of affirmative action programs is that medical care was provided to the previously ignored minorities and the poor. The argument that affirmative action lowers health care standards is of little concern to those who were denied medical care prior to preferential treatment for blacks and other minorities. Thus, those proponents of "sheer excellence" and "fairness" must recognize that their goals do not automatically meet the needs of all segments of society. Achieving individual rights must be accompanied by efforts to fulfill social responsibilities.

Another possible oversight is to assume that the use of race or ethnicity in job selection automatically implies preferential treatment. Shared racial or ethnic identities between therapist and patient may prove to be advantageous in mental health programs. Therefore, for a certain class of patients (e.g., blacks, Hispanics) race or ethnic identity combined with scores on a medical or graduate aptitude test may be a better predictor of job performance for aspiring psychiatrists or psychologists than aptitude test scores alone. When race or ethnicity has been demonstrated to enhance job performance, using them for personnel selection does not constitute preferential treatment. Instead, in such cases, race and ethnicity operate as causal variables in job performance. A similar problem occurs in the selection of police officers. A black patrol officer in a black ghetto may be more effective than a white patrolman. Reserving police positions to be filled by black applicants for patrolling black neighborhoods represents a procedure for identifying the most qualified applicants, not an example of preferential treatment. In a larger context, what is suggested is that race, ethnic identity, or gender can be employed as selective variables if they add to the predictive validity of an assessment procedure.

Is the principle of individual rights challenged and compromised by medical schools, such as Howard and Meharry that are designed to cater to black students? Do they not serve as preferential-treatment factories that allow blacks to bypass the competitive rigors involved in gaining admittance to a prestigious profession? Are they not practicing a form of segregation blacks fought hard to overcome? Should they be forced into setting race-blind admission standards that would force them to turn their backs on their own academic tradition? Does not any racial, ethnic, or religious group have the right to establish their own educational institutions to serve the needs of their constituents? But should public funds be permitted to support segregated goals?

These are not empty questions. In fact, they are weighty ones. They are designed to reveal the complexity of the problem. Viewing these policy questions solely as moral issues does little to resolve the under-lying social conflicts. In fact, one can suggest that pitting one moral belief against its opposite escalates the difference into an irresolvable conflict. When emotional reactions are put aside in favor of a detached analysis, then it becomes possible to perceive other ways of coping with the economic problems confronting certain minority groups, such as blacks. But such a detached, pragmatic orientation demands perceiving the conflicts created by preferential treatment programs directly and clearly, and not through an ideological mist.

Practically all social policies, such as affirmative action, have equiv-ocal outcomes: compatible with one goal and incompatible with another. The inverse relationship between the proportion of minority physicians and the average quality of medical care is a case in point. Keith, Bell, and Williams (1987) believe that the policy of preferential admission to medical school should continue, in spite of negative influ-ences on the quality of medical care. More important than the limita-tion, for them, is the increased minority representation in the medical profession. But it should be noted that they expect improved methods of educating minority students will wipe out the existing discrepancies between their performance and those of nonminority physicians, thus eliminating the need for preferential treatment. Regardless of whether this prediction comes to pass or not, it does raise the vexing question of whether preferential treatment programs should presently be con-sidered a temporary action or a permanent solution. Preferential treatment programs of the past can be accepted, if not approved, by many of their critics if their termination is generally supported. But if it is considered a basic civil liberty that cannot be denied to minorities and women, then a fierce battle will continue about the nature of individual rights.

Great debates about the meaning of a democratic ethic are not easily or quickly resolved. In the case of preferential treatment, the conflict is still intense and divisive. But persistent struggles have a way of encouraging new ideas and attitudes that hold promise of ameliorating the discord. The black community is shifting its position in important ways. It has become more acceptable for a black leader in public debates to stress the point that all black problems have not been created by white racism. This looking inwards has encouraged a reconsideration of the goal of a fully integrated society. Governmental efforts in busing and preferential treatment programs did not overcome the social barriers that isolated blacks to their "part of town." In addition, these efforts at social engineering increased the friction between whites and blacks. Instead of persistently seeking social acceptance from whites, some black voices are arguing that we should only demand fairness in the workplace while relying more on our own efforts in the struggle for economic justice. Black entrepreneurship with black workers in the black community can help blacks climb the economic ladder. This is not an unusual strategy for minorities who seek to elevate their socioeconomic position. Although black separatism need not be the specific goal sought, it can, in a diminished form, represent an effective strategy for improving the socioeconomic position of blacks. One of its advantages is that its success depends on the efforts of the black community, not on the handout of others.

In a similar vein, the black community can help solve one of its major problems. Bob Herbert (2006A), the black *New York Times* columnist who wrote eloquently about the pernicious effects of racism in 1994, recognizes the responsibility of the black community in coping with the current self-destructive pathology of black men. They "are laid low by this illness, don't snitch on criminals, seldom marry, frequently abandon their children, refer to themselves in the vilest terms (niggers, whores, etc.), spend extraordinary time kicking back in correctional institutions, and generally wallow in the deepest depths of degradation their irresponsible selves can find" (A27).

The education of blacks is a source of persistent conflict within and outside the black community. What should be the goal of their education? At one extreme is the tough-minded approach that encourages a demanding education consistent with both a child's ability and the child's future productivity as an adult. At the other extreme is the concern for the "damaged self-esteem" of black children resulting from "rampant racism." To compensate for their low self-esteem, black children, the argument goes, should be exposed to a positive view of their cultural heritage in the absence of any unnecessary threats of failures. The tough-minded response to such a proposal is that if concerns for self esteem and ethnic pride interfere with educational achievement, they should be ignored. The major need of the children of the black underclass, as well as all children, is hard work in a school that can provide an optimal learning experience. Effortful work toward academic goals will better prepare children to escape into the mainstream of society than will any superficial attempt to raise their self esteem (Dawes, 1994).

Many defenders of preferential treatment recognize its negative impact on social unity but, nevertheless, believe it should continue while reducing its divisiveness. The source of greatest resentment is a government policy that treats people unequally. For example, a case that triggered great resentment in Boston was the admission policy of the prestigious public high school, Boston Latin, the nation's oldest public school whose long list of distinguished graduates include five signers of the Declaration of Independence, as well as Ralph Waldo Emerson, Samuel Adams, and Leonard Bernstein. Minority students were admitted over whites who had superior records and test scores. Why should not all students compete equally and reward those who have been most successful? Those who fail to be admitted are not denied a high school education or an opportunity to overcome their failure to be trained at Boston Latin. Similarly, denial of admission to the most prestigious state university does not cut off the possibilities of higher education. Public colleges and community colleges are always available and everybody, by their own actions, can achieve their own level of competency. Throughout my academic career I have been surprised, and pleased, to see students from an undistinguished background, catch fire in graduate school and go on to a distinguished academic career.

Private colleges and universities are another matter. They have a right to decide their own academic philosophy and selection procedures. If they believe a diverse student body can provide a better education than one selected solely on academic ability, then they should be allowed to implement their idea. Some students will be attracted to a campus that provides the opportunity to mix with and learn from an ethnically diverse student body. In addition, such a campus might become more appealing if its academic program is multiculturally oriented. In contrast, a college emphasizing academic achievement more than ethnicity, would be more attractive to other students. Students with different interests–humanities, science, engineering, arts, social science–would be drawn disproportionately to one of the campuses with no one believing that they are being denied "equal treatment."

Recognizing the virtues and vices of preferential treatment redirects our attention toward the world of facts. The controversy has become chaotic because of the inability of the participants to establish a common framework for evaluating the consequences of preferential treatment. As a result, the debate has been polluted both by fact-free explanations and a willingness to accept simple lies in preference to complicated truths. If willingness could be created to have social policy, such as preferential treatment, and be guided by reliable and valid empirical evidence, then the chances of a productive interchange between opposing views will increase. Although agreement about policy choices would not necessarily follow, the points of disagreement should become clearer. In the give and take of informed exchanges, the likelihood of a widespread supported social policy would increase.

Chapter 6

MULTICULTURALISM:
EVOLUTION OR REVOLUTION?

Affirmative action and multiculturalism are like Siamese twins; they are intimately connected but individually distinct. Affirmative action set the stage for multiculturalism and multiculturalism served to justify affirmative action. Together they are perceived by some as necessary changes needed to make American society live up to its ideal of equal justice for all. For others, they are considered to be a drastic turnabout in United States' persistent effort, from its inception, to establish a truly democratic society in which individual equality is the guiding principle. The differences between multiculturalism and Eurocentric-Americanism, the reigning national philosophy that dominated the first two centuries of American history, will be reviewed in a debate format. Initially, the essence of each concept will be described and then their points of conflict will be highlighted and discussed. Finally, the social consequences of each viewpoint will be assessed.

A EUROCENTRIC VIEW OF AMERICAN CULTURE

The United States is a cultural offshoot of Europe, with England playing a major role. English, French, and Spanish initially settled the territories that were to become the United States. African blacks were brought as slaves to British settlements in North America in the early part of the eighteenth century. Soon after United States was created, European immigrants poured in with Germans, Scotch-Irish, and Irish being the largest groups. From 1820 to 1930 the United States accept-

161

ed about 60 percent of the world's immigrants, with Europeans from an expanding geographical base—Scandinavia, Italy, Greece, Poland, Russia—dominating the new arrivals. The continually increasing immigration met resistance by groups who had become "Americans" earlier but the powerful demands for new workers for industrial and agricultural expansion was too great to be thwarted. Opposition to some immigrants, for example the Chinese, led to immigration laws that expressed racial and ethnic prejudice. Similar political conflicts are currently a source of great contention, even though flagrant biases have been eliminated in favor of a system that assigns preference to certain groups (e.g., victims of persecution).

The relationship between one's ethnic background, ethnic identity, and being an American, can take many forms. A popular misconception is that the United States functioned as a melting pot, in which intermarriage among different ethnic groups occurred at a high rate, and within a span of a few generations everybody became a "Yankee-Doodle Dandy" American. Throughout the United States ethnic groups congregated together and maintained cultural traditions. While social interactions primarily took place in schools, the workplace, and armed services, intermarriages were suppressed by religious and racial differences. For the most part, European ethnic groups—Irish, Italians, Jews—maintained many of their ethnic traditions, while simultaneously seeking to become indistinguishable from established Americans. They were Jewish Americans, Italian Americans, and Irish Americans, with the emphasis on American. Sometimes a conflict arose between their competing allegiances, as was the case for some German Americans who resisted anti-Germany propaganda, as well as the declaration of war in World Wars I and II. Once the decision to enter the war was made, no significant opposition remained. But injustices happened. World War I, for example, created intense bias against German Americans who experienced job discrimination even in universities if they bore a German name like Karl Muenzinger. A dismal case of ethnic bias occurred with Japanese Americans during World War II. They were branded with the accusation that they were more emotionally committed to Japan than to the United States. In an act that was later recognized as a miscarriage of justice, Japanese American citizens on the West coast were interned to prevent them from assisting the enemy. Not only did this expectation prove wrong, but Japanese Americans performed brilliantly in the United States military as well.

The very nature of democracy dictates that a person has the freedom, the right, to form political opinions without being accused of sacrificing national to parochial interests. The Cuban American who favors economic restrictions on trade with communist Cuba, or the Jewish American who supports economic sanctions against Arab governments that sponsor terrorism, or the Irish American who advocates the unification of Ireland can argue that their position is in the national interest of the United States. The concept of "national interest" operates in the free market of political ideas and citizens of a democracy are entitled to interpret the concept as they see fit. At the same time, one must recognize that the unity of purpose a society will exhibit will be determined by the goals of its component parts. Extreme disunity occurred at the time of the Civil War and to a lesser extent during the Great Depression and the Vietnam and Iraq wars. In contrast, a high degree of oneness occurs when a decisive majority feels threatened by a common enemy, as Americans did during World War II.

United States, after World War II, had a clear vision of itself. It was a Eurocentric culture shaped by the European immigrants who created the new country and populated it throughout its development. This does not deny the impact of non-European influences, most notably that of the African Americans and Native Americans. In addition, the country's distinctive geography and history spurred a particular ingenuity and innovativeness. The ready availability of land combined with a labor shortage led to a pioneer spirit that conquered the vast continent and encouraged American individualism and resourcefulness. The fundamental character of American and Western European cultures shared a commitment to the ideals of political democracy that set them apart from most regions of the world following World War II. One distinguishing feature was an ethnic tolerance that allowed, in fact encouraged, the free expression of cultural traditions. Mexican Americans proudly demonstrated their own distinctive musical heritage, while jazz, with its black American origins, was enthusiastically incorporated into the musical culture of the United States as well as most of the world.

The educational curriculum in the United States was slanted toward Eurocentrism. Opportunities in colleges to study history of the United States, as well as English and European history, far exceeded those of other cultures. American literature was a vibrant field that recognized its English and European roots. The nonpareil position of many

English authors, most notably Shakespeare, was fully acknowledged. American science was continuous with European science, as demonstrated by the fact that doctorate students in the sciences during the middle of the twentieth century were required to exhibit some mastery in European languages, particularly German and French.

This Eurocentric orientation did not produce just another "European" country. Rather a distinctive American society was created that owed much to the diversity of European cultures. Essentially a mono-cultural American society was created with a multicultural character, but not without some ethnic friction and conflict. To varying degrees all immigrant groups suffered some prejudice and resentment. Certain minorities and women experienced limitations or even exclusion in their representation in university student bodies and faculties. But the Allied victory in World War II, with the recognition of the horrors of Nazism and the unjust treatment of Japanese Americans and African Americans, increased the sensitivities of Americans to democratic ideals.

A MULTICULTURAL VIEW OF AMERICAN CULTURE

Ostensibly, the conflict between Eurocentric culture and multiculturalism appears to be one of emphasis. Multiculturalism seeks recognition of a range of influences that the Eurocentric view ignores. Such an interpretation is off-target. Eurocentric America and multicultural America offer drastically different views of America's past and future. Multiculturalism is a revolutionary movement that seeks a fundamental restructuring of American society and culture.

Eurocentric America did not emerge inadvertently from the conditions that European explorers and settlers found in North America. Instead, according to the multiculturalist's view, three cultures–Native Americans, European, African blacks–converged in North America but one, the European, gained ascendancy in a series of clashes in which Native Americans, and later African blacks, were victimized and denied the freedom to pursue their own cultural traditions. This oppression of non-European cultures continued throughout the history of the imperialistic and racist American culture. In essence, American culture robbed minority cultures–blacks, Hispanics, Asians, American Indians–of their character and vitality by attempting to homogenize them into a single Eurocentric mold.

Multiculturalism offers a simple solution to the evils of Euro-Americanism. Right past wrongs by reorienting American society in the direction of multiculturalism and away from the Eurocentric view that idealized the achievements of white males. United States should become a multicultural society in which the various cultures can thrive without any one culture, Eurocentric, dominating all others. This ideal can only be achieved by recognizing that the Eurocentric domination of American culture, with white males occupying the seats of power, was a result of a systematic policy of discrimination against minorities and women.

In order to rectify the injustices created by a Eurocentric shaping of American culture, minorities and women had to gain access to the positions of power. This demanded affirmative action that assigned preferential treatment to minorities and women to empower them in their attempt to overcome past discrimination. But supplying a level playing field for the victimized to compete fairly is insufficient. Not only had they been mistreated by being denied equal opportunity in the economic and academic marketplace, but the "marketplace" itself was rigged by being distorted in favor of male-dominated Euro-American values. In such a culture, even if minorities and women could handle it, they would still be playing on a field that was tilted against their cultural and gender heritage and values. Affirmative action with preferential treatment was not enough; a revolutionary overhaul of American culture was needed to create a multicultural society that truly reflected the entire spectrum of the American population. In essence, a shift was sought from an American culture that emphasized its primary roots in western civilization to a multicultural society that sought fair representation and equal respect for all the diverse cultures represented in American society.

A Eurocentrist's Rejoinder

American-Eurocentrists would argue that the multiculturalists' agenda is based on historical distortions and a general failure to appreciate the consequences of a society based on multicultural principles. For example, the assumption that American society emerged equally from a tripartite foundation of Native Americans, Europeans, and African blacks is a historical myth. Democracy, freedom of speech and press, representative government, human rights, and due process of law are peculiarly European in origin. European influences were by far the dominant ones in shaping American society and culture.

American culture should not be judged against the standards of a utopia but instead in comparison to the achievement of other cultures. Of particular importance is its relative success in comparison to ideologically driven societies of the twentieth century whose loftiness of ideals could only be matched by the depth of their failures. Considering the overarching problems faced by the world's superpower, one can argue that the United States has been fairly successful in establishing a society that is relatively desirable, as demonstrated by the unmatched numbers of foreigners who seek admission. This neither implies a cultural superiority nor a level of social quality that is beyond improvement. It merely means that American society is attractive in comparison to others. And those cultures that many judge more appealing–Canadian, Australian, New Zealand, Western European countries–also have Eurocentric roots. And perhaps most importantly in evaluating these societies, they hold promise of improvement because of their commitment to democratic processes that encourage political disagreements.

A Eurocentric America does not perceive itself through rose-colored glasses. But neither does it belittle its achievements:

> We of the West have often failed catastrophically in respect for those who differ from us, as our dismal record of wars and persecutions may attest. But such respect is something for which we have striven as an ideal, and in which we have achieved some success, both in practicing it ourselves and in imparting it to others. . . . Imperialism, sexism, and racism are words of Western coinage–not because the West invented these evils, which are, alas, universal, but because the West recognized and named and condemned them as evils and struggled mightily, and not entirely in vain, to weaken their hold and to help their victims. If, to borrow a phrase, Western culture does indeed "go," imperialism, sexism, and racism will not go with it. More likely casualties will be the freedom to denounce them and the effort to end them. (Lewis, 1994, 51)

A Multiculturalist's Rejoinder

Multiculturalists reject this sanguine description of the Eurocentric view of American culture. They argue that the European influence has been exaggerated by ignoring the contributions of minority cultures and the exploitation of women. Not only does the designation of American culture as being Eurocentric overlook the contribution of other cultures, but it fails to note that its dominance was achieved at the expense of robbing minority cultures–Blacks, Hispanics, Native American–of their character and vitality by attempting to homogenize them into a single Eurocentric culture. The argument that the American Eurocentric culture is appealing to others and that progress has been made in coping with the triple evils of imperialism, sexism, and racism misses a basic point at issue. The goal of multiculturalism is not to make "progress" in dealing with these social blights but instead to eliminate them. Imperialism, sexism, and racism are built into Western European societies and the only way of extirpating their influence is to create a multicultural society in which diverse cultures are recognized as equal.

SOURCES OF CONFLICT

Eurocentrists and multiculturalists appear to be talking past each other. They perceive American culture in such contradictory ways that a meaningful discussion between the two appears impossible. Perhaps so, but at least the points of conflict can be highlighted in an effort to identify the sources of disagreement.

Cultural Diversity

One could easily get the impression from multiculturalists that the Eurocentric culture is opposed to cultural diversity. But such an accusation overlooks the ideal of democratic tolerance to which western civilization is committed. The history of the United States illustrated a steady progress, in spite of conflicts, to the ideal of freedom from ethnic and gender bias and bigotry. Diversity is the means by which Eurocentric America measured its progress in providing citizens, regardless of their ethnic or gender identity, the opportunities to pursue their goals free of discrimination. The freedom to express one's racial or ethnic allegiances without endangering one's perceived commitment to the United States is a sign that the democratic ideal of tolerance is being achieved. In other words, the dream of America was not a confederation of different cultures, a multicultural society, but a broad-based monoculturalism inhabited by ethnically diverse individuals. In contrast to the means-end-diversity of the Euro-American perspective, multiculturalism preaches a goal-end diversity in which no culture should dominate all others. A national sense of identity is being discarded in favor of a confederation of different racial, ethnic, and gender identities. A Eurocentric American culture encourages expressions of component cultures, but seeks to maintain the priority of the Euro-American cultural values that dominated American history.

A case that reflects the conflict between monocultural and multicultural America was a controversy in 1996 in Santa Barbara, California surrounding the use of a high school textbook in the ethnic study program for Chicanos, students of Mexican descent. The critics of the book took exception to the hypercritical manner in which it treated the actions of the United States in the war with Mexico in the 1840s. More importantly they objected to the book's political proposal that an open border be established between the United States and Mexico to achieve an equitable economic relationship between the two countries. Supporters of the textbook interpreted these criticisms to be a racist attack on their attempt to create a positive self-identity for Chicano students. Critics maintained that they were not attempting to eradicate ethnic attachments but, instead, were resisting the divisiveness the textbook encouraged by emphasizing Chicano identification at the sacrifice of American values and interests. The multiculturalist's response is that the past exploitation of Chicanos demands that they empower themselves by acting in concert to achieve political and economic equality. The critics posed the question, "Are you Mexican Americans or American Mexicans?" And so forth and so on!

Educational Policy

The major battlefield of the cultural war took place in education where multiculturalists tried to replace the dominance of Eurocentric programs with those representing minority cultures and women's studies. Before the advent of modern multiculturalism, ethnic studies existed but were not so designated. A student could specialize in the history of blacks and their influence on American culture or study the Jewish religion through a scholarly analysis of the Talmud and the Torah or major in German history and culture. But such ethnic specializations differed from the modern forms of multiculturalism in three important respects: (1) they occurred within traditional departmental structures; (2) they provided scholarly knowledge about various aspects of a particular culture without attempting to convey the phenomenological experience of being a member of that particular ethnic group; (3) teachers of these courses were selected for their scholarly achievements, not their ethnic identities. A white person could be an acknowledged scholar on the history of blacks, a Scandinavian could be an authority on Judaism, and a Frenchman could hold down the post of a professor of German history.

The emphasis on scholarly criteria for academic departments, subject matter of courses, and selection of faculty, distinguishes old-fashion American Eurocentric knowledge from new-fashioned multicultural fields such as black Studies and Women Studies. But admittedly this difference is difficult to define because some overlap in the scholarship of the two orientations can occur. At Harvard, for example, "Black Studies" is an undergraduate major that focuses on the black experience in contemporary America. The staff has joint appointments in established departments. One member, Wilson Julius Wilson, is a distinguished sociologist who has tried in a rigorous objective fashion to understand the influence of race in the American society and to develop more effective strategies to cope with inner-city poverty. Such a program is considered incomplete, if not superficial, by critics in the departmental program in African American studies at Temple University that offers graduate degrees in addition to an undergraduate major. A major theme of the Temple University program is that an Afrocentric approach is essential. One cannot understand American blacks without comprehending their African roots and heritage. And to do this successfully requires an appreciation of the uniqueness of African traditions and culture that cannot fully be revealed by Eurocentric scholarship that has been shaped by dead white males. Black Studies, as conceived by Temple University, encouraged African American history to be a mandated course for all Philadelphia high school students.

Factual disagreements took place in the debate between Eurocentrists and multiculturalists. For the most part Black Studies historians view the plight of present-day Africa as a product of a brutal European colonization that oppressed the native population, destroyed their social fabric, and exploited their natural wealth. American Eurocentrists (e.g., Wesseling, 1996) mostly offer a less persecutory view, suggesting that African colonization was not directed at enslaving Blacks but, instead, was a byproduct of European geopolitics combined with industrial and commercial expansion. A crucial factor in European successes was the collaboration of African black leaders, not only in the colonization, but also in the slave trade. At the extreme of Black Studies education are teachers like Leonard Jeffries who propose that Africans are "sun people" who are cooperative and communal, while Europeans are "ice people" who thrive on destruction and brutality. One suggestion is that African blacks were responsible for Egyptian civilization and Greek philosophy, conclusions that most historians vigorously reject (Lefkowitz, 1996).

The diametrically opposed views of history offered by Eurocentrists and multiculturalists immediately raise the question as to whether a golden mean can be achieved or whether one educational orientation must dominate. To some extent both conceptions are presently operating although in different spheres in academe. Although efforts have been made to undermine the Eurocentric foundation of natural science, their effects have been nil. The feminist critique argues that science expresses masculine values of achievement and objectivity, while ignoring feminist values of cooperation and subjectivity. This position may be ideologically appealing but is practically of no import. Natural science methodology, in practice but not in origin, is a universal form of inquiry designed to reveal empirical truths about nature that are independent of gender or culture.

> There can be no multicultural solution to the genetics of cystic fibrosis; the ozone hole cannot be deconstructed; there is nothing whatsoever relativistic or culturally contextual about the dopamine transporter molecule whose blockage by cocaine gives a rush of euphoria, the kind that leads the constructivist to doubt the objectivity of science. (Wilson, 1995, 74)

When it comes to art and literature, Eurocentrism and multiculturalism offer contrasting conceptions of excellence. Eurocentric education encouraged college courses designed to expose students to the great books of the western world. Although the authors selected varied from college to college, white men such as Aristotle, Homer, Kant, Hume, Shakespeare, Milton, Nietzsche, Rosseau, dominated the selection. Some women, like Jane Austen and Virginia Woolf, were included but with nothing approaching a balance between genders or among ethnic groups. Eurocentrists defended the choices because the selected authors represented the great ideas and vital stories of western civilization and conveyed what it means to be human as well. In contrast, multiculturalists questioned such choices because the reading lists failed to reflect the ethnic and gender composition of the student body. How could minority students and women resonate to the writings of dead white men who operated within a Eurocentric tradition? Therefore, the argument went, it became necessary to replace "Eurocentric authors" in a great books course with others who represent minority or feminine perspectives even though, from the Eurocentrist position, the literary quality would be reduced. Even among English majors in colleges the tide has turned against the "giants" of the past: Shakespeare, Chaucer, and Milton (Honan, 1996). Courses in popular culture–The Gangster Film, Melodrama and the Soap Opera, 20th-Century American Boxing Fiction and Film, Pornography–have replaced them in some prestigious institutions. The justification for this shift is to offer students more choices, including more diverse opportunities for them to learn about the times in which they live.

The argument between Eurocentrists and multiculturalists about literature is beyond resolution. Eurocentrists argue that their great books not only improve students' linguistic skills but also will enhance their esthetic and literary appreciation that will, in turn, elevate the quality of their lives. The shift away from the classics, Eurocentrists suggest, has been to serve the needs of political fashion that values ethnic and gender identification more than esthetic excellence. Multiculturalists view the choice differently. To overcome the negative effects of Eurocentric education, minorities and women must examine their self-worth and enhance their self-esteem.

The Psychology of Multiculturalism

Natural science psychologists, like physicists and biologists, view their empirical methodology as transcending cultural boundaries. But for one muticultural approach, cultural factors are supreme because natural science methodology itself is culturally biased, a product of "western tradition."

To presume Western concepts of the mind, along with its methods of study, not only lends itself to research of little relevance to other cultures, but disregards and undermines alternate cultural traditions. Against these tendencies toward a univocal science . . . a multicultural psychology [is proposed] . . . that celebrates the rich multiplicity of indigenous conceptualizations of the person along with varying means of acquiring knowledge. To realize such a psychology new forms of dialogue must be sought and the sharing made relevant to ongoing challenges of practical cultural significance. (Gergen, Gulerc, Lock, and Misra, 1996, 496)

This multicultural approach is not simply about the relative influence of cultural factors but, instead, about their interpretation. The interpretations offered are not within the tradition of scientific explanation. Instead, a complex web of interacting epistemologies is proposed that allows for knowledge claims to be offered in the absence of any clear-cut criteria by which to evaluate them. The cognitive processes that operate within these various epistemologies–phenomenological, hermeneutics, social constructionism, feminism, critical theory, to name a few–lead to a form of understanding that generates two conclusions that are at odds with natural science methodology: truth is an epistemological illusion because objective reality is a myth, and knowledge, however it may be described, has direct political implications. Concepts, for example, such as *intelligence* and *schizophrenia* that have their origins in western psychology are irrelevant, for example, to Maoiri culture because they have no indigenous meaning and carry the threat of being used as "instruments of politically motivated suppression" (Gergen, Gulerc, Lock, and Misra, 1996, 500). Multiculturalism demands that each culture should have its own independent psychological science.

If cultures are psychologically distinct, then students should be able to, even required to, learn about different cultures, especially their own. These opportunities are particularly important for those students who belong to ethnic, racial, or gender groups whose past histories have been distorted in the attempt to hide the abuses to which they have been subjected. Teaching them their true heritage not only exposes them to their real past, but also helps raise their self-esteem that had been damaged by Eurocentric history.

Eurocentrists consider such speculations to be more an outgrowth of ideology than of evidence. The assumption of a psychological unique-ness for each culture ignores the biological and psychological similar-ity that underlies all human societies. Consider such western con-structs as cognitive ability (e.g., intelligence) and brain diseases (e.g., schizophrenia) that have their origins in the observations of behavior and their roots in physiological processes. They are not merely sub-jective creations of a given culture, but instead are objective charac-teristics of human biology and behavior. Any culture, Maori or others, is free to ignore these concepts but that does not deny their existence in all cultures.

The conclusion that the Eurocentric view of history has damaged the self-esteem of minorities and women suggests a simple solution: Elevate the self-esteem of those whose self-worth has been damaged by Eurocentric education. Give big doses of praise to the individual and the ethnic group to which he or she belongs. But natural science psychology would question raising the self-esteem of a person without demanding compensating achievement. Raising self-esteem should not be an end in itself. High self-esteem can be harmful when it has no basis in reality (Baumeister, Smart, and Boden, 1996). Self-esteem enthusiasts raise another question that is at the heart of education. Should schools' concern for raising self-esteem compromise educa-tional standards (Sykes, 1995)? This question is not designed to quash consideration of students' self-esteem and related feelings of pride in one's race, ethnicity, and gender, but instead to suggest that the task should not conflict with the primary educational goals of knowledge acquisition and the improvement of cognitive skills. Failing students are "socially promoted" to the next grade for fear that their self-esteem would be damaged. Unfortunately, high self-esteem alone does not qualify a person for a job. Perhaps family and cultural organizations, not public schools, are best assigned the task of enhancing the stu-dent's ethnic and gender pride.

Finally, Eurocentrists raise the question whether special programs such as "Black Studies" or "Women Studies" were really needed? Could not prevailing academic organizations provide opportunities for students to pursue interests in scholarly topics associated with blacks, other minorities, and women? Limited course offerings and the number of qualified professors might create initial difficulties, but such obstacles could be overcome with time. The point is that at the time of the advent of multiculturalism the study of scholarly topics associated with race, minorities, and women was not outlawed. The educational issue separating the multiculturalist from the Eurocentrist was not educational subject matter but instead educational goals: cultural diversity versus traditional academic standards. But multiculturalists respond by suggesting that education, and living itself, should not be ruled by ivory-tower values but, instead, by the realities of life. White men may find it easy to live under conditions of subjugation of minorities and women, but the victims have difficulties. And so forth and so on!

Educational Diversity versus Academic Excellence

The goal of multiculturalism to achieve ethnic, racial, and gender proportionality in all occupations had important educational consequences. Education is the route by which people gain qualifications needed for a good job and a successful career. More or less by happenstance, a Supreme Court ruling in 1978 assigned value to the goal of student diversity that was effectively used by multiculturalists to promote expansion of ethnic programs in university education. The case, *Regents of the University of California vs. Bakke,* ruled on the admission policy of the medical school of the University of California at Davis, which used a quota system based on race and ethnicity (p. 124). The key issue was whether lower admission requirements, for example, for black applicants, are legal. One group of four justices ruled that the plan was illegal, a flagrant violation of the 1964 Civil Rights Act that prohibited discriminating against a person on the basis of race. Another group of four justices decreed the policy constitutional because it furthered the historic purpose of the equal protection clause of the Fourteenth Amendment that guaranteed civil rights to all citizens, including former slaves. Justice Lewis Powell, the swing vote, strongly sided with the ruling that lower standards was illegal, arguing that the admission policy not only violated the 1964 Civil Rights Act but also the Fourteenth Amendment. The ruling led directly to Bakke being admitted into the next class at the medical school.

In spite of his strong stand, Powell sought to reconcile the apparently irreconcilable views of the two groups by suggesting that race and ethnicity could be used, but not *exclusively,* in admission policies. His reasoning was that different ethnic viewpoints could encourage vigorous intellectual exchanges and thereby elevate the quality of university scholarship.

> Let us be clear. Never for a moment did Powell suggest that ethnic pro-
> portionality might be a legitimate goal in itself. On this point he could
> hardly have been more forceful: if the purpose of a university's special-
> admissions program was "to assure within its student body *some specific
> percentage* [emphasis added] of a particular group of its race or ethnic ori-
> gin," such a preferential purpose would be constitutionally invalid on its
> face. Only in pursuit of its proper intellectual business should a univer-
> sity be permitted to consider the race of applicants, along with other
> "diversity" factors, in making admission decisions. (Cohen, 1996)

Powell essentially brought diversity into university education through the back door, but multiculturalists took advantage of this opening to force it through the front door and make diversity a battle cry for establishing a diversified student body and a variety of ethnic study programs. But such successes have not quieted the strong opposition to multiculturalism as an educational philosophy. Legal and political efforts to eliminate preferential treatment in university admissions and faculty selection persist throughout the country. And within some educational circles the conviction prevails that multiculturalism's drive for diversity lowers academic standards for faculty appointments and for student graduation, and encourages grade inflation.

Eurocentrists accuse multiculturalists of substituting the academic criterion of cultural diversity for that of academic excellence. But multiculturalists offer the counter-argument that diversity itself is synonymous with excellence. Is this purely a semantic argument? In some ways it is, but in other ways, it is not. If the argument is reduced to competing definitions of excellence in the absence of any outside criterion, then the debate is semantic. But if the *consequences* of the different policies are considered, then the argument acquires empirical meaning. But estimating that empirical meaning would prove difficult, as would determining the consequences of different lists of books for a great literature course. Would the education of minority students and women profit more from reading Eurocentric classics or books that sought to capture the quality of their personal experience? What would be most beneficial to the entire society? Why can't minorities and women read "their books" on their own while learning about the culturally unifying Eurocentric classics? Why can't white males learn about "minority and women's literature" in college to understand how the less-advantaged live while reading the Eurocentric classics on their own? Although the choice of these alternatives probably has significant consequences (e.g., Denby, 1996) the selection of the books themselves would be determined primarily by Eurocentric or multicultural values.

Natural science education is a different matter. The claims of cultural distinct sciences—African or women's—cannot withstand critical examination. If society seeks to educate the best possible scientists, the focus of attention will be on individual aptitude and achievement and not on ethnic or gender membership. This conclusion in no way denies the possibility that the search for talent among minorities and women will prove productive, but it does deny the conclusion that the selection of a group of science trainees based on ethnic and gender proportionality will be more productive than a group of scientists who are selected on individual merit. Society will have to decide which is more important: scientific achievement or ethnic and gender diversity.

Powell's coupling of race with diversity influenced two Supreme Court affirmative action decisions in 2003. The University of Michigan's undergraduate admission program awarded 20 points on a rating scale to gain admissions to blacks, Hispanics, and Native Americans. This benefit was designed to reverse past racial injustices. The Supreme Court, in a 6–3 judgment declared the benefit unconstitutional because of the racial discrimination against whites. In a 5–4 decision the Supreme Court upheld the University of Michigan's law school affirmative action policy of giving minorities an advantage in gaining admission. The benefit to the minorities was not justified on the basis of previous injustices but, instead, on the creation of a diversified student body that was educationally advantageous to all students. This conclusion was encouraged by a manuscript to the Court that became known as the Gurin study that was later published (Gurin et al., 2002).

The Gurin defense offered evidence that students learn better in a diverse educational environment. Such evidence was sufficiently compelling to the Court to rule in favor of the admission requirements of the University of Michigan's law school. The evidence of educational benefits of racial and ethnic preferences was found wanting by Zuriff (2002). The Gurin study failed to distinguish between minority students who would have been admitted under a neutral racial/ethnic admission policy and those given preferences. In addition, East Asians, with their higher aptitude scores, were included in the minority group. No objective evidence was offered to demonstrate that education is advanced with a diverse student body. "For white students, grades were positively correlated with only one of the diversity activities, discussing racial issues–a diversity activity that does not require minority students. Even more shocking is the fact that for African American students, the one and only relationship between diversity activities and grades were *negative*–those who had taken the most ethnic studies courses earned the lowest grades!" (Zuriff, 2002, 280).

Cultural Equality: What Does it Mean?

At the core of the debate between Eurocentric and multicultural America is the idea that some cultures are superior to others. Do not Eurocentrists consider western civilization to be superior to the other cultures of the world? If there is one point that this book has tried to drive home it is that an abstract concept, such as cultural superiority, like the concepts of individual intelligence or moral truth, has no interpersonal meaning without a mutually acceptable definition. Utilizing concepts unanchored to modes of measurement guarantees misunderstandings and confusion. An answer to the question "What do you mean?" is a basic requirement for reasonable discussions.

According to Fowers and Richardson (1996, 609) ". . . multiculturalism is, at its core, a moral movement that is intended to enhance the dignity, rights, and recognized worth of marginalized groups." It is therefore both a moral and practical prescription that seeks to promote righteousness by encouraging multiculturalism while enhancing the self-esteem of minorities and women. Within the sphere of ethics Fowers and Richardson conclude that all cultures are morally equivalent because each contain a vision of the "good life" that is capable of being revealed by intercultural exchanges. Those who assume a dichotomy between facts and values cannot challenge such a conclusion about cultural equality. But Fowers and Richardson surreptitiously extend their analysis of equality from values to facts, from moral equality to cultural egalitarianism. They recommend that we should resist reflexively classifying alien cultural practices, such as ritual genital mutilation of girls "as primitive, barbaric, or immoral" (Fowers and Richardson, 1996, 619). Although the judgment of "immoral" would be inappropriate from the perspective of the fact/value dichotomy, the empirical characterizations of "female circumcision," as "barbaric" does not seem, for many, far off the mark. The consequences of the genital mutilation are threats to personal health, reproductive potential, and erotic pleasure. Cannot these empirical consequences be evaluated independently of the cultural tradition that had its origins among the pharaohs in ancient Egypt and presently operate among some Islamic communities in Egypt, the Sudan, and other African countries and even among some immigrant groups in the United States (MacFarquhar, 1996)? Although the Koran makes no mention of "female circumcision" the practice is justified because it helps guarantee a family's good reputation, while providing assurances to future husbands that their wives had not and will not "stray." Although many women resist the practice, others endorse it because their "good name" will be secured.

Multiculturalists argue that no culture is superior or inferior to another but instead all are equal. Their apparent tolerance is contradicted by their own intolerance to Eurocentric culture. Multiculturalism has been unstinting in its criticism of American racism, ethnocentrism, and sexism. Being an American white is synonymous with being a bigot; ". . . all whites are racists whether knowingly or unknowingly" (Sue and Sue, 1990, 113). In sharp contrast is the multiculturalist view of other cultures that condone oppressive behaviors far beyond that occurring in American society. Why the asymmetry? Multiculturalism is filled with internal contradictions. It simultaneously straddles a cultural relativism and a moral absolutism. While acknowledging that all cultural values are social conventions, we should simultaneously recognize that denying minorities and women human rights is morally wrong. Is it not inconsistent to preach an unqualified moral tolerance for all cultures except the only one, Euro-Americanism, that extols the ideals of liberty and individual equality?

The vague concept of cultural equality encourages respect, if not admiration, for all cultural traditions. One should nevertheless have no difficulty, even with unqualified moral tolerance, in recognizing vast cultural differences among styles of life, political freedom, material comfort, artistic expression, environmental degradation, technological sophistication, treatment of ethnic minorities and women, and in the condoning of such behaviors as terrorism, cruelty, sadism, and torture. Multiculturalism essentially suggests that mutual understanding of all cultures will work to the moral benefit of all societies. American Eurocentrism assumes a more critical stance because it is defined by such overarching concepts as the "unalienable rights" of "life, liberty, and pursuit of happiness" that automatically condemn cultural traditions such as the ritual genital mutilation of girls. The rejection of this practice may seem at first glance to be a purely moral judgment but within a historical perspective it can be perceived as part of the continuous effort to secure gender equality. And although disagreement prevails as to how close to that goal American society has reached, it has been relatively successful when compared to non-Eurocentric cultures.

American Eurocentrists argue that the advantages of multiculturalism are basically extensions of the American democratic tradition, while its disadvantages are self-imposed. Eurocentrism encourages cultural diversity as long as it stays within the boundaries of individual rights and freedom. American Eurocentrism is not ethnocentric in ignoring the values of foreign cultures. In actual fact, Eurocentrism has been receptive to outside influences. Egyptian, African, and Japanese art, for example, have not only been appreciated, but are also influential in Eurocentric art. But equal respect for cultural expressions does not imply equal admiration. Some artistic expressions are favored over others. For the most part, Native American dance is not judged as esthetic, as is Asiatic Indian dance. Nor is Eurocentric culture, for the most part, as receptive to Australian aboriginal art as it is to Aztec art. Other cultures also exhibit cultural preferences. Japan has not only been able to admire western classical music, but also to practice it with a skill that matches that of the culture from which it emerged. In sum, multiculturalists automatically respect all cultural efforts, whereas for the Eurocentrists the respect must be earned.

Eurocentric versus Multicultural Society: Consequences

It should be obvious why multicultural education has an enormous appeal. Ethnic identification has a powerful hold on human behavior, as witnessed by the "tribal wars" that have sprung up throughout the world. Threats against one's group encourage identification and support, especially with memories of the group's past victimization. But while recognizing the power of racial, ethnic, and gender identification, one also can resonate to the democratic ideals of equality before the law and equal educational and economic opportunities. While acknowledging the appeal of both multiculturalism and Euro-Americanism one must face up to their mutual incompatibility.

Euro-Americans do not deny the facts of past or present discrimination against minorities and women. But they insist that great progress has been made in reducing the prejudice and, more importantly, continued progress is needed and possible. But prejudice in the marketplace can be eliminated without abandoning the principle of equality of treatment that is the moral keystone of American Eurocentrism. In contrast, multiculturalists consider this proposed Eurocentric scenario to be detached from reality. Emotional commitment to a democratic ethic is insufficient to restrain prejudice against minorities and women that are built into Eurocentrism by centuries of discrimination. Only a multicultural society can eliminate the evils of racism and gender bias. Only by converting a Eurocentric democracy into a multicultural society will it be possible to achieve a true democracy.

If one is pessimistic about the practical value of engaging in debates about the moral righteousness of American Eurocentrism versus multiculturalism, then one can try to shift attention to their social consequences. The ideal arrangement would be to base decisions about the competing policies on reliable evidence about their outcomes. But this ideal is difficult to approach by the participants in the debate because of their incompatible views of what constitutes "reliable evidence." Nevertheless, it should prove useful to focus in a general manner on two fundamental issues: social unity and economic productivity.

Social Unity

One attribute of a society is its social unity, the cohesiveness of its various subgroups in pursuit of common goals. In trying to reduce the ambiguity of social unity, it may prove helpful to describe the end points of a hypothetical dimension. One endpoint would be the disunity in the United States created by the Vietnam and Iraq wars while the other would be the cohesion that occurred throughout World War II. Whereas a sharp disagreement prevailed about what constituted the common good in the Vietnam and Iraq wars, general agreement about its meaning held sway during World War II.

Numerous variables impact social unity. Two that are particularly relevant to the Eurocentric-multicultural debate are the degree of ethnic diversity within a society and the number and intensity of ethnic conflicts between groups. It is probably more difficult to achieve unity in a society with a population consisting of many ethnic groups (e.g., United States) as compared to one that is culturally homogeneous (e.g., Japan). The potential for divisiveness would likely be greater when an ethnic conflict has a long duration; witness the recent history of the former Yugoslavia, Ireland, Rwanda, Sri Lanka, Canada, and the Xinjiang region of China.

From this perspective, the United States is particularly susceptible to forces that create social disunity. Does multiculturalism represent a solution to the ethnic and gender conflicts in America or is it a product of them? However that question may be answered, multiculturalism is perceived by many minority and women's organizations to be an effective program for redressing past wrongs. And they have little faith in the capacity of the American Eurocentric society to emancipate them from discriminatory attitudes and practices. They ask "How can a system that created discrimination and victimization eradicate them?" One does not have to deny the effects of past discrimination in order to criticize multiculturalists' efforts to correct them. Although persuasive in its appeal, multiculturalism must be judged by the cultural separatism it preaches. Does multiculturalism contain the seeds of its own destruction? This is not to imply that if multiculturalism achieves its goals the United States will go the way of Yugoslavia. What it does suggest is that multiculturalism's effort to rectify past wrongs can backfire by increasing social disunity—destroying a sense of national identity—with its effort to rectify past sins.

When dealing with past injustices, two issues come to the fore: how the unfairness is to be measured and whether it should be redressed. If the victims are dead, should their descendants be compensated? Although Native Americans and blacks stand out in the extent of their past mistreatment, practically every immigrant group has been victimized by prejudice and economic discrimination. If all the sins of the past are to be redressed, most Americans would be eligible for victimhood. The other alternative is to acknowledge the difficulty, if not impossibility, of overcoming past wrongs, and shift attention to the task of ridding society of bias and discrimination in schools and in the workplace. These opposed modes of dealing with past injustices highlight the difference between multiculturalism and Eurocentrism.

Multiculturalists argue that redressing past wrongs is a necessary first step in assisting minorities and women to overcome the disadvantages resulting from their past victimization. The step selected was affirmative action with preferential treatment. Eurocentrists interpreted this proposal as being diametrically opposed to the democratic ideal of equality of treatment for all persons. Multiculturalists disagreed, insisting that equal treatment demands preferential treatment for those that society had disadvantaged. This linguistic circus surrounding the meaning of equality of treatment prevents rational agreement being reached, leaving the resolution to other means.

Preferential treatment policies have stirred up the political and legal pot, while the boiling point has been reached in university life. What is not fully appreciated is that the problem of preferential treatment expanded beyond its apparent limits. It served as the link to create cultural diversity in the curriculum to serve the needs of minorities and women. Eurocentric education was sufficiently flexible to include new offerings as long as traditional academic standards are not compromised. But courses planned to meet the need for cultural diversity were frequently designed to raise the self-esteem and group identification of minorities and women students, as well as to provide easy courses for poor students. Education took a back seat to cultural politics and the result was that academic standards were compromised, if not corrupted.

Whatever one might think of these arguments and rebuttals, preferential treatment and multiculturalism have contributed to social strife. Although sophisticated techniques to measure social unity could help clarify the amount of social disunity, numerous political and legal conflicts that gain public attention suggest that it is increasing. Similar debates involve bilingual education for Latinos. Strident disputes are occurring within and outside academe about the goals of university education. Even the dramatic arts have been rocked by controversy about whether a racial divide should separate white from black theater (Goldberger, 1997). August Wilson (1945–2005), the best-known black playwright who limited his writings to the African American experience, had urged a black separatism designed to prevent white culture from contaminating the Black voice in the American theater. He objects to all-black production of "white" plays, such as *The Death of a Salesman,* or color-blind casting in which Romeo and Juliet would be played by actors of different races. Richard Brustein, the artistic director of the American Repertory Theater and long-time theater critic, judges Wilson's proposal as a step backwards to the days of black segregation and replacing esthetic standards with political criteria.

Is it fair for Brustein to accuse Wilson of cultural separatism when the origins of the difficulty have been the failure of the white community to fully accept blacks? But the purpose of the present analysis is not to assign blame, but to try to reveal the consequences of the influences on American society of Eurocentrism and multiculturalism. True, the black community has not been fully integrated with the white community, but certainly the arts and entertainment segment of American culture has been receptive to Black artistic expression. Most of August Wilson's ten plays have been produced on Broadway, with two of them being awarded Pulitzer Prizes. On the most fundamental level, multiculturalism represents a threat to the Euro-American tradition because it eliminates a cultural core and threatens a Balkanization of American society.

Economic Productivity

To contrast broad social views as Eurocentrism and multiculturalism on the basis of their economic productivity will appear to many as a crude attempt to reduce the quality of a culture to a dollar sign. Such a reaction overlooks the point that economic success can pave the road for cultural achievements in the arts and sciences. Countries strongly influenced by western European culture, such as the Czech Republic, were not only more successful than eastern European countries, such as Romania, in recovering from Communist state-controlled economies, but also in creating a cultural renaissance.

Multiculturalism does not deny the importance of economic productivity, but argues that western civilization has failed to achieve a fair distribution of wealth. American Eurocentrists would not deny the criticism, but would note that other cultures have fared worse. And perhaps, more importantly, would be the recognition that fairness, morally or economically, can never be defined to the satisfaction of all. Ultimate goals are never harmonious; they inevitably compete and conflict. But the argument can be advanced that western democratic market economies have made progress in achieving a more acceptable distribution of wealth. And if gradual progress has been made in the past, why can it not be extended into the future? One can consider the western-styled market economies throughout the world as being engaged in a variety of experiments designed to determine how economic productivity and communal responsibility can best be combined. Denying the possibility of a utopian solution may prove to be the first step in shaping a policy that approximates an "equitable" distribution of wealth.

Multiculturalism has economic implications. Those organizations, minorities and women, that favor a multicultural agenda, argue that Euro-Americanism discriminated against them, resulting in their economic hardships. In support of their contention they quote evidence of statistical underrepresentation in the work force as well as lower median incomes. Preferential treatment, therefore, becomes essential to overcome the effects of past discrimination in order to achieve social and economic equity. One cannot deny that discrimination against minorities and women lowered their economic welfare. But that does not mean that multiculturalism and preferential treatment will solve these problems. Negative side effects could outweigh their possible beneficial consequences.

The comparison between Euro-Americanism and multiculturalism in the economic sphere cuts across many lines. Two major lines are the economic security of individuals and the economic health of the entire society. In regard to the first, the United States, since the time of Franklin Roosevelt's New Deal, sought to provide everybody who was willing to make the effort with opportunities to live a dignified, economically rewarding life. Although progress was made in that direction, most notably for the elderly, the aspirations exceeded the achievements. The most glaring failures in the quest for a reasonably fair society are the urban centers of poverty where minorities dwell. The current debate between Euro-Americanism and multiculturalism revolves about the contributions of past and present discrimination to these impoverished conditions and the kinds of remedies that are needed.

One might think that the economic health of all individuals would automatically produce the highest possible level of economic prosperity for the entire society. Not necessarily, if we compare the United States economy with that of the western European countries near the end of the twentieth century. During the latter part of the nineteenth century social welfare programs were instituted in western European countries to ward off the threat of socialism. The United States trailed behind Europe in welfare legislation, but was expected to catch up after Roosevelt's New Deal. Since that time there has been much disagreement about the influence that social welfare programs had on economic productivity. After World War II western Europe maintained its lead in social welfare and began to approach the United States in economic productivity. But once global free trade began to dominate the economic landscape, the United States drew away from its European competitors. It appears the combination of nearly full employment and low social welfare costs made the United States a more effective competitor in the global economy than the western European countries that suffered a persistent unemployment problem and greater welfare costs. One possible explanation is that a country that aspires to be a successful economy for global free trade requires an elimination of *inessential* costs resulting from primitive technology, unproductive workers, and social welfare programs. The downsizing of corporations and lower welfare costs gave the United States a competitive edge over its European rivals in the global economy.

If true, the above analysis suggests important differences in the Euro-American and multicultural views about the economic policies and welfare programs and their interactions. Social welfare programs have been a source of great debate in American society. Some, like the Social Security Act of 1935, which initiated old-age retirement and unemployment insurance, have been readily accepted because they are considered to be needed, just, and essential for maintaining workers' productivity and morale. Others, like child support for unmarried mothers, have triggered criticism and resentment, because they are judged to reward irresponsibility and "immorality." The expansion of welfare programs, particularly in western European countries, such as the 35-hour work week in France, is considered by many economists to exert a drag on the economy because they divert funds from capital investment to economically unproductive behavior. The United States, as noted, is considered to have a competitive edge over western European countries because it is not burdened by "excessive" welfare costs. The other side of the coin is America's increasing gap between the rich and poor, which threatens social turmoil. These discrepancies between the United States and western European countries–breadth of welfare coverage and extent of income gap between rich and poor–raise the issue as to whether a country is well-advised to enter the brutal global competition full force or whether economic productivity should be modulated by human welfare considerations.

The United States has been a prime player in, and a major beneficiary of, the global economy. From the perspective of the American version of the Eurocentric tradition, it would appear impossible for the United States to back off from competing full force in the global market place. The price of withdrawal would be a tremendous loss of financial wealth and prestige. The only alternative for the United States would seem to be to continue its role as an economic superpower, while striving to achieve the goal of being a reasonably fair society. To do so requires an appreciation of the fact that economic productivity and social welfare need not be considered as opposed processes that operate to the disadvantage of each other. For example, increases in economic competitiveness need not be achieved at the expense of social welfare. The Euro-American tradition does not embrace (in fact it denies) the Marxist concept of the class struggle in which economic advantages accruing to one side, capital or labor, is achieved at the expense of the other. Increasing economic productivity can work to the advantage of the entire community, although a source of conflict will remain as to what constitutes a reasonably fair distribution of wealth.

The American economy would benefit if welfare recipients shifted to the work force, where their income and productivity would increase, presumably along with their self-respect. Of course, certain social welfare expenses cannot be eliminated or reduced or even prevented from increasing. But a pragmatic approach, or what John Dewey preferred to call "experimentalism," would search for evidence that would assist in the shaping of a socially acceptable welfare policy. The Euro-American tradition, in essence, operates within a framework that considers economic productivity of prime importance and seeks solutions to policy questions, such as welfare, with a pragmatic bottom-up approach. Multiculturalism, in contrast, represents a top-down vision of what a society should be. In this conception, economic productivity takes a backseat to ideologically driven principles that emphasize diversity in education and the workplace. Such a policy can be criticized as having a dampening effect on the economy by imperiling the educational needs of an advanced technological society. It encourages a self-defeating economic dependency among those who perceive themselves as victims of discrimination, while it Balkanizes society into hostile racial, ethnic, and gender groups.

One cannot discuss educational practices without specifying goals. If one purpose of education is to serve the needs of an advanced technological society by providing a sophisticated work force, then multiculturalism can be faulted for several reasons. Muticulturalism goes counter to the major structural changes that have occurred in the American economy. Close to half the students who enter college require remedial courses (Schemo, 2006). This automatically bars students in New York City from admission to the colleges of the City University of New York, the largest urban university. California State University seeks to limit unprepared freshman to 10 percent by testing them as high school juniors and requiring them to make up deficiencies before they graduate. Half of the present-day high school graduates are unqualified to become production workers in an automobile factory (Murnane and Levy, 1996). Decades ago an automobile production worker, a good paying blue-collar job, did not require a secondary education, but merely the capacity to do a repetitive task on an assembly line. Today, only a worker with effective communication skills, some familiarity with computers, and a capacity to understand training manuals can get a job as an automobile production worker. Without technological skills, a high school diploma entitles a person to a lifetime of low wages.

Multiculturalism, in its effort to rectify past wrongs by increasing minority representation in college, contributes to the economically unproductive idea that a college degree is needed to "make it" in American society. This assumption debases high schools by ignoring their ability and responsibility to provide skilled workers for a technologically advanced society. And it debases colleges by assuming that everybody is academically qualified to get a college degree. The result is the lowering of the academic standards of both high school and college education by ignoring the boundary between the two. Presumed victims of past ethnic and racial discrimination are encouraged to seek a college education even with poor qualifications. To accommodate these marginal students, remedial courses are added to the college curriculum to make up for their academic deficiencies. The availability of such courses relieves high schools of their responsibility to offer a college-preparatory curriculum. Many students who receive an ethnic or racial pass to get into college have a difficult time in meeting academic standards. Grade inflation comes to their rescue, as well as college courses "dumbed down" to help those students experiencing academic difficulties. A sizable number do not graduate, thus making their college experience a double waste of time; time that could have been better spent in acquiring economic skills that should have been obtained in high school but was wasted in an unsuccessful pursuit of a college degree.

While the need for basic cognitive and technical skills increases, multiculturalists concentrate on ethnic identity and self-esteem as goals of education. While complaining about their disproportionate representation in the lower socioeconomic level, some Hispanic groups, their critics claim, are pursuing policies, such as bilingual education, that exacerbate their economic disadvantages. Communication skills in English are needed for success in the labor market and delaying their acquisition is self-defeating. The younger one is when learning a second language, the easier it becomes (Blakeslee, 1997). Economic disadvantages can also result from majoring in ethnic studies programs in colleges. Blacks who major in Afrocentric studies, designed primarily to convey the experiences of being black, will be at a competitive disadvantage when they enter the commercial world.

There is no doubt that preferential treatment has been economically advantageous to many people, but the question can be raised as to whether these benefits outweigh the social divisiveness and damage to the economic and cultural productivity of the entire society. Perhaps the frustrations experienced by minorities and women, that led them to support multiculturalism and affirmative action can be more effectively managed with alterations of our legal and economic systems. Improved legal methods of identifying ethnic and gender discrimination in the academic and commercial marketplace can open up job opportunities presently unavailable to qualified individuals. Such an effort would be more in tune with the original conception of affirmative action that was designed to identify qualified individuals who have been overlooked. And of equal, if not greater, importance is the modification of our economic system to increase job opportunities by reshaping jobs themselves.

One cannot and should not ignore the economic disadvantages of minorities and women, as well as other groups, including white males, who have difficulties in getting or retaining a foothold in the economic sphere of life. This problem has been exacerbated by the tremendous progress in computer technology combined with the development of a global economy that has eliminated mid-level administrative jobs and those for workers with low skills. These changes can simply be accepted as an inevitable consequence of fierce competitiveness of the global economy or they can serve as a challenge to the entire society to cope creatively with these economic problems. The first step is to acknowledge the need for reform so that every individual will be treated fairly. The next step is to provide the opportunity for all to realize their potential. But, recently, with the increasing gap between economic "winners" and "losers" and the increasing cognitive demands being made on the work force, it becomes incumbent upon the entire society to create job opportunities for all to achieve a dignified existence. Human ingenuity, combined with the enormous needs to improve various components of contemporary society—education, the environment, economics, health services, commerce, communication, entertainment, science, arts—should make possible the creation of jobs for all levels of competency.

A FINAL COMMENT

Achieving an economically just society requires a general strategy. A common belief is that some rationally constructed global plan fed by ideological principles, can do the job. Perhaps the complexities of human behavior and contemporary technological societies make it impossible to formulate an a priori plan guaranteed to succeed. A more strategic approach might be pragmatically driven programs, with an inherent degree of uncertainty about the success of each, designed to achieve a series of limited objectives.

Multiculturalism proposes to eliminate group prejudice by force, via preferential treatment programs designed to achieve proportional representation of racial, ethnic, and gender groups in various economic slots in society. The alternative is to persist in the effort to eliminate group bias, while living up to the democratic principle of equal treatment for all individuals. Such an effort must recognize that its objections to preferential treatment programs become more forceful if progress is achieved by elevating the economic condition of those who reside at the lower level of the economy.

Chapter 7

FINAL THOUGHTS

James Conant, when president of Harvard University, asserted that we need "a widespread understanding of science in this country, for only thus can science be assimilated into our secular pattern" (Conant, 1947). His book extends this idea to the problems of public policy in a democratic society. While expressing agreement with Conant's general sentiment, one must be aware of the ease with which the so-called scientific method is misused or misunderstood. In addition, general suspicion reigns about the capacity of the behavioral sciences to meet the standards of scientific knowledge. And finally, confusion prevails among all, including scientists, about the interrelationship between science and morality.

While seeking to clarify the meaning of natural science methodology and its particular implications for psychology and morality, two important topics were put aside until a satisfactory foundation for their discussion was achieved: the social value of science and moral pluralism.

THE SOCIAL VALUE OF SCIENCE

A basic operating assumption has been that natural science methodology is an effective method for revealing the nature of the world and for providing means for controlling events. However true that may be, the question can be raised as to whether the potential merits of a natural science psychology may be offset by disadvantages that accrue from science itself. Scientific methodology especially when applied to human psychology, according to some critics, corrodes human dignity and dulls social compassion.

Science is an unqualified success if its value is limited to its achievements in revealing the nature of the physical and biological world. From its origins in the distant past as a problem-solving technique needed for survival in a hostile world, science has developed into a sophisticated methodology that has exposed nature's most intimate secrets. The requirement that scientific explanations be logically consistent with empirical evidence has provided an objective measure of scientific success and a perpetual inducement to further scientific progress.

When science is judged not on its home turf but, instead, from the perspective of social value, criticisms abound on three fronts. The first two, *antiscience* and *antiscientism* are broad in conception, with each condemning in its own way science's impact on society. Antiscience argues that the natural sciences have victimized society with abnormal creations such as the atomic bomb. Antiscientism suggests that a scientific view of life demeans the human spirit. The third criticism questions whether science, in general, and psychology, in particular, can enhance human welfare. Can the clarity of the laboratory be transferred to the fogginess of the social world? Or must all reliable scientific information be distorted and perverted by political forces so that social planning is denied the benefits of empirical truth? Or is it impossible to maintain the clarity of laboratory findings when they are transferred to the complexities of the "real world." One can precisely predict the rate of the fall of a feather in a vacuum but find it difficult, if not impossible, to estimate the time required for it to hit the ground in a hurricane. Predicting the operation of a simple scientific principle becomes difficult when it interacts with other phenomena. In sum, can scientific integrity be maintained when science is shaped, perhaps misshaped, by social forces?

The answers to these questions are complex, but a response becomes possible when a distinction is made between two kinds of explanations that differ in their level of precision. Whenever a spark is passed through a mixture of oxygen and hydrogen gas, the gases disappear and water is formed. It always occurs under given conditions. In contrast to "causal" laws are "probabilistic" ones that can predict future events on a likelihood basis. One can predict that a group of students entering college with IQs of 125 will achieve a higher grade point average and graduation rate than a group with IQs of 110. This expectation is probabilistic. Some lower IQ students will do better, both in terms of grades and graduation rates, than some members of the higher IQ group. Nevertheless, the overall success rate of the higher IQ group will be greater.

A theory can also be probabilistic. A simple example from economics is the hypothesis of Robert Rubin, the former Treasury Secretary in President Clinton's administration, that deficits in the national budget have negative consequences on the entire economy. Not being able to control all other budgetary factors, the theory is reduced to the probabilistic estimate that the health of the economy will be inversely related to the size of the deficit. Consequently, uncertainty prevails as to whether efforts to control deficits would automatically result in a healthy economy. Thus, in economic planning one should try to control deficit spending even though all relevant variables are not known. The situation is similar to that of a clinical psychologist whose patient is sensitive to the depressogenic effects of stress. Although other variables are involved, a reasonable therapeutic effort would be to minimize the threat of stress.

Antiscience

The unending debate about the moral justification of the atomic bombing of Hiroshima and Nagasaki during World War II clearly illustrates the problem of blaming science for its creations. Was it science's fault that these cities suffered more than 225,000 casualties and massive radiation damage? Obviously this tragedy could not have happened if physicists and engineers had not invented the bomb. But atomic bombs are not needed for such devastation. During the "rape of Nanking" in 1937, more than 300,000 Chinese civilians were brutally murdered in an old-fashioned way by Japanese soldiers (Chang, 1997). And early in 1945, when the defeat of Germany in World War II was assured, 100,000 German civilians were killed in an Allied bombing raid that destroyed the beautiful city of Dresden. Although science has enhanced the efficiency of mass killings, disasters on a lesser scale have occurred throughout history.

If one were looking for a culprit for mass killings one would have to look beyond science. Science does not act alone. Truman had the final responsibility in the bombings of Hiroshima and Nagasaki. His decision cannot be impugned simply by the destruction wrought. Facts are ethically neutral, even when mass killings are involved. Moral judgment must be based on criteria other than the empirical event itself. One can, for example, condemn Truman's actions because of ethical sanctions against mass killings of civilians. But one can defend Truman by other ethical criteria, e.g., ending the war immediately in an effort to save the lives of masses of soldiers and civilians, the belief that the decision to bomb Japan was the final product of democratic processes, Japan was morally responsible for the war, and so forth. Today similar moral conflicts are confronting governments that seek to cope with the threat of terrorism.

Obviously these moral debates can go on interminably. The reason is simply that these debates are irresolvable. No evidence and no logical analysis can reconcile the opposed moral judgments. One can conceivably understand why competing moral views are adopted, but the contrasting conceptions are impotent in resolving the moral dispute. One cannot argue that one moral position (e.g., civilians should not be military targets) is superior to another (e.g., civilians are morally responsible for the actions of their governments). The Israeli-Lebanon War in 2006 illustrates this conundrum. Lebanese citizens were responsible for their government breaking international law by firing rockets at Israelis and kidnapping their soldiers. Israel was wrong in retaliating by bombing large numbers of Lebanese civilians. In sum, moral positions in ethical debates, such as the killing of civilians and use of the atomic bomb, cannot be validated by empirical evidence or ethical principles.

One can easily get the impression that the above analysis, cold-blooded to the hilt, conceptualizes moral judgments as arbitrary decisions, a view in line with an ethical nihilism that denies the existence of any possible base for establishing a moral philosophy. Denying a logical linkage between facts and values does not trivialize moral judgments but, instead, forces one to recognize the complex origins, structure, and function of moral codes. Moral codes can be conceptualized as social instruments designed to resolve ethical disputes.

Democracy, in particular, provides opportunities for settling conflicts by encouraging one value to give way to a more basic one. In some cases the moral conflict is hidden by technical details. For example, in the late 1960s, a fierce debate occurred in the United States Congress between those who favored and opposed continuing funding for the development of an American-built supersonic transport plane (SST). After hearing numerous experts in government, business, science, and finance estimate the consequences of building or not building the SST, Congress canceled additional funding. Those who supported building the SST accepted the verdict because their commitment to technological advancements yielded to their allegiance to democratic values. In other cases the moral core of policy conflicts is transparent. Prejudice springing from religious beliefs and heterosexual bias against homosexual behavior has yielded, for many, to more tolerant views encouraged by the democratic principle of individual rights. The significant point is that the rejection of the notion that facts cannot simply resolve ethical disputes need not leave society helpless in the face of such conflicts. Established conflict-resolving procedures within an entrenched and accepted political tradition appear to be the first line of defense against the possibility that moral conflicts will spin out of control, as they have so often done in the past and are now doing in the present world.

Antiscience, the view that science is morally impoverished, has taken a variety of forms, ranging from specific allegations that science has converted the world into a technological dump site to the general criticism that science misleads humankind into believing that only science can explain the true nature of the world. Because science is not an autonomous entity but is, instead, an agent of society, the message that science is morally bankrupt should be forwarded to society, not science.

Science is also attacked for its responsibility in creating technologies that have backfired: pollution caused by automobiles and industry, depletion of the ozone layer by chlorefluocarbons that replaced hazardous chemical refrigerants, methods of forest fire prevention that reduced their incidence but later unwittingly led to enormous conflagrations not previously experienced, and finally global warming. Tenner (1996) has labeled these unintended consequences as "revenge effects" of scientific solutions that sought instant benefits. Although revenge effects may not be completely controllable, they need not be considered as inevitable consequences. Society's efforts to achieve quick fixes must give way to greater consideration of possible side effects.

An alternative to an antiscience attitude is to view the total effect of science: the state of humankind before or after the advent of science and its technologies. Although some might yearn for the past, most probably would not. But that estimate, if true, indicates only a preference, not a moral validation. And the fact that humankind has persistently supported scientific efforts suggests that science, in some manner, serves the needs of humanity. But in the final analysis, the debate that the antiscience view encourages may properly be dismissed. Humankind is stuck with the scientific method; there is no way of putting "the genie back in the bottle." Science is here and must be dealt with, not as an enemy to be destroyed, but as an ally to serve the needs of society.

Antiscientism

The belief that a scientific attitude corrupts humanity (Passmore, 1978) suffers from the same deficiencies as the view that science is inherently bad. It appears to be more of a peevish negativism than a well-thought-out critique. Nevertheless, antiscientism does raise interesting and significant questions. Let us first examine the opposite viewpoint, proscientism. Richard Feynman, a physicist of enormous intellectual talents and achievements (Gleick, 1992), viewed the entire intellectual world through the eyes of a scientist and found nonscientific realms to be inferior. He held a general contempt for the sloppiness of humanistic scholarship. Can such arrogance be justified? Yes and no, depending on the frame of reference employed to evaluate the charge. If one uses an epistemological framework consistent with natural science methodology, then questions such as "What is beauty?" "What is the underlying philosophy of Anthony Trollope's novels?" "What is justice?" "What were Hamlet's true motivations?" and the like, will inevitably produce sloppy thinking when judged by the logical rigor and empirical restraints of natural science standards.

At the same time, it should be appreciated that not being able to answer a question scientifically does not mean the question is unanswerable. Similar questions have been answered and even though none has achieved the degree of acceptance attained by "scientific truths," some are nevertheless considered valuable cultural contributions. But there should not be any doubt, regardless of their influence and fame, that they do not meet the demands of science. To be specific, when, ethical theories (e.g., Rawls, 1971) are confronted with the two questions that capture the essence of science (Feigl, 1949) "What do you mean?" and "How do you know?" the ethical formulations are found wanting. They lack the empirical content and logical organization required to substantiate scientific explanations either in regard to the meaning of concepts or theoretical conclusions. Thus, if the scientific method is the epistemological litmus test used to evaluate ideas, then it would be justified to conclude that the literary interpretations of Hamlet's motivation or philosophical conceptions of justice fall short, as Feynman suggests, of being rigorous. In other words, Feynman cannot be faulted for employing the standards of natural science to evaluate knowledge claims, but can be criticized for his attempt to superimpose natural science values on art and humanism. It is possible that Feynman was a closet artist as revealed by his comment, "What I cannot create, I do not understand."

Obviously, Feynman was a controversial character, who no doubt enjoyed baiting the nonscientific academic community. At the same time, a humanist presumably should recognize Feynman's humanness. An amazingly creative physicist and mathematician, whose achievements earned him a Nobel Prize, a strong opponent of social cant and snobbishness, and a person who coped with his impending death with courage, dignity, and wit. When dying of cancer, *The Los Angeles Times* offered him the draft copy of its proposed obituary. He thanked the author but refused; "I have decided it is not a very good idea for a man to read it ahead of time: it takes the element of surprise out of it" (Gleick, 1992, 437).

Is proscientism any more justified than antiscientism? Can either or both be judged to be reasonable? In the larger context of society they each reflect a contrasting world view. George Kennan (1992), for example, a distinguished diplomat and political philosopher, bemoans those aspects of modern life that have emerged from perceiving the world through the restricted confines of science. Feynman's and Kennan's views of science serve their own individual needs by contributing to their distinctive creativity. These comments are not intended to support a wishy-washy tolerance or eclecticism of both antiscientism and proscientism. They are intended instead to forcefully reject the idea that either position is automatically good or bad. Proscientism and antiscientism represent general attitudes that cannot be judged in isolation but must be considered in terms of their consequences.

A common reproach of the scientific view of life is that the scientific method forces one to treat humans as objects, thereby depriving them of their humanness. Roszak (1972), a persistent critic of science, refers to the recommendation of Clark Hull (1884–1952), a noted psychologist, who suggested the seemingly callous strategy of viewing a "behaving organism as a completely self-maintaining robot, constructed of materials as unlike ourselves as may be" (Hull, 1943, 27). Roszak apparently thought he hit the bull's-eye in this criticism of the scientific outlook, but his accusation was off target. He failed to understand the special context underlying Hull's recommendation. Hull was not expressing a philosophy of everyday life but, instead, a methodological prophylaxis against rampant subjectivism that he thought prevented psychology from becoming a mature natural science. Hull believed that when a psychologist begins to empathize with the experimental subject—subhuman or human—"all his knowledge of his own behavior, born of years of self-observation, at once begins to function in place of the objectively stated general rules or principles which are the proper substance of science" (Hull, 1943, 27). It is a far cry from a narrow methodological suggestion to a broad social policy to treat all humans as robots.

Another common criticism directed at the scientific mode of thinking is that it destroys beauty. The magnificent rainbow loses its majesty when understood as a consequence of the refraction of the sun's rays in raindrops. Although similar censures are directed at scientific interpretations of natural phenomena, no evidence is offered to demonstrate the point that scientific understanding diminishes esthetic reactions. My personal impressions are the opposite. Esthetic reactions are enhanced when their scientific bases are comprehended: "truth is beauty." In any case, the accusation that the scientific way of thinking interferes with the joys of life appears far-fetched considering that the word "beauty" and other positive descriptions have so frequently been applied to the experience of scientific creativity. Those who believe that scientific analysis and esthetic appreciation are incompatible are basing their conclusions on their own personal experience. In addition, they make the mistake that the scientist in all aspects of life thinks like a scientist. Some creative scientists have been known to behave like existentialists, humanists, and even hedonists when not coping with scientific problems.

Antiscientism commits the fundamental error of extending the meaning of science beyond its proper boundaries. Limitations or failures of science are not due to its intrinsic properties but, instead, results from how science is interpreted or applied. Every human problem cannot be solved by science alone. First, to truly appreciate science and understand what it can do, requires an understanding of what it cannot do. Although science has been successful in interpreting empirical events, one must realize that in the absence of factual underpinnings science is incapable of proposing valid knowledge claims. Science, for example, cannot offer a general answer to what many people yearn to know: "Does God exist?" or "What is the meaning or purpose of life?" or "What is morally right?" For example, the accusation that science fails to satisfy the spiritual needs of humans can be judged to be a fair criticism if science is considered to be a world view designed to deal with the human condition. If, however, science is considered a method that humans created to understand their world, then the criticism is off the mark because the satisfaction of spiritual desires is not part of science's agenda. Second, science is not the only method by which humans seek to "understand" the world in which they live. Humans in search for answers to life's problems resort to rational and intuitive conclusions that cannot, or need not, approach the epistemological demands of science. It appears strikingly clear to many that reason alone justifies the existence of an Almighty. Science is neither capable of disputing or confirming that claim.

Scientific Integrity

The enormous growth in scientific knowledge has led to the belief that all important world problems would ultimately succumb to scientific research. Such optimism was misplaced for a variety of reasons, most notably the inability of science to validate moral principles. But another factor, commonly overlooked, is that the scientific method, the general problem-solving technique that emerged from a combination of a naturalistic view of the world and human cognitive ability, does not operate in an autonomous mode that precludes errors and ambiguities. Science is a tricky enterprise that demands constant surveillance if its conclusions are to be trusted. Society, if it is to profit from science, must guard against scientific misrepresentation and junk science.

Science, to repeat myself (pp. 8–9), is not an exact discipline. It does not always provide an accurate and precise picture of "reality." Measures of physical or biological events, such as the speed of a falling body or a person's blood pressure, can vary from time to time. But the history of physical and biological sciences reveals remarkable improvements in the technology of measurement and a consequent increase in the reliability of measuring instruments. Such improvement has not eliminated all fluctuations in measurement, nor should that be expected. The tendency for psychological test scores to vary does not deny either their scientific status or usefulness. Measurements are not made for measurement alone. They serve the larger scientific purpose of aiding in the discovery and formulation of empirical laws between independently defined concepts: the strength of the earth's gravitational field as a function of different altitudes, the relationship between blood pressure and subsequent heart attacks, the score on an intelligence test and academic performance. By knowing one measure—altitude, blood pressure, IQ—one can estimate the second measure—strength of gravitation, probability of heart attack, academic performance. In other words, knowledge of one (independent) variable has predictive validity in estimating the other (dependent) variable.

The life of scientists would be much easier if they could accept the veracity of all claims of empirical laws. Instead of willingly accepting such assertions, scientists must view them with suspicion. Several years ago physical scientists reported the production of energy by the method of atomic fusion in a relatively simple laboratory set-up (Taubes, 1993). Subsequent research finally revealed that the data were misinterpreted; atomic fusion had not occurred. In 2006 a South Korean scientist, Hwang Woo-Suk, confessed to having fabricated stem cell research that he reported to have led to the cloning of cows, dogs, and humans. The fact that evidence offered by scientists cannot be fully trusted is neither a condemnation of science nor of scientists. Honest mistakes can occur. But so can unintentional or deliberate falsifications. Thus, society is confronted with a paradox; scientific evidence can help social planning but scientific evidence cannot always be trusted. There is no prescription that can guarantee society's ability to distinguish between valid facts and distorted evidence. But there are ways to minimize scientific misrepresentations. First, is the general cautionary view that data and theoretical conjectures should, at best, be considered as approaching, but not quite achieving, truth status. A persistent critical view is the proper attitude for scientists. Second, is the recognition that the scientific method, if practiced effectively, is a self-correcting enterprise that sifts out empirical and theoretical errors.

Attempts at replicating results, an essential requirement in science, is a powerful tool for revealing empirical falsehoods. Broadly testing theoretical implications helps to evaluate the verisimilitude of theories. Finally, the best advice for enhancing the quality of scientific knowledge is to replace poor scientific practices with good ones.

Facts must be pinned down before they can be used productively in social planning. Factual disagreements can occur in all sciences, including physics, as illustrated in the controversy about atomic fusion. Such clashes occur frequently in the behavioral sciences, especially when questions of social policy are posed. Apparently simple questions such as "Is bilingual education effective?" and "Does gender bias operate in the education of mathematicians?" can be answered in the affirmative or negative with ample evidence being offered in either case. Why cannot a definitive and convincing answer be forthcoming? Many interrelated factors prevent a clear response. The phenomena are exceedingly complex, being products of an enormous number of interacting variables. In addition, no agreement prevails as to how the crucial variables are to be measured. Bilingual education has numerous meanings both in conception and practice, and effective education depends on one's judgment about the purpose of education. Gender bias is defined in many different ways, varying from specific cases of discrimination to the discrepancy between the proportion of women in the population and their membership in professional organizations, such as mathematicians. Another factor adding to the confusion is the lack of systematic research that is required to unravel the influences of the numerous variables involved. Available evidence is usually a product of one-shot efforts designed to offer a definitive answer or studies that are planned to prove an ideological conclusion for or against bilingual education.

Two general reactions to the confusion surrounding research relevant to social policy are possible. One is to throw our hands up and admit that science cannot operate in a political jungle. Social policies belong to the political realm of life and must be left there. The other choice is to recognize the overwhelming difficulties, and then surmount them. History repeatedly shows the capacity of science and scientists to overcome numerous obstacles that blocked efforts to understand the world. Rather than succumb to the difficulties, efforts must be made to conquer them.

Elevating the Quality of Research

From the scientific vantage point it seems obvious that scientific efforts can throw light on the consequences of social policies, such as bilingual education and gender bias in the education of mathematicians. At the same time, it must be recognized that controversial issues in the behavioral sciences are not usually resolved in any simple, step-by-step manner. In fact, scientific progress in the behavioral sciences can border on the haphazard when social policy questions are involved. Poorly designed research, conflicting findings, frustrated efforts at replicating studies, theoretical imprecision and disagreements, clashes over the proper procedure for measuring behavior, statistical errors, and other confounding factors result in an enormous amount of data with no consensus about their meaning. The important scientific question is whether these studies have any practical use in formulating social policy. The answer obviously depends on the scientific quality of the evidence and the ability of those who evaluate the information. It would seem that this critical task could only be done effectively by sophisticated scientists. The recommendation that aspirin reduces the chances of a heart attack was a conclusion drawn by medical experts and statisticians after they examined evidence meeting their scientific standards. Numerous bodies of experts (e.g., National Academy of Sciences) offer advice on broad issues associated with science and technology, as well as specific recommendations for medications, foods, building materials, fire alarms, and so forth. Is it not therefore possible for recognized experts in the behavioral sciences to evaluate the scientific status of behavioral evidence, such as the effectiveness of bilingual education, and convey their conclusions to society? If it can be done for the physical and biological sciences, why can't it be done for the behavioral sciences, assuming, of course, that the available evidence can lead to a scientifically justified conclusion? If not, then further, better designed research may be needed. The operating assumption behind this view is that psychological research, in principle, is capable of yielding reliable empirical knowledge about educational practices.

Accurate Reporting of Socially Relevant Research

In addition to the problems of discovering and evaluating relevant empirical data is the task of transmitting such knowledge in an accurate and unbiased fashion in order that the public will have an opportunity to make informed decisions about social policies. History provides repeated evidence that science is capable of replacing erroneous interpretations of nature with valid conceptions. Distinguished scientists who are committed to seek empirical truth without regard to ideological goals have, time after time, been successful in offering accurate descriptions of the empirical world. And when distortions occur, subsequent corrections can be made. Science is not error free but its persistent scrutiny can ultimately lead to empirical truth. And when democracy and science operate in a mutually respectful and responsible manner their combined efforts can yield shared benefits.

Natural Science Psychology and Society

Natural science psychology can provide information about the consequences of competing social policies and, thus, assist society in making informed policy decisions. But this suggested advantage is dependent upon two important requirements being met by psychology and psychologists: the employment of natural science methodology in behavioral research and the ability to separate research procedures and data from value judgments and political contamination. Although these stipulations are easy to state, they are difficult to implement. Natural science methodology cannot be described in an exact fashion and the borderline between science and nonscience is hazy. In spite of this, it is still possible to establish procedures and standards by which a society can evaluate the relevance of empirical information for the formulation of social policy. In a similar fashion one can admit that although the ability to separate empirical relationships from political contamination is not clear-cut, it is nevertheless possible to minimize, and even to eliminate, sources of bias.

To achieve scientific respectability, psychology must overcome obstacles not shared by other sciences. Perhaps the major one is that a large segment of the population is convinced they know more about human behavior than do scientific psychologists. I am amazed and annoyed when some physicist friends arrogantly reject reliable psychological knowledge in favor of their own personal intuitions. Scientific standards employed in physics are readily abandoned when these physicist friends (former friends if they read this book!) pontificate about human behavior. Of course, the reliance on one's experiences in interpreting psychology is not limited to physicists but, instead, applies to most people. The reason for referring to the *chutzpah* of these physicists is to dispel the notion that reliance on personal intuition to explain behavior is not simply a consequence of a lack of scientific training. From childhood on, all of us are forced to explain our behavior in the absence of any guidance but our conscious experience.

Another obstacle in psychology's path to gain social acceptance is that psychology is not a unified science in the sense that physics, chemistry, and biology have become. The conceptual wars in the physical and biological sciences have been won with natural science methodology achieving victory. Although the triumph of natural science methodology may be attributed either to its capacity to reveal a true picture of "reality" or to provide useful knowledge, or some combination of both, the victory is practically complete. Today natural-science physical and biological disciplines are challenged only by those anti-scientists who, for a variety of reasons ranging from ideology to quirkiness, are willing either to ignore empirical evidence or to interpret it irrationally. However, one cannot so easily dismiss those psychologists who reject a natural science approach to behavior because, for them, such an orientation is inappropriate for the study of human consciousness, a position that is being challenged by neuroscientists with advanced biotechnological procedures (e.g., Hardcastle, 1996). And there are those humanists who argue that only literature and art can offer a veridical account of human consciousness.

History has shown that the major question confronting natural-science psychology is not whether such a science is possible but, instead, how successful can it become. Presently it is a growth industry with the resulting progress unevenly distributed throughout its empirical range. The search for broadly-based behavioral theories has not been as successful as hoped for, but that is not surprising considering the complexity of psychology and its relatively brief history. At the same time, solid advances have been made in numerous areas with expectations of greater progress, especially within the neurosciences with its sophisticated biotechnology. Even the slippery phenomena of human consciousness, as just noted, are being examined productively within a natural science approach.

The age-old nature versus nurture problem has been clarified both methodologically and empirically. Environment and heredity do not operate as separate and opposed forces but, instead, are inextricably interdependent. The influence of one cannot be understood without understanding the other. A simple example of this reciprocal interaction comes from the bodily changes the snowshoe rabbit undergoes with changes in season. In summer the snowshoe rabbit is the same color as its brownish environment. But when autumn comes and the weather grows colder, the snowshoe rabbit gradually changes color until in winter, when snow covers the ground, the animal becomes entirely white. Genetic factors are responsible for the color of the snowshoe rabbit's fur, but the actual color is influenced by the animal's environment. This example, as many others in psychopathology—major depression, generalized anxiety disorder, alcohol abuse, bulimia—dramatically illustrates the futility of trying to interpret any form of behavior as being caused exclusively by either heredity or environment (K. S. Kendler and Prescott, 2006).

The relatively new field of behavior genetics has approached the problem of unraveling nature-nurture interactions with new and powerful methodological and statistical techniques. As noted previously, behavior geneticists insist their efforts to understand genetic influences cannot achieve fruition without comprehending environmental inputs. Nevertheless, critics seek to equate such a research program with the political slogan "heredity is destiny," in an attempt to discredit it as being undemocratic and resistant to environmental solutions for social problems. The difference between the approaches of the behavior geneticists and their critics can be highlighted by competing educational policies for one of society's most important natural resources: gifted children. Those who criticize behavior geneticists' hypothesis of a hereditary involvement in children of exceptional talents suggest that imaginative educational procedures could raise the level of ordinary children to match the achievements and potential of the gifted child (Benbow, 1998). But the evidence fails to lend support to this hypothetical degree of human malleability (Winner, 1996). Achieving the future potential of the gifted, as well as all children, demands educational programs geared to a child's talent. This does not imply a lock-step education that limits a child's future to a rigid tracking that is beyond change. The system can be sensitive to possible misdiagnoses of a child's potentials, while still retaining the principle that the most effective educational procedures are designed for students who can profit from them.

Within this debate between genetic interactionists (behavior geneticists) and environmental determinists parading under the banner of "democratic equality" lies the crucial issue of how a society should spend its economic resources. Although it is generally accepted that the education of children is a basic social responsibility that should not be compromised, reality demands recognition that resources are limited. What should be the relative assignment of funds throughout the educational hierarchy? How should educational resources at the elementary school level be divided among the slow learners, the average, the above average, and the exceptionally talented? Understandably, compassion reigns supreme when the needs of the slow learners, including the physically handicapped, are considered. But if self-interests and the future of society are considered, it should be obvious that ignoring the needs of the gifted in favor of unrealistic programs for the below average could be counterproductive (Benbow and Stanley, 1996). When optimism distorts reality, subsequent reality will suffer. Would not slower learners comprehend better and be happier if their instruction were geared to their talents?

The basic question is whether educational planning will be more effective when guided by the model of genetic interactionists that stresses the importance of the reciprocal influence between heredity and training or the upbeat claim that all children have unlimited or equally limited potential for all forms of learning. The facts favor the behavior genetics model and it is up to society to choose between the two. If knowledge about the consequences of the competing policies is clear, then a democratic society will be able to make a more informed choice. When it comes to the selection and training of Olympic and professional athletes, the genetic interactionist model reigns supreme!

MORAL PLURALISM

Moral pluralism can be considered as a reaction to the inability of any one ethical system to gain the allegiance of all people. It would follow, therefore, that some form of pluralism, a choice among different ethical systems, is required for a democratic society that aims to serve the needs of all its citizens. But does not pluralism invade the rights of individuals to pursue absolute moral beliefs? Where does moral pluralism end and anarchy begin?

Moral pluralism emerges from the failure of moral monism. Isaiah Berlin a powerful philosophical voice in the advocacy of a moral pluralism pinpointed its psychological relevance.

> If, as I believe, the needs of men are many and not all of them are in principle compatible with each other, then the possibility of conflict—and of tragedy—can never be wholly eliminated from human life, either personal or social. The necessity of choosing between absolute claims is then an inescapable characteristic of the human condition. (Berlin, 1958, 34)

In illustrating his point, Berlin referred to Machiavelli's juxtaposition of Christian morality of virtue with that of the pagan vision of a good life (Berlin, 1979). The adoption of one vision would automatically exclude the possibility of the other. The value of these competing systems is impossible to determine in the absence of an independent ethical scale to measure their relative worth.

Moral pluralism is both an attractive and repelling concept. It implicitly preaches tolerance, while it simultaneously threatens anarchy. Depending on one's moral orientation, moral pluralism generates enthusiastic support or violent condemnation. Moral pluralism is anathema to moral absolutism and moral monism. For example, Orthodox Judaism, in its struggle to retain religious control in Israel against the more open-minded Conservative and Reform conceptions, offers a simple justification for its monistic position. It claims that there is no other form of Judaism than Orthodox Judaism. The concept of moral pluralism is not to be found in Jewish theology. There is only one Jewish religion, and that is Orthodox Judaism, based on the 3,000-year-old religious tradition expressed in Halacha, the entire body of Jewish theology.

Absolutist interpretations of a religion, like that of Orthodox Judaism, are doomed to fail if success is to be measured by the adherence of followers of a given religious tradition. The facts of history illustrate how monism—Christianity, Islam, Judaism—inevitably splits into pluralism. Two fundamental factors seem to be operative in the failure of absolutist positions to be maintained: human cognitive ingenuity and absence of an objective measure of moral truth.

Human cognitive ability is so flexible and creative that every conceivable moral principle generates opposition and counter-principles. If one God is proposed, another God, or no God, will inevitably be suggested. Human contrariness is not limited to religion. It exhibits itself in every cognitive activity from religion to science, from art to politics. But whereas oppositional thought in science is checked by empirical constraints, it goes unimpeded in ethics. Ethics, unlike science, as repeatedly noted, has no extrinsic criterion to judge the validity of moral principles. Moral truths are restricted to the domain of the ethical system that endorses them. They fall by the wayside when extended beyond their home base. Thus, those who seek universally accepted moral truths have a choice of persisting in the face of failure or admitting defeat. Thus, moral pluralism appears to be a psychological end product of a society whose members are free to express their ethical views. This conclusion, it must be emphasized, does not validate moral pluralism in preference to a moral monism; it only explains its historical ascendancy.

Moral pluralism, as an alternative to moral monism, raises more of an ethical problem than a solution. Although it rejects an autocratic morality, it does not suggest a clear alternative. There is no compelling principle that describes how a pluralistic society should be or what, if any, moral restrictions should be imposed. Moral pluralism is not equivalent to a moral neutralism that condones all forms of morality, including those that preach antisocial violence and destruction. Moral pluralism must be fashioned to preserve its own integrity to prevent it being overturned by a moral monism or a moral anarchy. To be successful, moral pluralism must offer a range of appealing and acceptable choices. If not, the integrity of the society will be constantly threatened as occurs in communities (e.g., Iraq, Lebanon) that are constantly under incompatible ethical pressures.

Moral Pluralism: Problems and Solutions

Now that a psychological rationale for moral pluralism has been described, it is time to analyze its impact and consequences. Is the goal of moral pluralism unlimited freedom or ethical tolerance? Can every moral principle thrive in a pluralistic society: free speech should reign, "immoral speech" should be restrained, comments that are offensive to any group should be restricted, shouting down speakers in a public forum should be a punishable crime, and so on. It should be obvious that moral pluralism cannot succeed if the pluralism lacks boundaries. But it should also be recognized that clear-cut boundaries threaten the implicit tolerance of moral pluralism. The paradox that confronts moral pluralism dissipates when moral pluralism is recognized not as a complete, self-contained ethical system that is applied wholly to a society but instead is viewed as an ethical orientation that is modifiable, open to changes that will enhance its approval and effectiveness. The transformation of this orientation into a specific moral guidance system is a complex task, far more difficult than the formulation of a rigid ethical code. The reason is that moral guidelines are needed in an ethically pluralistic society, but they cannot be set in stone. They require constant evaluation to determine their consequences so that the functional value of moral pluralism will not be endangered, either by disruptive moral conflicts or intolerant restrictions. One must realize that the delineation of moral boundaries in a pluralist society can be approached, but never finalized. A continuous surveillance of the consequences of the guiding moral principles, supported by reliable empirical evidence, will be needed to improve social policies. But the goal of a moral pluralistic society should not be utopia but instead one that is in tune with the realities of human capacities.

Social Harmony and Moral Diversity

In the ongoing effort to set reasonable and workable boundaries for contrasting ethical systems, the law serves as the first line of defense in protecting moral pluralism from the predatory inroads of monistic moralities and socially destructive agendas. The United States Constitution, embedded in a complex political and legal framework, infiltrated by religious and philosophical traditions, and surrounded by social conventions, essentially endorses moral pluralism. But its history clearly illustrates that the forces that encourage moral pluralism are the same forces that demand moral restrictions. The religious freedom clause of the First Amendment–"Congress shall make no law respecting an establishment of religion, or prohibiting the free exercise thereof"–appears to allow unfettered religious commitments. In fact, history suggests that restraints are needed for a "reasonable" freedom to operate. Inevitably, orthodoxy of one religion will contradict the moral imperatives of others. American history has been marred by intense and frequently vicious religious conflicts, especially over the use of artificial birth control methods and the practice of abortion. Sometimes these conflicts are pinpointed in excruciatingly painful detail, as occurs when a mother's life is threatened during pregnancy. Jewish theology assigns priority to the mother's life while Roman Catholicism reverses the order. A core belief of Christian Science is that prayer can achieve salvation from illness, but members of that faith risk criminal prosecution when medical assistance is denied to save the life of a child. Mormon theology initially accepted polygamy, but a man who actively sought such a marital status would run the risk of criminal penalties in practically all parts of America. A moral pluralistic society continuously struggles with the problem of identifying boundaries between morality and immorality.

One might suggest that the participants in a pluralistic society have a moral obligation to tolerate views other than their own. One can be convinced about the validity of one's own moral commitments without feeling compelled to impose them on others. But that is easier said than done. If one is convinced that God judges an abortion to be morally wrong, then is one not obligated to stop the "the murder of an innocent child in the womb?" When the evil of abortion is contrasted with the "greater iniquity" of denying abortion to a rape victim or a woman carrying a deformed fetus, it becomes clear why a moral reconciliation between pro- and antiabortion groups is impossible. Recognition of an unbridgeable moral gap encourages one to look beyond morality to deal with ethically divisive issues.

The history of the moral conflict surrounding the sale of contraceptives designed to prevent pregnancy is worth reviewing. The main opposition to their use was the Roman Catholic Church that fought to defend anti-contraceptive laws in an effort to preserve the sanctity of marriage and procreation. Their struggle finally failed in 1965, when the United States Supreme Court struck down the last state law (Connecticut) that forbade the sale of contraceptives. Without abandoning their moral objection to artificial modes of birth control, the Church finally yielded to the power of public opinion. The threats of world overpopulation, the tremendous economic drain on all members of large families, the increase in women's desires to have their own careers, and the freer acceptance of erotic pleasures, all operated to transform the issue of contraceptives use from the moral to the practical. Even a majority of Catholics used artificial birth-control methods, in spite of the Church's disapproval. A Catholic political scientist

(Canavan, 1995) perceives the moral issues associated with contraceptive use confronting the Church as follows:

> Since the law sooner or later must reflect public opinion, the mission of Catholics in debates about public morality is not adequately defined as one of advocating or defending laws that embody sound moral principles. In the long run, it is far more important to influence the public conscience from which laws spring. . . . In a religiously divided and partly de-Christianized society we cannot appeal to the authority of the Church or of God Himself. This is not to say that we should disguise the religious source of our moral convictions or pretend that we believe in the viability of a purely secular morality. . . . But we can hope, and certainly we should try, to restore to the men of today an insight that they are losing: the Catholic vision that life is good and is a great gift from God. Because life is good, marriage is good, procreation is good, and the life that is procreated is good. (15–16)

Thus, the case for Catholic theology can be presented full force in a moral pluralistic society with the recognition that it will not, and need not, be accepted by all. Canavan's comments illustrate three important points. First, in a moral pluralistic society a monist theology can be practiced without being compromised by the majority views of society. Second, a monist morality can thrive within laws that are incompatible with its principles. Third, a monist morality can stick to its principles and persist in its political efforts to shape laws in line with its own theology.

The battle over the legalization of artificial methods of birth control illustrates the difficulties of retaining an ethical imperative while bucking overwhelming practical concerns. Outlawing birth control methods has no chance of achieving social acceptance when it imposes such hardships on everyday living. Justifying moral principles without considering their consequences can be the most effective way of discouraging their acceptance as a social policy in a democratic society. Detaching ethical principles from their social impact, as was done in the fight over birth control and is presently shaping the debate about abortion, tends to freeze the conflict between extreme, irreconcilable positions. Possible sources of compromise become hidden from view.

Although Catholic theology outlaws artificial birth control and abortion because they both distort human procreation, the relative merit of these practices in the eyes of the public is strikingly different.

Artificial birth control methods are considered by most to be a necessity in modern life, primarily for adolescents, even if they do raise complex moral and practical problems. But abortion resides on a different moral plane because, for the most part, it seeks to rectify a past mistake. Planned Parenthood fiercely defends free-choice, but simultaneously strives to reduce the number of abortions to a minimum. They argue that, with effective educational techniques, the rate of abortion in the United States could be drastically lowered to the level of the Scandinavian countries. Many pro-choicers would readily acknowledge their personal antipathy toward abortions but, nevertheless, insist that freedom to have an abortion is a moral imperative for a compassionate society.

If the past acceptance of contraceptives serves as a guide to the future, it would appear highly unlikely that a pluralistic society would outlaw all abortions. In light of the fact that American society has a strong desire to reduce the incidence of abortion, would it not be more productive to shift the debate from the moral to the practical? As was the case for contraceptives, once it was recognized that contraceptives could not be banned, the problem became one of regulating their availability. If the question of the moral justification of abortion could be put aside, it should be easier to formulate a policy that would govern the practice of abortion. Again, it should be noted that accepting a social policy does not force its moral acceptance. While accepting the strength of public opinion, one could personally accept the ethical imperative that condemns abortion as a fundamental sin. Social harmony and moral diversity need not operate in opposition to each other.

Although moral pluralism preaches tolerance, the disturbing question can be raised as to whether excessive tolerance can lead to the destruction of the core social values required to bind a society together. Contemporary American culture, according to one view, is constantly expanding individual rights while simultaneously eroding social responsibilities. But how can "core social values" and "social responsibilities" be defined or determined? In the case of *Bowers vs. Hardwicke* in 1986, the Supreme Court upheld in a 5 to 4 decision the Georgia law that criminalized sodomy. The majority view argued that for centuries homosexual relationships had been considered immoral and a state had every right to legislate morality. The minority disagreed, contending that denying individuals the right to express their intimate feelings in privacy was a much greater threat to Constitutional values than were unconventional sexual practices. In sum, society is not permitted to have a public morality that governs all forms of moral pluralism. Such a view is supported by the philosopher of law, Ronald Dworkin:

> . . . political decisions must be, as far as possible, independent of any particular conception of the good life, or of what gives value to life. Since the citizens of a society differ in their conceptions, the government does not treat them as equals if they prefer one conception to another. (Dworkin, 1984, 64)

A hint as to where this view can lead is contained in Justice William Douglas's opinion that constitutional protection applies to publications "of value to the masochistic community or to others of the deviant community" (quoted in Canavan, 1995, 101). The next possible extension of the "good life" is to provide constitutional protection for the masochistic community to practice violent sex, even when leading to bodily harm or permanent injury. But would that be allowed in a society fashioned by Dworkin's principle that no moral conception of a "good life" has precedent over all others? The answer would depend on the interpretation of the qualifying phrase "as far as possible" as it applies to restrictions on the choice of meaning of a "good life." One could suggest that Dworkin's principle, including the key phrase "as far as possible," represents the legal and political procedures contained in laws of the land. Although the interpretation does not offer an answer to the hypothetical question about the latitude of behavior permitted by the masochistic community, it does indicate from where the answer would be forthcoming. According to Dworkin, the law, not religion, represents the moral core of a pluralistic society.

The threat that competing and conflicting views of the "good life" holds . . . for a society is expressed in Canavan's insistence that a pluralistic society must maintain a religious core if a unity is to be preserved:

> There is undeniably ample evidence that the division of society into a small number of strong and cohesive communities can tear the society apart. But if we carry liberal individualism to its logical term in order to preserve unity through pluralism, we shall learn that this solution, too, carries a price. The constant disparagement of particular communities

and their beliefs, and the steady subordination of their cherished ideals to the unity and stability of the political society end by robbing the political society itself of vitality and drying up the springs of political loyalty and love of country. . . . But without communities that have strong bonds of belief and affection, there will be no soil out of which the consensus may grow. Without them, society may indeed be pluralistic in the sense of being made up of rootless individuals. But such people will not regard society and its political system as anything more than a utilitarian convenience. . . . Pluralism does not require that the communities and their moral belief be sacrificed to the equality of all individual preferences. The larger and sounder part of society must have the right and power to determine the moral limits of permissible action. If the larger part is in fact not the sounder part of society, then society will certainly be in peril—but it will not escape the danger by resorting to an unrestrained liberal individualism. . . . Some relationship between the state and religion more nuanced than neutrality between religion and irreligion is needed . . . [to prevent] a steady degeneration of pluralism into mere individualism. (Canavan, 1995, 102–104)

Dworkin identifies legal procedures contained in the Constitution as the cement that can bind a democratic society together. Canavan denies that law itself can do the job; a super morality must be adopted to prevent pluralism ultimately leading to a moral anarchy. And that super morality must reflect the religious values that served as the foundation of the American democracy. In his farewell address, George Washington (1796/1991) warned that "reason and experience both forbid us to expect that National morality can prevail in exclusion of religious principle" (p. 19) while John Adams declared that "Our constitution was made only for a moral and religious people" (cited in Howe, 1966, 185). Such admonitions appear inconsistent with the principle of religious freedom. But freedom of religion, according to Canavan, is not equivalent to freedom *from* religion.

From the perspective of this irreligious writer, the fundamental issue at stake is psychological. Although one can respect Washington's and Adam's convictions, one also must recognize that American society has changed since their time. The population has expanded to include a much wider range of ethnic and religious groups. Keeping the church and state separate is a powerful force in American politics. Individual freedom, for many, is threatened by the policies of those who expound a conservative religious agenda. And the world provides too many examples of religious persecutions and religious-based autocratic regimes to permit the barrier between church and state from being lowered. At the same time, when one views the current scene in which traditional moral principles appear to be losing their grip, one cannot avoid speculating about the effectiveness of God-given moral convictions as compared to secular ethical principles in controlling behavior. "No human society has been a religious vacuum" (Schoenfeld, 1995, 183). Would not social stability in contemporary American society be enhanced if those religious beliefs that guided our founding fathers could reassert their influence?

One could easily get the impression that the opposed positions of Dworkin and Canavan—moral pluralism based on law versus a moral pluralism with a religious core—are being simultaneously supported. In some sense they are, but only as possible options for a democratic society to consider in maintaining social unity. What is often overlooked is that religious groups, like secular ones, have every right to push their political agendas. This is evident in the current conflict about homosexual rights, the issue that is dividing the American middle-class into two warring moral camps (Wolfe, 1998). From the viewpoint of a secular democracy, homosexuality is a matter of civil rights, but for most religious orientations, homosexuality is sinful. Homosexuals have made great strides in having their sexual orientation accepted and their cultural contributions recognized. At the same time, social conflict has erupted over their efforts to share legal options that are available to heterosexuals, such as marriage, rights to adopt children, and memberships in certain social organizations such as the Boy Scouts.

Although science cannot legislate morality, it can offer neutral information that can help formulate social policy. The view of society toward homosexuality will be influenced by whether it is shown to have a genetic involvement or is a chosen lifestyle. Research suggests that homosexuality has a genetic involvement. It is moderately heritable, but no specific gene or genomic region has been reliably identified. Although this evidence would encourage tolerance of homosexual behavior, it would not automatically justify a wide range of policies that vary from homosexual marriages to the inclusion of "queer sex" courses in colleges. The attempt to expand pluralistic "rights" will always be countered by those who perceive such extensions as threatening to the core beliefs of society. Each position has the right to be heard and evaluated. Although moral pluralism encourages the expansion of individual and group rights, it does not automatically justify the elimination of all restrictions that might threaten the integrity of the entire society. If society can be exposed to reliable estimates of the consequences of the conflicting policies, then the political and judicial procedures would be in a better position to contain the inevitable stresses that moral pluralism generates. A case in point is the conflict surrounding the issue of whether lesbian and gay parents should be allowed to adopt children. When the moral issue is set aside to allow empirical investigations to determine whether the sexual orientation of a parent affects child development, then democratic processes can help a society formulate a policy decision. A recent study (Patterson, 2006) that spanned twenty years concluded that the quality of the family relationship, not the sexual orientation of the parents, influenced the development and adjustment of children. Important differences were not found between children of heterosexual and homosexual parents. These conclusions, needless to say, require replication.

INTERNATIONAL RELATIONS

Can the methodological analysis of the intersection of science, psychology, and ethics within an established democracy, such as the United States, be extended to the world stage? If one presumes an epistemological similarity between natural science methodology and historical analyses, then an affirmative response would be forthcoming. The flow of history is postulated to be a consequence of interacting variables similar to those operating in laboratory experiments. The epistemology is the same but the application is much more difficult because of the greater number of variables and the inability to control them. At best, predictions about future historical events, such as the outcome of the conflict between political democracies and Islamic fundamentalism, should be expressed in probabilistic estimates instead of precise forecasts. In other words, historical extrapolations should be set forth in a cautious and tentative manner. This maxim is particularly important when policy decisions are based on historical analysis. A more pragmatic approach, rather than adopting a complete plan with a goal in the distant future, would be to set short-term targets that would reveal whether the effort is going in the right direction. Awareness that all relevant variables are not known should prepare one to modify decisions in an effort to avoid potential failures.

Viewing historical explanations within a probabilistic framework should guard one against *single-cause* explanations. George W. Bush did not solely cause the Iraq War. A host of other variables–the founding of Iraq, 9/11, Islam, Middle East oil, Rumsfeld, Saddam Hussein– and numerous other factors contributed to the onset of the conflict. Single-cause historical interpretations are rarely complete.

The Conflict Between Political
Democracies and Militant Islam

The term *democracy* has its roots in the Greek word *demos,* which means, "rule by people." Representative democracy is the contemporary form of this kind of political organization. Four basic features distinguish it from other forms of government. First, although citizens do not vote directly, they do, in principle, participate via elections in governmental decisions. Second, modern democracies seek to maintain a separation between religion and the state. Third, to qualify as a democracy, the society must abide by democratic principles that include voting rights, judicial fairness, and freedom of speech. Admittedly, democratic governments are not immune from criticisms of their lack of adherence to these ideals, and in some cases the judgment appears justified. Such deviations are slight in comparison to the vast discrepancy between totalitarian states that lack representative traditions. Fourth, to qualify as a democracy requires the society to maintain its political traditions over a significant period of time. A political democracy is not simply created by the occurrence of an election. Political democracies are established by strong cultural traditions adopted by those who govern and are governed.

An abstract way of treating democracy is contained in Karl Popper's *The Open Society and Its Enemies* (1945) that focuses on the moral conflicts raging among nations in the recent past. As Popper's title implies, the conflict occurs between open and closed societies, which he defined generally as between democracies and totalitarian states. Not only did democracies triumph over their opponents during World War II, but they also helped convert them to open societies. Later the struggle was repeated between the former Allies and the dictatorial Soviet Union, following the dissolution of the association. Many of its member states moved in the direction of an open society with various degrees of success. Today a major Popperian conflict is between Islamic societies and representative democracies.

A number of historical forces have operated to encourage the development of democracies in Western Europe and its subsequent export to other parts of the world. The European Enlightenment, with its rejection of dogmatic faith and espousal of reason and freedom, inaugurated major cultural changes. Democracy, itself, offered a political organization that was appealing and rewarding to the majority of its citizens. Although a democracy suffers from many hurly-burly influences, especially during elections, Winston Churchill wryly noted its outstanding virtue: "It has been said that democracy is the worst form of government except for all the others that have been tried."

Democracy provides personal and political freedom that encourages a variety of social benefits. Of primary importance is the advantageous effect freedom has on the growth of science and technology, which in turn accelerates economic development and progress in the health and welfare of the population. To further this progress, educational support is required to supply needed scientists, engineers, doctors, technicians, and skilled workers. Such support for scientific development can be misdirected or aborted by incompatible ideological commitments. The racial views of Nazi Germany and anti-heredity conceptions in the Soviet Union are examples from the past. Today, theological creationism operates as an obstacle in the training of biological scientists. More than fifty percent of biology teachers in secondary education in Turkey fail to fully accept Darwinian evolution. A lavish 768-page book on Islamic creationism is being produced in Turkey and sent unsolicited to countries in Western Europe that have sizable Muslim populations (Enserink, 2007). Scientific freedom is sometimes stymied in political democracies, as is the case for stem cell research in the United States. Overcoming opposition to scientific restrictions is accomplished much more easily in a democracy than in a theocracy.

If a closed society is defined negatively as the absence of democratic procedures, then Popperian conflicts between open and closed societies are being replicated throughout the world, particularly between Western democracies and Islamic Fundamentalism. In comparing the two, one important point, emphasized throughout the book, cannot be ignored. The *moral goodness* of contrasting cultures cannot be proven by empirical means. The contrast between living in an open society and being a member of an Islamic country is so extreme that a citizen raised in a democracy cannot imagine making a free choice in favor of an Islamic government. The fact/value dichotomy and the naturalistic fallacy (pp. 26–27) deny the possibility that a moral conviction, such as a preference for an open society or an Islamic theocracy, can be empirically validated. The present world situation demonstrates that both have their supporters, with the majority of the people of the world not clearly committed to any one world view. Thus, the relative merits of these social organizations will ultimately be decided by the attractiveness and consequences of their value systems.

An interesting psychological question is whether humankind has a genetic predisposition to prefer a certain kind of social organization, democratic versus totalitarian, or whether humans are so malleable that environmental pressures can encourage acceptance and adjustment to any form of government? Another possibility is that certain psychological characteristics (e.g., ethical commitments, ethnic identification, cognitive ability) of human beings or social groups will predispose them to certain social organizations.

Does history *suggest* that humans prefer open societies to closed ones? The historical development in Western Europe and its influence in North America, Australia, New Zealand, and parts of Asia, intimate that a democracy has sufficient appeal to replace authoritarian forms of governments. In some cases, countries with a Western European foundation–Spain, Germany–strayed from their tradition, only to return.

An unqualified preference for political freedom is not the sole factor in determining the preference for an open society. A host of variables may be operating, including the higher standard of living that democracies generate from their scientific and technological friendly environments. Did the dominance of Christian religion play a role in the development of open societies in Western Europe and their offshoots in other parts of the world? Although Christian countries did not originally support democracies, did Christianity have a greater potential tolerance than Islam? Is it possible that the differences between the symbolic Christ and Muhammad play a role in the development of political democracies? The lives led by the two, as history suggests, encourage a fundamental ethical difference in the monotheistic religion they each served as originator.

Jesus and Muhammad led markedly different lives: The former

steeped in religion, the latter an ordinary man who, in middle age, experienced the voice of God and subsequently became a prophet. Although Jesus was always a devout Jew, his historical legacy provided a foundation for the new religion of Christianity. He was a charismatic teacher and prophet, leading a small band of disciples, some of whom played a major role in developing the new religion of Christianity. The New Testament represents the theological core of Christianity, containing narratives of Jesus Christ ministry in the early Church prepared by the four Apostles: Matthew, Mark, Luke, and John. In addition are advice, instructions, and prophecies. Muhammad (570–632) was born in Mecca to a family of traders. At the age of 25 he married an older widow who had hired him to manage her caravans. At 40 he heard God's voice reveal Holy Scriptures that Muhammad, an illiterate, was unable to record. Muhammad shared his experiences with his family and friends and he soon attained the status of prophet. His revelations were recorded and formed the basis of the Koran (Armstrong, 2006).

The question had been raised as to whether Christianity was more amenable to a democratic ethic than Islam. One can speculate about several differences that would increase the probability of a Christian society being transformed into a political democracy. Of paramount importance was the influence of Greek rationality on western thought. A more specific factor is the Golden Rule that was expressed in both a negative and positive form. The essence of Judaism, as described by the sage, Hillel, who lived in Jerusalem before the birth of Christ, is "That which is hateful to you, do not do to your neighbor." A positive principle, with more general "righteous" implications, is Jesus' "Do unto others as you would have them do unto you." Both propositions characterize important features of a democracy, with the negative form being interpreted as a basic value of criminal law and the positive form reflecting a principle of equal rights.

Muhammad's personal life was unlike that of Jesus. His original attempts to convert the people of Mecca to Islam were unsuccessful. He then traveled to nearby Medina where his efforts were rewarded. He returned to Mecca and achieved success, which previously had been denied, by combining his roles of prophet with that of military tactician. Combining his missionary zeal with military support enabled Muhammad to extend Islam to parts of the Arabian Peninsula and the Syrian Desert. The legacy of Muhammad's missionary style is testified to by Muslim's armies being in Spain only 100 years after the Prophet's death and 350 years before the First Crusade.

The proposal has been offered that Christianity is more adaptable to democracy than Islam. Islam means *submission,* suggesting that converting to Islam is a more passive act than the positive acceptance of Christianity. In addition, the gender inequalities in Islam are greater than in Christianity. Polygamy, for Muhammad, was consistent with Islam, with four wives being an appropriate limit. The fact that Muhammad exceeded this number, after taking his adopted son's wife, did not suggest any hypocrisy. Instead, he was admired for his virility (Armstrong, 2006). The capture of women when spreading Islam through military means was an added incentive to the missionary zeal of his followers. The sensuous and militaristic Muhammad contrasts sharply with the ascetic and pacifist Jesus. For some, the greater violence of contemporary Islam is a reflection of the character of their founder. Others believe that Christianity was equally brutal in its early years, as exhibited by the Crusades and hostilities toward some nonbelievers. Perhaps Islam will become mellower with age?

The unity of every religion is disturbed by theological disagreements. In the sixteenth century Christianity experienced the Protestant reformation in western Europe, challenging the dominance of the Catholic Church. Five centuries later numerous sects of Christianity prevail in the absence of violent clashes. Following the death of Muhammad in 632 a dispute occurred in Islam as to who should serve as the successor to the Prophet. The resulting Sunni-Shia split persists today in the Middle East and has repercussions throughout the entire world. The theological views of each group have impacted their secular influences. Worldly success is a powerful incentive for Sunnis, while moral victories are a goal of Shias (Nasr, 2006).

The relationship between Muslims and their views of democracy can be represented by four general categories. A *fundamentalist* believes that Islamic society ought to be governed by God, in contrast to the belief that humans should rule in a democracy. Thus, the religious laws of Islam, Sharia, derived from the Koran, should be the laws of Islamic states. *Traditional* Muslims also reject democracy, believing the west's emphasis on human rights is a devious attempt to undermine the supremacy of Islam. At the same time, these traditionalists recognize that modern societies require political changes to function effectively. Political administration is required to supervise civil activities, but at all times it ought to be subservient to the rulings of religious leaders. *Moderate* Muslims acknowledge the need to retain Islamic traditions, but believe they can be reformulated to meet the demands of modern times. *Secular* Muslims seek to imitate Western democracies in their social progress and technological advancement. They favor religious freedom and the separation of church and state, without necessarily rejecting a personal faith in Islam.

The Future

Suggesting that historical development is a product of interacting variables in a manner similar to laboratory experiments raises the challenge of identifying some of the major factors influencing the present conflict between western democracies and Islamic Fundamentalism. An important first step is to recognize that a complete understanding of this cultural collision is beyond possibility because of the inability to identify all historical variables. At best, a set of major influences can be hypothesized along with their individual impacts and interactions. The following trial run seeks to briefly exemplify this approach. The discussion will be conducted in an amoral fashion to avoid contaminating empirical analyses with ethical biases. The interacting historical variables—religious, economic, educational, political—will be reviewed in an integrated manner to estimate the future.

A fundamental theological question is whether human behavior is governed by free will or is predetermined. This conflict has been expressed in two forms. The first refers to the thesis that free will and determinism are mutually exclusive assumptions. Either God has given people a free will to act as they desire or they have been created in a deterministic mold that forces behavior consistent with God's plan. The free will assumption implies people are morally responsible for their actions, whether it be saving or taking the life of another person. Some theologians have argued that the concept of free will is an illusion. If an omnipotent and omniscient God created humans, then their future conduct is dictated by the Creator's creative design. If true, heinous acts, such as rape and murder, are not the responsibility of the offender but can be attributed to God's design. Theologians who contemplate the potential operation of free will and determinism do not have to view the two as being mutually exclusive. They can be considered as interactive, operating on some principle that enables humans to operate freely outside the framework of God's will.

The theological disputes involving free will and determinism have taken many forms, limited only by the inventiveness of theologians. Although religiously significant, the conflict, from a natural science viewpoint, is incapable of any resolution because of the absence of empirical operations that could provide definitive answers. In spite of the lack of scientific meaning, the dispute can have a psychological impact on those who assume a free will or unqualified deterministic assumption. The assumption of a free will encourages serious deliberations before making an important decision, such as choosing a course of political action or medical treatment. If one believes the future is predetermined, rational decision-making appears unnecessary. One can also suggest that people who operate under the assumption of free will favor a democratic form of government. Seeking personal goals will be more successful in an open than in a closed society where correct forms of behavior are rigidly dictated.

Is the distinction between free will and determinism relevant to the dispute between western democracies and Islamic fundamentalism? A reasonable and cautious conclusion would be that Islamic societies, as contrasted with democratic ones, are definitely tilted toward a deterministic view of life. As noted, Islam means submission, an attitude that appears to be expressed in a variety of ways, from the general willingness to accept government dictates to the extreme act of becoming a suicide bomber. As noted, Islamic societies did not experience the equivalent of the Enlightenment with the consequences of democratization and secularization.

The economic productivity of democracies, as compared to Islamic states, is not the direct outgrowth of political freedom, but rather its consequences. Democratic capitalism, or what some would designate as a market economy, has proven to be the most successful society as measured by the standard of living produced. This achievement depended on the educational resources providing the necessary personnel from workers to top executives. A continuing debate occurs within a democracy over the economic policies that should be pursued, particularly in relation to the distribution of financial resources to various segments of society such as business, science, social welfare, military, education, agriculture, communication, and others.

The September 11, 2001 destruction of the twin towers of the World Trade Center in New York City initiated the "War on Terrorism." This characterization is ambiguous because the concept of war during most of the twentieth century implied an *inter*state conflict, as occurred in World War II between United States versus Japan and Germany. Recently *intra*state clashes, involving irregular forces employing violence to gain political ends, have become more common as exemplified by the revolutionary efforts of Algerians and Vietnamese to achieve independence from France. A similar conflict presently rages between *Militant Islam* and their host society (D. Pipes, 2003): Hezbollah in Lebanon, Hamas in Palestine, the Muslim Brotherhood in Egypt, the Islamic Action Front in Jordan, and other militant groups sponsoring Jihad, violence justified by a Muslim's religious duty. Militant Islam does not represent all of Islam. Secular Muslims, as in Turkey, believe they can achieve a democratic society without abandoning their religious commitments.

The conflict within Islam, between Sunnis and Shiites, destabilizes the Middle East. Neither fully accepts the other as being authentic Muslims while each contends they are the true descendents of Muhammad. After the minority Sunnis governed Iraq under the dictatorship of Saddam Hussein, the majority Shiites sought to control the country. This civil war has brought into focus the question of whether there is an irreconcilable conflict between militant Islam and the democracies. Do the democracies face a situation comparable to that existing with Nazi Germany that could only be resolved by military action? Or can strategies be adopted that would weaken militant Islam, in a manner similar to the loss of power of the Communists in the Soviet Union, and lead, ultimately, to political democracy among some of the component states? Although from the present vantage point a definitive answer cannot be unqualifiedly endorsed, some of the influential variables can be discussed and analyzed.

The topic of violence of militant Islam can be perceived from many different perspectives. Morality is one. Suicide bombers murdering victims in their vicinity, kidnappers severing the heads of their prey, roadside bombs spraying death, all seem frightening, repellant, and unnecessary to members of an open society. Such moral judgments are rejected by Islamic militants who note, with scorn, the number of their victims is minute compared to the consequences of aerial bombs and nuclear weapons. Is the conflict basically moral or a disagreement about acceptable forms of violence?

A related question is whether militant Islam is currently more violent than Christianity, the dominant religion in the democracies. This issue was brought to head by Pope Benedict XIV's recent remarks on Islam (Fisher, 2006). In a stated effort to encourage dialogue with the Muslim world, the Pope offered a theological thesis that violence is contrary to God's nature. The concept of *jihad* (holy war) was offered by the Pope as an example of an apparent inconsistency with his own view of God and that of Muslim theology. In addition, the Pope referred to the comments of the fourteenth-century Persian, Byzantine Emperor Manuel II Paleologus: "Show me just what Mohammed brought that was new, and there you will find things only evil and inhuman, such as his command to spread by the sword the faith he preached." Muslims questioned the Pope's desire to further dialogue by employing a negative view of Islam. One leader accused him of being a "charlatan" intent on initiating another Crusade against Muslims. The Pope expressed regret for offending Muslims, adding that he did not share the Byzantine Emperor's views. The controversy did not facilitate meaningful discourse between Christian and Islamic leaders.

Is Islam presently racked by uncontrollable violence? Daily facts, weekly reports, yearly summaries, all testify to the nihilistic violence embedded in contemporary Islam, particularly as it is practiced in the Middle East and in parts of Europe, where some Muslim immigrants and their relatives have adopted a militant stance. This point was illustrated in the Netherlands, an extremely liberal democracy. A 27-year-old Muslim brutally murdered Theo Van Gogh, the great grandson of the painter's brother, who had produced a 10-minute film, entitled *Submission,* which pictorially criticized the Muslim's treatment of women. The assassin testified that Islamic law compelled him to murder anyone who insulted Allah and the Prophet. Similar conflicts have occurred in England, where native-born Muslims have committed terrorist attacks on British society. Muslims in Sudan have killed more than one million Christians and animists. One should also note the mayhem and slaughter that Muslims visit on their co-religionists.

On the simplest level, a conflict rages between open societies and militant Islam. One can perceive the battle as collisions between contrasting world views: modernity versus the past and secular tolerance versus theological truth. Regardless of the values associated with the alternatives, one can suggest a strategy that might achieve victory for one world view. The present concern will be with a general plan that would encourage the triumph of open over closed societies. Two major tactics can be employed. One is to impair Militant Islam by reducing and, ultimately, eliminating its appeal. The second would be to weaken the enemy in interstate and intrastate conflicts by military means.

The higher standard of living that emanates from freedom has an appeal to many Muslims. Consumerism for all sorts of goods, from popular music to sensual apparel to flashy cars, is popular in conservative Saudi Arabia and United Arab Emirates. A liberal education of the sort that occurs in democracies opens up attractive careers unavailable to those who pursue a rigid Islamic education. Muslim boys, when beginning schooling, first learn about their religion and, from that point on, all future learning has to be integrated with their faith. They spend their day from 8 a.m. to 5 p.m. in religious schools, memorizing the 6,200 verses from the Koran. The task usually requires two to three years, with the successful student receiving the title, *hafiz*, which entitles him entrance into heaven, assuming all other religious obligations have been met at the time of death. From the perspective of education in a democratic society, this kind of religious training interferes with the acquisition of scientific, engineering, and commercial skills, a good understanding of which cannot be acquired by rote learning.

A variable that has potential for undermining militant Islam is the goal of gender equality. The exact meaning of the concept in democracies is admittedly open to debate. However, throughout the world women activists are expressing their desire for an end to their subservient role in society, including access to educational and career opportunities (Ali, 2007; Lempinen, 2007). Their voices are reaching a receptive audience even in Islamic societies. Some undemocratic practices are worth noting. A traditional Islamic law is that a woman must produce four male witnesses to prove that she has been raped. If she cannot, she can be prosecuted for adultery. In some parts of the Muslim world, young men are raised to believe that their religion instructs them to murder their unchaste sisters. "Honor killings" have occurred in a Bedouin clan in Israel because a young woman rejected an arranged marriage. A question that the future will answer is whether Islamic fundamentalism will be able to resist a worldwide trend toward gender fairness when the presumed victims approximate half the population?

Turkey

Turkey can be perceived as a trial case in estimating the interactions between democracy and Islam. It is not a pure example of the present conflict between an open society and militant Islam because Turkey is neither Arab nor do Shiites play a crucial political role as they do in parts of the Middle East. The history of Turkey does mirror the conflict between open and closed societies, while exhibiting modest signs of reconciliation.

The introduction of democracy into Turkey was a result of the failure of the economic structure of the Ottoman Empire. While western Europe was developing free market capitalism leading to industrialization, the Ottoman Empire Islam was burdened with an agricultural economy saddled with a variety of ethnic groups seeking independence. The leader of Turkey's quest for self-rule was Mustafa Kemal (1881–1938), who was born in the Greek city, Thellosiki, which at that time was in the Ottoman Empire. His family had fled to Greece at the end of the fifteenth century to escape the Spanish Inquisition, and presumably passed down to members of successive generations a desire to live in secular society free of religious domination. Kemal, motivated by the ideals of political independence and humanistic values, played a key role in the founding the Republic of Turkey in 1923. He served as the first president of the country earning the title, *Ataturk,* "Father of the Turks."

Kemal's military education began when he was 12 and soon exhibited extraordinary scholarly talents, especially in mathematics. Later in his education he joined secret revolutionary societies opposed to the Ottoman Empire's restrictive rule in Turkey. The Empire collapsed following the end of World War I in 1918. He graduated at 24 as a lieutenant and two years later attained the rank of captain and became a leader of the Young Turks who helped found the Republic of Turkey in 1923. Some of his political achievements accelerated contacts between Turkey and world democracies. The Turkish alphabet was converted from Arabic to European lettering, Islam's religious law, Shariah, was replaced with the Swiss civil code, and women were discouraged from wearing the veil while men were forbidden to wear the fez. He is honored in Australia for his chivalry as an opponent in the Battle of Gallipoli in 1915. His only error appears to be the overriding of the Islamic ban against consuming alcoholic drinks. He died at the age of 58 from cirrhosis of the liver.

Today, Turkey is at a crossroad between an Islamic society and a European-style political democracy. Ataturk's secular reforms are currently being challenged by the prime minister of Turkey, Erdorgan, who assumed this office in 2003. In contrast to Ataturk, Erdogan is a pro-Islam leader whose religious attitudes have been shaped by a conservative Islamic education. His experiences in the secular world as a professional football player with a university education in management, prepared Erdogan to become a widely acclaimed corruption-free mayor of Istanbul. His success was achieved without abandoning his Islamic commitments. As mayor, he banned alcohol drinks in the cafes of Istanbul. As Prime Minister, he refused to take his wife, who wears a religiously required headscarf, to government functions where such items, a remnant of Ataturk's secular ideology, are banned by law.

A representative example of the ongoing conflict between Ataturk's democratic heritage and Islamic fundamentalism was the assassination of Hrank Dink, in 2007. Dink was the editor of Turkey's only Armenian-language newspaper and had been convicted of insulting the Turkish state because of his comments of the mass killings of Armenians in Turkey during World War I. Many historians recognize this event as genocide by the Ottoman army. The Turkish government denied the accusation and passed a law, still in operation, making "insulting Turkishness" a crime. The reaction to the killing reveals significant changes in the ongoing conflict between political democracy and Islam. The assassin was a Turkish high school dropout who confessed to murdering Dink because of the insult he directed against Turkey. He was part of an ultranationalist Islamic group that was isolated from the world by its ideology and poverty. Violence was idealized and played a recreational role in everyday life. Prime Minister Erdogan applauded the swift capture of the assassin and noted that the crime was a direct attack against political freedom that had the effect of isolating Turkey from the rest of the world. At the same time, Erdogan supports governmental policies inconsistent with political freedom, such as freedom of the press. Publishers have been jailed for producing books reporting events related to the conflict between the Turks and Armenians during World War I.

During 2007 the Turkish conflict between the political conceptions of Ataturk and Erdogan came to a critical head. According to the polit-

ical descendents of Ataturk who have controlled the government since
its founding in 1923, Turkey can only maintain its democratic features
by retaining a strict division between religion and the state. Erdogan
and his political associates reject such a position, assuming that the
religious beliefs and practices of governmental leaders need not interfere with a democracy. The religious convictions of George
Washington and John Adams in the founding of the United States can
be cited in defense of their position (p. 213). The relevance of this
defense depends upon whether a democracy can thrive in an Islamic
culture as it had in the Christian society of the United States.

This debate surrounding the role of Islam in a democracy is occurring against a backdrop of Turkey's attempt to gain entrance into the
European Union. Those who favor this affiliation believe it would
enhance the economy and freedom of expression. At the same time,
political forces are operating to prevent Turkey from abandoning its
Islamic roots. At the extreme are those Turks who believe their future
belongs not to Europe, which represents only three percent of
Turkey's landmass, but to Islamic nations throughout Asia, particularly its neighbors Syria, Iraq, and Iran. What will Turkey's influence be
on the worldwide conflict between Islam and democracy? Will Turkey
help attenuate the cultural conflict between Islamic countries and
open societies? Or is Turkey a peripheral agent to the main battle that
is localized in the Middle East, where militant Muslims are creating a
new kind of political organization involving a loose federation of violent groups whose goal is to establish fundamentalist Islamic societies?

FINAL COMMENTS

This book attempts to create a frame of reference that would illu-
minate the manner in which psychologists and other behavioral scientists could contribute to the resolution of moral conflicts in a democratic society, among democratic states, and in international relations.
Although the task is simple in conception, the problem is overwhelmingly complex in execution. At the root of the difficulty is the perpetual threat of confusion and misinformation. Ordinary language is
intrinsically ambiguous thus encouraging conflicting, and even contradictory, interpretations of basic concepts. Two notable examples,
already discussed, are the ideas of *equality* and *science*. The "equal pro-

tection clause" of the Fourteenth Amendment has been interpreted to both reject and endorse preferential treatment in affirmative action programs. By applying different referents to the demand for equal treatment, individuals versus groups, the plea for equality leads to divergent consequences. Science also lends itself to clashing conceptions. Natural science and human science are similar only in the common word *science* that they share. Although they each yield systematic knowledge, the knowledge claims differ in their epistemological characteristics. Knowledge claims of natural science methodology are required to meet objective standards, while those of human sciences seek the indefinable essence of being human. Although natural science methodology, at a given time, does not guarantee agreement about empirical facts and theoretical assumptions, its persistent application resolves disputes and promotes scientific progress. In sharp contrast are the debates within the human sciences that endure because of the inability to resolve conceptual disagreements. The characterization of the differences between natural science and human science methodology does not imply an intrinsic superiority of one over the other. Neither one can claim priority for the simple reason that they seek diverse ends. But their knowledge claims are not equally useful. Natural science information can be exploited to shape the future in order to achieve desired social goals. Human sciences, for the most part, offer interpretations that vary in their existential appeals but lack effective procedures for achieving preferred ends.

The value of natural science methodology can be oversold or undersold. Its successes are not unlimited nor are its purviews unrestricted. All human and social problems will not automatically succumb to scientific solutions. At the same time, the great successes of science in solving physical, biological, and social problems illustrate its value in planning the future. In this effort, only ignorance about and prejudice against natural science psychology can dispute its actual and potential achievements in contributing reliable and useful information about human behavior.

Everybody, including scientists, must recognize that the successes of natural science methodology are limited to the world of facts. Moral truths, the nature of right and good, are beyond the capacity of science to determine. Thus, nature itself will be unable to reveal the rules of right conduct. Human creativity, either stimulated by divine dictate or secular ingenuity, is required to devise a moral code that binds a community together. But such an achievement cannot be accomplished without dissent. Whatever moral principles are proposed, no matter how compelling they appear, will fail to achieve universal acceptance. Moral laws for some will surely collide with the moral convictions of others. Although arguments will persist, the underlying reality of such debates is that ethical clashes are inevitable and cannot be resolved by logic alone.

How can society cope with humanity's inclination to be in a perpetual state of moral conflict? The first step in dealing with moral conflicts is to abandon the idea that they can be resolved. They can only be contained. The second step is to realize that a democratic form of government is geared, not only instrumentally but also morally, to cope with the discord produced by ethical clashes. Democracy provides the political procedures for settling moral disputes and the ethical justification for the resolution to be accepted. This does not mean a passive acceptance, because democratic change is an ongoing option. Throughout American history the law has been challenged and many times reversed. Nevertheless, a legal verdict at a given time exerts a moral pressure to be obeyed by committed members of a democracy.

History suggests that a symbiotic relationship integrates democracy, science, and moral pluralism. All three share a tolerance for a multiplicity of ideas in their respective areas. The triumvirate thrives in an open society that allows free discussion and unfettered pursuit of truth, however it may be defined. Individual views within each framework are judged from a common perspective. They all interact in mutually beneficial ways. A democracy profits more from formulating public policy in light of reliable scientific evidence than from ignorance, or worse, myth. The awareness of the inevitability of moral pluralism encourages tolerance, not only for a range of ethical positions but also for highly restrictive monistic views. In sum, the constantly changing interactions among democracy, science, and moral pluralism, can create a climate in which social problems can be more effectively solved.

These final comments encourage the view that an attempt should now be made to offer a few methodological principles and psychological insights that would alert behavior scientists to the pitfalls of their disciplines and the public to the misinformation to which they are exposed. I have no illusions that these principles would be generally approved. But such an effort would encourage a more perspicacious evaluation of empirical evidence and moral and political arguments.

The hope is that a critical atmosphere can be created that will work to the benefit of society in exploiting the potentially synergistic relationships between science and democracy. Within this perspective the following 15 Commandments are proposed.

THE 15 COMMANDMENTS

1. There is a reality.
2. Reality does not always stare you in the face. It must be discovered.
3. Reality can be a bitch.
4. Facts are facts and values are values and never can the two become one.
5. It is easier to believe than to know.
6. You are entitled to your own opinion but not to your own facts.
7. Moral pluralism dovetails with democracy.
8. The ethical principles governing a moral pluralistic society can be approximated but never finalized.
9. Let society seek socially effective moral principles but defend it from those who have found moral truths.
10. Don't reify socially constructed concepts.
11. Life has meaning but it can't be found; it must be created or chosen.
12. All social policies will have unintended consequences.
13. The strenuous pursuit of a utopia will backfire.
14. Know what you don't know.
15. A good question is better than a bad answer.

REFERENCES

Ali, A. H. (2007). *Infidel*. New York: Free Press.

Anastasi, A., & Foley, J. P. (1958). *Differential Psychology* (3rd ed). New York: Macmillan.

Armstrong, K. (2006). Seeing Muhammad as both a prophet and politician. *The New York Times, 155,* p. B12.

Atkinson, R. C. (1977). Reflections on psychology's past and concerns about its future. *American Psychologist, 32:* 205–210.

Baker, J. R. (1974). *Race*. New York: Oxford University Press.

Balter, M. (2007). Brain evolution studies go micro. *Science, 315:* 1208–1211.

Barinaga, M. (1994). From fruit flies, rats, mice: Evidence of genetic influence. *Science, 264:* 1690–1693.

Baumeister, R. F., Smart, L., & Boden, J. M. (1996). Relation of threatened egotism to violence and aggression: The dark side of high self-esteem. *Psychological Review, 103:* 5–33.

Beer, W. R. (1992). Affirmative action: Social policy as shibboleth. In P. Suedfeld & Tetlock, P. E. (Eds.), *Psychology and social policy,* pp. 137–147. New York: Hemisphere Publishing Corp.

Benbow, C. P. (1988). Sex differences in mathematical reasoning ability in intellectually talented preadolescents: Their nature, effects, and possible causes. *Behavioral and Brain Sciences, 11:* 169–232.

Benbow, C. P. (1998). Psychological aspects of giftedness. *Contemporary Psychology, 43:* 13–15.

Benbow, C. P., & Stanley, J. C. (1996). Inequity in equity: How current educational equity policies place able students at risk. *Psychology, Public Policy, and Law, 2:* 249–292.

Benbow, C. B., Lubinski, D., D. Shea, D. L., & Eftekhari-Sanjani, H. (2000). Sex differences in mathematical reasoning ability at age 13: Their status 30 years later. *Psychological Science, 11:* 474–480.

Berlin, I. (1958). *Two concepts of liberty*. London: Oxford University Press.

Berlin, I. (1979). *Against the current*. London: The Hogarth Press.

Blakeslee, S. (1997). When an adult adds a language, its one brain and two systems. *The New York Times, 146,* July 15, p. B13.

Blum, D. (1997). *Sex on the brain: The biological eifferences between men and women*. New York: Viking.

Bolick, C. (1996). *The affirmative action fraud.* Washington, D.C.: Cato Institute.

Bouchard, T. L., Jr. (1982). Review of identical twins reared apart: A reanalysis. *Contemporary Psychology, 27:* 190–191.

Bouchard, T. L., Jr. (1983). Do environmental similarities explain the similarity in intelligence of identical twins reared apart? *Intelligence, 7:* 175–184.

Bouchard, T. J., Jr. (1993). Genetic architecture of human intelligence. In P. A. Vernon (Ed.), *Biological approaches to the study of human intelligence,* pp. 33–93. Norwood, NJ: Ablex Publishing Corporation.

Bouchard, T. J., Jr., Lykken, D. T., McGue, M., Segal, N. L., & Tellegen, A. (1990). Sources of human psychological differences: The Minnesota study of twins reared apart. *Science, 250:* 223–228.

Bouchard, T. J., Jr., & McGue, M. (1981). Familial studies of intelligence: A review. *Science, 250:* 223–238.

Bowen, W. G., & Bok, D. (1998). *The shape of the river: Long term consequences of considering race in college and university admissions.* Princeton: Princeton University Press.

Bragg, R. (1995). Fighting bias with bias and leaving a rift. *The New York Times,* 144, August 21, pp. A1, A8.

Brody, N. (1992). *Intelligence,* 2nd ed. New York: Academic Press.

Brown, F. A. (1944). A comparative study of intelligence of Jewish and Scandinavian kindergarten children. *Journal of Genetic Psychology, 64:* 67–92.

Browne, J. (1995). *Charles Darwin. Voyaging. Vol. 1 of a Biography.* New York: Knopf and London, Cape.

Bruner, J. S., & Postman, L. (1949). On the perception of incongruity: A paradigm. *Journal of Personality, 18:* 206–223.

Burt, C. *The backward child,* 5th ed. London: University of London Press, original work 1937, 1961.

Burt, C. (1961). Intelligence and social mobility. *British Journal of Statistical Psychology, 14:* 3–24.

Burt, C. (1966). The genetic determination of differences in intelligence: A study of monozygotic twins reared together and apart. *British Journal of Psychology, 57:* 137–153.

Canavan, F. (1995). *The pluralist game: Pluralism, liberalism, and the moral conscience.* Lanham, MD: Rowman and Littlefield Publishers.

Carroll, J. B. (1993). *Human cognitive abilities: A survey of the factor-analytic literature.* New York: Cambridge University Press.

Chang, I. (1997). *The rape of Nanking.* New York: Basic Books.

Chorney, M. J., Chorney, K., Seese, N., Owen, M. J., Daniels, J., McGuffin, P., Thompson, L. A., Detterman, D. K., Benbow, C., Lubinski, D., Eley, T., & Plomin, R. (1998). A quantitative trait locus associated with cognitive ability in children. *Psychological Science, 9:* 159–166.

Clinton, H. R. (1996). *It takes a village and other lessons children teach us.* New York: Simon and Schuster.

Cohen, C. (1996). Race, lies, and "Hopwood." *Commentary, 101* (No. 6): 39–45.

Cohen, J. (1994). The earth is round (p < .05). *American Psychologist, 49:* 997–1003.

Conant, J. (1947). *On understanding science.* New Haven: Yale University Press.

Couzin, J., & Unger, K. Cleaning up the paper trail. *Science, 312:* 38–43, April 7, 2006.

Darwin, F., & Seward, A. C. (Eds.). (1903). *More letters of Charles Darwin, vol. I.* London: John Murray.

Dawes, R. M. (1994). *House of cards: Psychology and psychotherapy built on myth.* New York: Free Press.

Dawkins, R. (1986). *The blind watchmaker.* New York: Norton.

Denby, D. (1996). *My adventures with Homer, Rousseau, Woolf, and other indestructible writers of the western world.* New York: Simon and Schuster.

Desmond, A., & Moore, J. (1992). *Darwin.* New York: Warner.

Deutscher, M., & Chein, I. (1948). The psychological effects of enforced segregation: A survey of social science opinion. *Journal of Psychology, 26:* 259–287.

Dickens, W. D., & Flynn, J. R. (2006). Black Americans reduce the racial IQ gap: Evidence from standardization samples. *Psychological Science, 17:* 921–922.

Ding, W. W., Murray, F., & Stuart, T. E. (2006). Gender differences in patenting in the academic life sciences. *Science, 313:* 665–667.

Dworkin, R. (1984). Liberalism. In Sandel, M. (Ed.), *Liberalism and its critics.* New York: New York University Press.

Eaves, L. J., Eysenck, H. J., & Martin, N. G. (1989). *Genes, culture and personality.* New York: Academic Press.

Enserink, M. (2007). In Europe's mailbag: A glossy attack on evolution. *Science, 315:* 925.

Farber, S. L. (1981). *Identical twins reared apart: A reanalysis.* New York: Basic Books.

Feigl, H. (1949). Logical empiricism. In H. Feigl and Sellars, W. (Eds.), *Readings in philosophical analysis.* pp. 3–26. New York: Appleton-Century-Crofts.

Fischman, J. (1996). Evidence mounts for our African origins-and alternatives. *Science, 271:* 1364.

Fisher, I. (2006). Muslims condemn Pope's remarks in Islam. *The New York Times,* 155, September 15, p. A1.

Fishman, D. B. (1999). *The case for pragmatic psychology.* New York: New York University Press.

Fletcher, R. (1991). Intelligence, equality, character, and education. *Intelligence, 15:* 441–461.

Fowers, B. J., & Richardson, F. C. (1996). Why is multiculturalism good? *American Psychologist, 51:* 609–621.

Fox, D. R. (1993). Psychological jurisprudence and radical social change. *American Psychologist, 48:* 234–241.

Garber, H. L. (1988). *The Milwaukee Project: Preventing mental retardation in children at risk.* Washington, D.C.: American Association on Mental Retardation.

Gergen, K. J., Gulerce, A., Lock, A., & Misra, G. (1996). Psychological science in cultural context. *American Psychologist, 51:* 496–503.

Gilligan, C. (1982). *In a different voice: Psychological theory and women's development.* Cambridge: Harvard University Press.

Gillie, O. Crucial data was faked by eminent psychologist. London: *Sunday Times,*

24, October, 1976.

Glazer, N. (1998). For racial dispensation in admissions. *Academic Questions, 11* (3): 22–31.

Glater, J. D. (2006). Straight 'A' student? Good luck making partner. *The New York Times,* 155, December 3, p. 3 (News of the Week).

Gleick, J. (1992). *Genius: The life and science of Richard Feynmann.* New York: Pantheon.

Goble, F. (1971). *The third force.* New York: Pocket Books.

Goldberger, P. (1997). From page to stage: Race and the theater. *The New York Times,* 146, January 22, pp. B1, B4.

Gootman, E. (2006). Despite New York's efforts, Black and Hispanic students in its elite schools decline. *The New York Times,* 155, October 18, p. A16.

Gottfredson, L. S. (1994). The science and politics of race norming. *American Psychologist, 49:* 955–963.

Gould, S. J. (1981, 1996). *The mismeasure of man.* New York: W. W. Morton.

Gray, S. W., & Klaus, R. A. (1965). An experimental pre-school program for culturally deprived children. *Child Development, 36:* 897–898.

Greenhouse, L. (1995). Justices say lower courts erred in order in desegregation case. *The New York Times,* 144, June 13, pp. A1, A9.

Gross, J. (1967). *Learning readiness in two Jewish groups.* New York: Center for Urban Education.

Gurin, P., Dey, E. L., Hurtado, S., & Guin, G. (2002). Diversity and higher education: Theory and impact on educational outcomes. *Harvard Educational Review, 72:* 330–366.

Gurr, T. R. (1970). A comparative study of civil strife. In Graham, H. D., and Gurr, T. R. (Eds.), *The history of violence in America.* (Rev. Bantam ed.), New York: Bantam.

Handler, P. (1980). Public doubts about science. *Science, 208:* 1093.

Hardcastle, V. G. (1996). *How to build a theory in cognitive science.* Albany: State University of New York Press.

Harrington, A. (1996). *Reenchanted science.* Princeton: Princeton University Press.

Harrington, H. J., & Miller, N. (1992). Overcoming resistance to affirmative action in industry. In Suedfeld, P. and Tetlock, P. E. (Eds.), *Psychology and social policy,* pp. 121–135. New York: Hemisphere Publishing Corp.

Hartigan, J. A., & Wigdor, A. K. (Eds.). (1989). *Fairness in employment testing: Validity generalization, minority issues, and the general aptitude test battery.* Washington, D.C.: National Academy Press.

Hauser, M. D. (2006). *How nature designed our universal sense of right and wrong.* New York: Ecco/Harper Collins Publisher.

Havighurst, R. J. (1970). Majority subcultures and the law of effect. *American Psychologist, 25:* 313–322.

Hearnshaw, L. S. (1979). *Cyril Burt: Psychologist.* Ithaca: Cornell University Press.

Heber, R., Garber, H., Harrington, S., Hoffman, C., & Falender, C. *Rehabilitation of families at risk for mental retardation: Progress report.* Rehabilitation Research and Training Center in Mental Retardation. Madison, University of Wisconsin, December, 1972.

Herbert, B. (1994). In America: Throwing a curve. *The New York Times,* 143, October 26, p. A17.

Herbert, B. (2006). A triumph of felons and failure. *The New York Times,* 155 August 24, p. A27.

Herrnstein, R. J., & Murray, C. (1994). *The Bell Curve.* New York: The Free Press.

Honan, W. H. (1996). Alas, poor Shakespeare: No longer a 'Must Read' at many colleges. *The New York Times,* 145, December 29, p. 13.

Howe, J. (1966). *The changing political thought of John Adams.* Princeton: Princeton University Press.

Hull, C. L. (1943). *Principles of behavior.* New York: Appleton-Century-Crofts.

Hull, C. L. (1952). *A behavior system.* New Haven: Yale University Press.

Humphreys, L. G. (1994). Intelligence from the standpoint of a (pragmatic) behaviorist. *Psychological Inquiry, 5:* 179–192.

Hunt, E. (1995). The role of intelligence in modern society. *American Scientist, 83:* 356–368.

Hunter, J. E., & Schmidt, F. L. (1990). *Methods of meta-analysis: Correcting error and bias in research findings.* Newbury Park, CA: Sage Publications.

Ibrahim, Y. M. (1995). Muslim edicts take on a new force. *The New York Times,* 144, February 12, p. 4.

James, W. (1890). *The principles of psychology,* vols. I and II. New York: Henry Holt.

Jencks, C., Smith, M., Acland, H., Bane, M. J., Cohen, D., Gentis, H., Heyns, B., & Michelson, S. (1972). *Inequality: A reassessment of the effects of family and schooling in America.* New York: Basic Books.

Jensen, A. R. (1973). *Educability and group differences.* New York: Harper and Row.

Jensen, A. R. (1989). Raising IQ without increasing g? A review of the "Milwaukee Project: Preventing mental retardation in children at risk." *Developmental Review, 9:* 234–258.

Jensen, A. R. (1998). *The G factor: The science of mental ability.* Westport, CT: Praeger.

Jensen, A. R., & Sinha, S. N. (1993). Physical correlates of human intelligence. In Vernon, P. (Ed.), *Biological approaches to the study of human intelligence,* pp. 139–242. New York: Academic Press.

Johnson, T. C., Scholz, C. A., Talbot, M. R., Kelts, K., Ricketts, R. D., Ngobi, G., Beuning, K., Ssemmanda, I., & McGill, J. W. (1996). Late Pleistocene desiccation of Lake Victoria and rapid evolution of cichlid fishes. *Science, 273:* 1091–1093.

Juel-Nielsen, N. (1965/1980). *Individual and environment: Monozygotic twins reared apart.* New York: International Universities Press.

Joynson, R. B. (1989). *The Burt Affair.* London: Routledge.

Kamin, L. J. (1974). *The science and politics of IQ.* Potomac, MD: Erlbaum.

Kamin, L. J. (1976). Heredity, intelligence, politics, and psychology: I. In Block, J. J. and Dworkin, G. (Eds.), *The IQ controversey: Critical readings,* pp. 242–264. New York: Pantheon Books.

Keith, S., Bell, R., & Williams, A. (1987). *Assessing the outcome of affirmative action in medical schools.* Santa Monica, CA: Rand.

Kemelman, H. (1976). *Wednesday the Rabbi got wet.* New York: Morrow.

Kendler, H. H. (1963). *Basic psychology.* New York: Appleton-Century-Crofts.

Kendler, H. H. (1974). *Basic psychology,* 3rd ed. Menlo Park, CA: W. A. Benjamin.

Kendler, H. H. (1981). *Psychology: A science in conflict.* New York: Oxford.

Kendler, H. H. (1987). *Historical foundations of modern psychology.* Pacific Grove, CA: Brooks Cole Publishing Company.

Kendler, H. H. (2002). A personal encounter with psychology (1937–2002). *History of Psychology, 5:* 52–84.

Kendler, H. H. (2005). Psychology and phenomenology. *American Psychologist, 60:* 318–324.

Kendler, H. H., & Kendler, T. S. (1962). Vertical and horizontal processes in problem solving. *Psychological Review, 69:* 1–16.

Kendler, H. H., & Kendler, T. S. (1975). From discrimination learning to cognitive development: A neobehavioristic odyssey. In Estes, W. K. (Ed.), *Handbook of learning and cognitive processes,* Vol. 1. Hillsdale, NJ: Erlbaum Associates, pp. 191–247.

Kendler, K. S., & Prescott, C. A. (2006). *Genes, environment, and psychopathology.* New York: The Guilford Press.

Kendler, T. S. (1995). *Levels of cognitive development.* Mahwah, NJ: Erlbaum.

Kennan, G. G. (1992). *Around the cragged hill: A personal and political philosophy.* New York: W. W. Norton.

Kessel, F. S. (1969). The philosophy of science as proclaimed and science as practiced: "Identity" or "dualism"? *American Psychologist, 24:* 999–1005.

Kinder, D. R., & Sears, D. O. (1981). Prejudice and politics. Symbolic racism versus racial threats to the good life. *Journal of Personality and Social Psychology, 40:* 414–431.

Kirp, D. L. (2006). After the Bell Curve. *The New York Times,* 155, Section 8, 15–16. July 23.

Kohlberg, L. (1971). From is to ought: How to commit the naturalistic fallacy and get away with it in the study of moral development. In Mischel, T. (Ed.), *Cognitive development and epistemology,* pp. 151–235. San Diego: Academic Press.

Kohlberg, L. (1981). *Essays on moral development: Vol 1. The philosophy of moral development.* New York: Harper and Row.

Kohlberg, L., Levine, C., & Hewer, A. (1983). *Moral stages: A current formulation and a response to critics.* Basel, Switzerland: Karger.

Kuhn, T. S. (1962). *The structure of scientific revolutions.* Chicago: University of Chicago Press.

Kuncel, N. R., & Hezlett, S. A. (2007). Standardized tests predict graduate students' success. *Science, 315:* 1080–1082.

Kurtz, A. L. (1944). *The prediction of code learning ability.* OSRD Report No. 4059. New York: The Psychological Corporation.

Lack, D. (1947). *Darwin's finches.* Cambridge: Cambridge University Press.

Lakatos, I. (1970a). History of science and its rational reconstruction. In Buck, R. C. & Cohen, R. S. (Eds.), *Boston studies in the philosophy of science,* vol. 8. Dordrecht, Netherlands: Reidel.

Lakatos, I. (1970b). Falsification and the methodology of scientific research programmes. In Lakatos, I. & Musgrave, A. (Eds.), *Criticism and the growth of knowledge,* pp. 91–196. Cambridge: Cambridge University Press.

Lander, E. S., & Schork, N. (1994). Genetic dissection of complex traits. *Science, 263:* 2037–2047.

Lefkowitz, M. (1996). *Not out of Africa: How Afrocentrism became an excuse to teach myth as history.* New York: Basic Books.

Lempinen, E. (2007). AAAS News & Notes. *Science, 315:* 1090–1091.

Leroi, A. M. (2005). A family tree in every gene. *The New York Times,* 154, March 14, p. A23.

Lewis, B. (1994). Eurocentrism revisited. *Commentary, 98,* No. 6: 47–51.

Lewontin, R. C. (1987). The irrelevance of heritability: Resisting the hereditarian agenda. *Science for the People, 19,* No. 36, 23, and 32.

Lewontin, B, C., Rose, S., & Kamin, L. (1984). *Not in our genes.* New York: Pantheon.

Linn, M. C. (2007). Can evidence inform the debate? *Science, 317:* 199–200, 317.

Lippman, W. (1955). *The public philosophy.* Boston: Little, Brown.

Locurto, C. (1990). The malleability of IQ as judged from adoption studies. *Intelligence, 14:* 275–292.

Losee, J. (2001). *A historical introduction to the philosophy of science.* 4th ed. New York: Oxford University Press.

Lykken, D. T. (1982). Research with twins: The concept of emergenesis. *Psychophysiology, 19:* 361–373.

Lykken, D. T., McGue, M., Tellegin, A., & Bouchard, T. L. (1992). Emergenesis: Genetic traits that may not run in families. *American Psychologist, 47:* 1565–1577.

MacFarquhar, N. (1996). Mutilation of Egyptian girls: Despite ban, it goes on. *The New York Times,* 145, August 8, p. A3.

Mackintosh, N. J. (1995). *Cyril Burt/Fraud or framed?* New York: Oxford University Press.

Major, B. (1998). Beyond choice: Myths and facts about adjustment to abortion, 1–35. Wellness Lectures. Oakland, CA.

Mann, C. C. (1994). Behavior genetics in transition. *Science, 264:* 1686–1689.

Martin, N. G., & Eaves, P. G. (1977). The genetic analysis of covariance structure. *Heredity, 38* (1) 79–95.

Mascie-Taylor, C. G. N., & Gibson, J. B. (1978). Social mobility and IQ components. *Journal of Biosocial Science, 10:* 263–276.

Maslow, A. H. (1954). *Motivation and personality.* New York: Harper and Row.

Maslow, A. H. (1961). Eupsychia–the good society. *Journal of Humanistic Psychology, 1*(2): 1–11.

Matarazzo, J. D. (1972). *Wechsler's measurement and appraisal of adult intelligence.* New York: Oxford University Press.

McCartney, K., Harris, M. J., & Bernieri, F. (1990). Growing up and growing apart: A developmental meta-analysis of twin studies. *Psychological Bulletin, 107:* 226–237.

McClearn, G. E., Johansson, B., Berg, S., Pedersen, N. L., Ahern, F., Petrill, S. A., & Plomin, R. (1997). Substantial genetic influence on cognitive abilities in twins 80 or more years old. *Science, 276:* 1560–1563.

McGue, M., Bouchard, T. J., Jr., Iacone, W. G., & Lykken, D. T. (1993). Behavior genetics of cognitive ability: A life-span perspective. In Plomin, R. & McClearn, G. E. (Eds.), *Nature, nurture, and psychology,* pp. 59–76. Washington, D.C.:

American Psychological Association.

Medawar, P. B. (1993). Unnatural science. *The New York Review of Books, 24* (1): 13–18.

Meehl, P. E. (1993). Philosophy of science: Help or hindrance? *Psychological Reports, 72:* 707–733.

Murnane, R., & Levy, R. (1996). *Teaching the new basic skills: Principles for educating children to thrive in a changing world.* New York: Free Press.

Nasr, V. (2006). *The Shia revival.* New York: W. W. Norton & Co.

Neisser, U. (1997). Rising scores on intelligence tests. *American Scientist, 85:* 440–447.

Newman, H. H., Freeman, F. N., & Holzinger, K. H. (1937). *Twins: A study of heredity and environment.* Chicago: University of Chicago Press.

Nichols, R. C. (1978). Twin studies of ability, personality, and interests. *Homo, 29:* 158–173.

Osborne, R. T. (1980). *Twins, black and white.* Athens, GA: Foundation for Human Understanding.

Osborne, R. T., & McGurk, F. C. J. (Eds.). (1982). *The Testing of Negro Intelligence,* vol. II. Athens, GA: Foundation for Human Understanding.

Passmore, J. A. (1953). Can the social sciences be value free? In Feigl, H., and Brodbeck, M. (Eds.), *Readings in the philosophy of science,* pp. 674–676. New York: Appleton-Century-Crofts.

Passmore, J. A. (1978). *Science and its critics.* New Brunswick: Rutgers University Press.

Patterson, C. J. (2006). Children of lesbian and gay parents. *Current Directions in Psychological Science, 15:* 241–244.

Pedersen, N. L., Plomin, R., Nesselroade, J. R., & McClearn, G. E. (1992). A quantitative general analysis of cognitive abilities during the second half of the life span. *Psychological Sciences, 3:* 346–353.

Penniski, E. (1999). Genetic study shakes up out of Africa theory. *Science, 283:* 1828.

Pipes, D. (2003). Dr. Pipes' views on Islamic terrorism and Turkey: Voice of Ataturk. March (Daniel Pipes.org).

Pipes, R. (1990). *The Russian revolution.* New York: Knopf.

Pipes, R. (1993). *Russia under the Bolshevik regime.* New York: Knopf.

Plomin, R., De Fries, J. C., & Loehlin, J. C. (1977). Geneotype-environment interaction and correlation in the analysis of human behavior. *Psychological Bulletin, 84:* 309–322.

Plomin, R., & Thompson, R. (1987). Life-span developmental behavior genetics. In Baltes, P. B., Featherman, D. L., and Lerner, R. D. (Eds.), *Life-span development and behavior: Vol. 8,* pp. 111–123. Hillsdale, NJ: Erlbaum.

Polkinghorne, D. (1983). *Methodology for the human sciences.* Albany: State University of New York Press.

Popper, K. R. (1945). *The open society and its enemies.* UK: Routledge.

Popper, K. R. (1965). *Conjectures and refutations: The growth of scientific knowledge,* 2nd ed. New York: Harper and Row.

Posthuma, D., & de Geus, Eco J. C. (2006). Progress in the Molecular-Genetic Study of Intelligence. *Current Directions, 15:* 151–155.

Puka, B. (Ed.). (1994). *An ethic of care: Feminist and interdisciplinary perspective.* New York: Routledge.

Ramey, C. T. (1992). High-risk children and IQ: Altering intergenerational patterns. *Intelligence, 16:* 239–255.

Ramey, C. T., MacPhee, D., & Yeates, K. O. (1982). Preventing mental retardation: A general systems model. In Jofee, J. M., and L. A. Bonds, (Eds.), *Facilitating infant and early childhood development,* pp. 343–407. Hanover, NH: University Press of New England.

Rawls, J. (1971). *A theory of justice.* Cambridge: Harvard University Press.

Rawls, J. (1993). *Political liberalism.* New York: Columbia University Press

Ree, M. J. (1992). Intelligence is the best predictor of job performance. *Current Directions in Psychological Science, 3:* 86–89.

Riley, B. P., & Kendler, K. S. (2006). Molecular genetic studies of schizophrenia. *European Journal of Human Genetics, 6:* 669–680.

Roberts, S. (2006). Hands-on approach to studying the brain, even Einstein's. *The New York Times,* 155, November 14, p. 4.

Robinson, N. M., Abbott, R. D., Berninger, V. W., Busse, J., & Mukhopadhyay, S. (1996). The structure of abilities in mathematically precocious young children: Gender similarities and differences. *Journal of Educational Psychology 88:* 341–352.

Robinson, N. M., Abbott, R. D., Berninger, V. W., & Busse, J.: Developmental changes in mathematical precocious young children. *Gifted Child Quarterly, 41:* 145–158.

Roszak, T. (1972). *Where the wasteland ends.* Garden Grove, NY: Doubleday.

Rushton, J. P. (2000). *Race, evolution, and behavior.* Port Huron, MI: Charles Darwin Research Institute New Brunswick, Transaction.

Rushton, J. P., & Jensen, A. R. (2006). The totality of available evidence shows the race IQ gap still remains. *Psychological Science, 17:* 921–922.

Sabeti, P. C., Schaffner, S. F., Fry, B., Lohmueller, J. Varilly, P., Shamovsky, O., Palma, A, Mikkelsen, T. S., Altshuler D., & Lander, E. S. (2006). Positive natural selection in the human lineage. *Science, 312:* 1614–1620.

Sackett, P. R., & Wilk, S. L. (1994). Within-group norming and other forms of score adjustment in preemployment testing. *American Psychologist, 49:* 929–954.

Scarr, S. (1992). Developmental theories for the 1990s: Development and individual differences. *Child Development, 63:* 1–19.

Scarr, S., & McCartney, K. (1983). How people make their own environments: A theory of geneotype-environment effects. *Child Development, 54:* 424–434.

Scarr, S., & Weinberg, R. (1976). IQ test performance of Black children adopted by White families. *American Psychologist, 31:* 726–739.

Schemo, D. J. (2006). At 2-year colleges, students eager but unready. *The New York Times,* 155, September 2, A1, A9.

Schmidt, F. L. (1988). The problem of group differences in ability test scores in employment selection. *Journal of Vocational Behavior, 33:* 272–292.

Schmidt, F. L., Ones, D. S., & Hunter, J. E. (1992). Employment testing. *Annual Review of Psychology, 43:* 627–670.

Schoenfeld, B. (1995). The loneliness of being white. *The New York Times Magazine,* 144, May 14, pp. 34–37.

Schoenfeld, W. N. (1993). *Religion and human behavior.* Boston: Authors Cooperative,

Inc.

Scott, D. M. (1997). *Contempt and pity: Experts, social policy, and the black psyche.* Chapel Hill, NC: University of North Carolina Press.

Shields, J. (1962). *Monozygotic twins brought up apart and brought up together.* New York: Oxford University Press.

Shuey, A. M. (1966). *The testing of Negro intelligence,* 2nd ed. New York: Social Science Press.

Smith, M. B. (1991). *Values, self, and society: Toward a humanist social psychology.* New Brunswick, NJ: Transaction Publishers.

Smith, S. (1942). Language and nonverbal test performance of racial groups in Honolulu before and after a 14-year interval. *Journal of General Psychology, 26:* 51–93.

Sowell, T. (1990). *Preferential policies: An international perspective.* New York: William Morrow.

Spelke, E. S. (2005). Sex differences in intrinsic aptitude for mathematics and science: A critical review. *American Psychologist, 60:* 950–958.

Spitz, H. H. (1986). *The raising of intelligence: A selected history of attempts to raise retarded intelligence.* Lawrence Erlbaum Associates.

Spitz, H. H. (1992). Does the Carolina Abecedarian Early intervention project prevent socialcultural mental retardation? *Intelligence, 16:* 225–237.

Sternberg, R. J. (2004). Culture and intelligence. *American Psychologist, 59:* 325–338.

Sternberg, R. J. (2006). The Rainbow Project: Enhancing the SAT through assessments of analytical, practical, and creative skills. *Intelligence, 34:* 321–350.

Sternberg, R. J. (2006). Personal communication.

Stevenson, H., Stigler, J. W., Lee, S., Lucker, G. W., Kitamura, S., & Hsu, C. (1983). Cognitive performance of Japanese, Chinese, and American children. *Child Development, 61:* 1053–1066.

Stoddard, G. (1943). *The meaning of intelligence.* New York: Macmillan.

Sue, D. W., & Sue, S. (1990). *Counseling the culturally different: Theory and practice.* New York: Wiley.

Summers, L. H. (2005). Excerpts from remarks by Harvard University president Lawrence H. Summers at conference on Diversifying the Science and Engineering Workforce. *The New York Times,* February 18, 2005.

Sykes, C. (1995). *Dumbing down our kids: Why American children feel good about themselves but can't read, write, or add.* New York: St. Martin's.

Taubes, G. (1993). *Bad science. The short life and weird times of cold fusion.* New York: Random House.

Taylor, H. F. (1980). *The IQ game: A methodological inquiry into the heredity-environment controversy.* New Brunswick: Rutgers University Press.

Tenner, W. (1996). *Why things bite back. Technology and the revenge of unintended consequences.* New York: Knopf.

Terman, L. M. (1916). *The measurement of intelligence.* Boston: Houghton Mifflin.

Thernstrom, S., & Thernstrom, A. (1997). *America in black and white: One nation indivisible.* New York: Simon & Schuster.

Tolman, E. C. (1922). A new formula for behaviorism. *Psychological Review, 29:*

44–53.

Tolman, E. C. (1932). *Purposive behavior in animals and men.* New York: Century.

Tuddenham, R. D. (1962). The nature and measurement of intelligence. In Postman, L. (Ed.), *Psychology in the making: Histories of selected research topics,* pp. 469–525. New York: Knopf.

Turkheimer, E., Haley, A., Waldron, M., D'Onofrio, B., & Gottesman, I. I. (2003). Socioeconomic status modifies heritability of IQ in young children. *Psychological Science, 14:* 623–628.

Vandenberg, S. G. (1968). The nature and nurture of intelligence. In Glass, D.C. (Ed.), *Genetics.* New York: Russell Sage Foundation.

van der Dennen, J. M. G. (1987). Ethnocentrism and in-group/out-group differentiation. In Reynolds, V., Falger, V. S. E., and Vine, I. (Eds.), *The sociobiology of ethnocentrism,* pp. 1–47. London: Croom Helm.

Vernon, P. A. (1982). *The abilities and achievements of Orientals in North America.* New York: Academic Press.

Volkogonov, D. (1994). *Lenin: A new biography.* Trans. by Shukman, H. (Ed.). New York: Free Press.

Wade, N. (1976). Sociobiology: Troubled birth for a new discipline. *Science, 191:* 1151–1155.

Waller, J. H. (1971). Achievement and social mobility: Relationships among IQ score, education, and occupation in two generations. *Social Biology, 18:* 252–259.

Washington, G. Washington's Farewell Address. Senate Document # 3, U. S. Senate, 1020 Congress, 1st Session, 1796/1991, pp. 1–30.

Watson, J. B. (1913). Psychology as a behaviorist views it. *Psychological Review, 20:* 158–177.

Watson, J. B. (1926). What the nursery has to say about instincts. In C. Murchison, (Ed.), *Psycheies of 1925.* Worchester, MA: Clark University Press.

Wechsler, D. (1958). *The measurement and appraisal of adult intelligence,* 4th ed. Baltimore: Williams and Wilkens.

Weinberg, R. A., Scarr, S., & Waldman, I. (1992). The Minnesota transracial adoption study: A follow-up of IQ test performance at adolescence. *Intelligence, 16:* 117–135.

Wertheimer, M. (1945). *Productive thinking.* New York: Harper.

Wesseling, H. L. (1996). *Divide and rule: The partition of Africa, 1880–1940.* Trans. Pomerans, A. J. Westport: Praeger.

Wickelgren, I. (1999). Nurture helps mold able minds. *Science, 283:* 1832–1834.

Wilson, E. O. (1995). Science and ideology. *Academic Questions, 8,* No. 3: 72–81.

Wilson, J. Q. (1993b). *The moral sense.* New York: The Free Press.

Winner, E. (1996). *Gifted children: Myths and realities.* New York: Basic Books.

Wolfe, A. (1998). *One nation, after all.* New York: Viking.

Woodward, J. (2003). Making things happen. New York: Oxford University Press.

Zuckerman, M. (1990). Some dubious premises in research and theory on racial differences: Scientific, social, and ethical issues. *American Psychologist, 45:* 1297–1303.

Zuriff, G. (2002). Is racial and ethnic diversity educationally beneficial? *World and I, 17:* 271–287.

NAME INDEX

SUBJECT INDEX

251

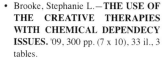

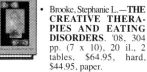